PROVINCIAL
LIBRARY
MANITOBA

DISCARDED
LIBRARY
515 Portage Avenue
Winnipeg, Manitoba R3B 2E9

COMMITTEE FOR ECONOMIC DEVELOPMENT
RESEARCH STUDY

# SMALL BUSINESS: ITS PLACE AND PROBLEMS

## *COMMITTEE FOR ECONOMIC DEVELOPMENT RESEARCH STUDIES*

PRODUCTION, JOBS AND TAXES
*By Harold M. Groves*

POSTWAR TAXATION AND ECONOMIC PROGRESS
*By Harold M. Groves*

AGRICULTURE IN AN UNSTABLE ECONOMY
*By Theodore W. Schultz*

INTERNATIONAL TRADE AND DOMESTIC EMPLOYMENT
*By Calvin B. Hoover*

CONTROLLING WORLD TRADE
*By Edward S. Mason*

SMALL BUSINESS: ITS PLACE AND PROBLEMS
*By A. D. H. Kaplan*

*Studies That Dealt with the Transition Period from War to Peace*

THE LIQUIDATION OF WAR PRODUCTION
*By A. D. H. Kaplan*

DEMOBILIZATION OF WARTIME ECONOMIC CONTROLS
*By John Maurice Clark*

PROVIDING FOR UNEMPLOYED WORKERS IN THE TRANSITION
*By Richard A. Lester*

FINANCING BUSINESS DURING THE TRANSITION
*By Charles C. Abbott*

JOBS AND MARKETS
*By CED Research Staff*

## *SUPPLEMENTARY RESEARCH PAPERS*

WORLD POLITICS FACES ECONOMICS
*By Harold D. Lasswell*

THE ECONOMICS OF A FREE SOCIETY*
*By William Benton*

PERSONNEL PROBLEMS OF THE POSTWAR TRANSITION PERIOD*
*By Charles A. Myers*

* *Published by CED*

COMMITTEE FOR ECONOMIC DEVELOPMENT
RESEARCH STUDY

# SMALL BUSINESS: ITS PLACE AND PROBLEMS

By A. D. H. KAPLAN

FIRST EDITION

NEW YORK TORONTO LONDON
McGRAW-HILL BOOK COMPANY, INC.
*1948*

SMALL BUSINESS: ITS PLACE AND PROBLEMS



THE MAPLE PRESS COMPANY, YORK, PA.

The Trustees of the Committee for Economic Development established the Research and Policy Committee "to initiate studies into the principles of business policy and of public policy which will foster the full contribution by industry and commerce in the postwar period to the attainment of high and secure standards of living for people in all walks of life through maximum employment and high productivity in the domestic economy." (From CED By-Laws.)

The studies are assigned by the Research Director to qualified scholars, drawn largely from leading universities. Under the by-laws, "all research is to be thoroughly objective in character, and the apporach in each instance is to be from the standpoint of the general welfare and not from that of any special political or economic group."

The reports present the findings of the authors, who have complete freedom to express their own conclusions. They do not purport to set forth the views of the Trustees, the Research and Policy Committee, the Research Advisory Board, the Research Staff, or the businessmen affiliated with the CED. This report on the place of small business in a free-enterprise economy, its position and its needs today, is the fourteenth study in the CED series.

The Research and Policy Committee draws on these studies and other available information in formulating its recommendations as to national policy for the problems examined. Its policy statements are offered as an aid to clearer understanding of steps to be taken to reach and maintain a high level of productive employment and a steadily rising standard of living. The statements are available from the national CED headquarters.

# FOREWORD

THE POLITICAL ORATOR can conjure with "small business." It is a symbol of opportunity, enterprise, innovation, and achievement. It is an independent way of life. It stands for something essential to our freedoms.

Although much has been written and declaimed to extol small business and plead its cause, comparatively little has been done to analyze its role in our economy or to appraise its problems. This the present study does. The author makes evident, among other things, the interdependence of big and little business as well as the areas of competition between them. And he shows some of the lines of action that will enable small business better to help itself.

This CED research report is part of a program of research into the problems crucial to the maintenance of high, productive employment in a free-enterprise system. A description of this program appears on pages 262 to 268.

THEODORE O. YNTEMA
*Research Director*

# PREFACE

TREATING SMALL business as a subject of inquiry by one person has obvious limitations. Small-scale enterprise is widely diversified as to lines of industry, relative size, financial strength, and character of management. This diversity is reflected in the attitudes of small enterprisers on issues of common concern. The experience of a single individual and his own opportunities for observation are hardly extensive enough to insure a balanced sampling of the field as a basis for definitive generalizations.

The giant corporation can readily see that its decisions and method of doing business affect the whole market of which it is a part. It is much more difficult for the small-scale enterpriser to visualize the bearing of his individual conduct on the soundness of the whole business community. The individualism of small businessmen may be in the fine tradition of free enterprise, but it means that it does not help in finding common ground for their cooperation on the plane of national policy.

In these circumstances, I was fortunate to have the benefit of a close association with CED's Special Committee on Small Business. Its members provided a broad range of business experience and outlook. They were instrumental in opening up areas of inquiry that might otherwise have been overlooked. As the manuscript progressed there was opportunity to expose my tentative findings to their seasoned judgment. Individual members of the Small Business Committee gave careful and critical reading to the successive installments of the manuscript.

Thus, whether or not they would be happy in being so identified, the members of the Small Business Committee have in a very real sense participated in the preparation of this study. Manifestly they cannot be blamed for its shortcomings, nor be held responsible for some of the controversial judgments which it expresses. Their helpful suggestions have carried no implication of pressure for the adoption of their views. This opportunity to express my grateful appreciation of the intellectual fellowship they afforded is welcomed. I am indebted to them for increasing my confidence in the general validity of the conclusions reached.

There is room here for only a general acknowledgment of obligation to businessmen, bankers, and trade representatives, as well as to those in the government service who contributed to my education for this study.

Joseph K. Wexman, who served as regular staff member during the earlier stages of the project, collaborated in planning and summarizing the sample study of small-scale enterprises made for the CED by the National Opinion Research Center, in November, 1944; he also assisted in the organization of materials for the first draft completed in the fall of 1945. Postwar developments called for revision of the manuscript at a time when I was involved in commitments that shared priority with the Small Business study. The understanding, patience, and encouragement of Theodore O. Yntema, Director of Research for CED, during this rather trying period, leaves me very much in his debt. There is also a large obligation to Sylvia Stone for substantive counsel as well as expert editing in advancing the manuscript to press. Thanks are due to Esther Payson, who, in addition to her full-time secretarial duties, cheerfully managed the additional job of putting together and checking the manuscript. Robert Lenhart lightened my work by his skillful digests of the regular sessions with the Small Business Committee.

As in the previous study undertaken for the Committee for Economic Development, I have profited by fruitful comment and suggestions from members of the Research Advisory Board and the CED staff.

A. D. H. Kaplan

Washington, D. C.
*July*, 1948

# CONTENTS


Foreword . . . . . vii

Preface . . . . . ix

I. WHY THE CONCERN FOR SMALL BUSINESS? . . . . . 1

War Impact on Small Enterprise . . . . . 2
Traditional Symbol of Independence . . . . . 3
Self-employment Opportunity . . . . . 4
The Waste of Small Business? . . . . . 5
A Trend to Be Reversed . . . . . 6
The Need for New Small Business . . . . . 7

II. WHAT IS SMALL BUSINESS? . . . . . 10

Definition by Size . . . . . 10
Department of Commerce Classification . . . . . 10
Bureau of Labor Statistics (BLS) Definition . . . . . 11
Size by Assets and Income . . . . . 14
Limitations of the Size Classification . . . . . 15
Position in the Industry . . . . . 16
Organization and Operation . . . . . 17
Yardsticks of Public Spokesmen . . . . . 19
The Composite Definition . . . . . 21

III. PREWAR AND POSTWAR PATTERN . . . . . 23

Business Population by Size . . . . . 23
Number of Firms . . . . . 23
Number of Employees . . . . . 24
Business Population by Industry and Size . . . . . 26
Volume of Business . . . . . 26
The Areas of Small Business . . . . . 28
Distribution . . . . . 28
Retail Trade . . . . . 28
Wholesale Trade . . . . . 30
Services . . . . . 32
Transportation, Communication, and Public Utilities . . . . . 34

Finance, Insurance, and Real Estate . . . . . . . . . . . 35
Production—Manufacturing, Construction, Mining . . . . . . 36
Manufacturing . . . . . . . . . . . . . . . . . . . . . 36
Industrial Concentration . . . . . . . . . . . . . . . . 38
Construction . . . . . . . . . . . . . . . . . . . . . 39
Mining and Quarrying . . . . . . . . . . . . . . . . . 41
Prewar Trend of the Business Population . . . . . . . . . . . 41
Population Shifts in Industry . . . . . . . . . . . . . 44
War Impact on Small Business . . . . . . . . . . . . . . . 44
Postwar Prospects for Small Business . . . . . . . . . . . . 47

IV. VITAL STATISTICS OF SMALL ENTERPRISE . . . . . . . . 54

Characteristics of Small-business Mortality . . . . . . . . . . 55
Business Failures . . . . . . . . . . . . . . . . . . . . 58
Reasons for Business Failure . . . . . . . . . . . . . . . 64
Life Span of Small Business . . . . . . . . . . . . . . . . 68
Retail Survival . . . . . . . . . . . . . . . . . . . . 68
Manufacturing Discontinuances . . . . . . . . . . . . . 71
Long-term Mortality Trend . . . . . . . . . . . . . . . 72
Summary . . . . . . . . . . . . . . . . . . . . . . . . 74

V. RELATIVE EFFICIENCY OF SMALL BUSINESS . . . . . . . 77

Summary of Efficiency Comparisons . . . . . . . . . . . . . 79
The Evidence on Relative Costs . . . . . . . . . . . . . . . 81
Rate of Profits . . . . . . . . . . . . . . . . . . . . . . 87
Hidden "Efficiency" Factors . . . . . . . . . . . . . . . . 100
Small Business Efficiency and the Investor . . . . . . . . . . . 101

VI. MANAGEMENT AND RESEARCH . . . . . . . . . . . . . 103

Why Small Business Needs Guidance . . . . . . . . . . . . . 103
Management Factor in Survival . . . . . . . . . . . . . 104
Rising Caliber of Competition . . . . . . . . . . . . . 105
Public Pressure on Small Business . . . . . . . . . . . . 106
Factors Retarding Management Guidance . . . . . . . . . . . 106
Problem Areas in Small-business Management . . . . . . . . . 108
Rebuilding Lines for Postwar Markets . . . . . . . . . . 109
Organizing for Control of Performance . . . . . . . . . . 111
Technological Progress . . . . . . . . . . . . . . . . . 114
Safeguarding Continuity . . . . . . . . . . . . . . . . . 115
Approach to a Guidance Program . . . . . . . . . . . . . 118
Sources of Management Guidance . . . . . . . . . . . . . . 119

Counsel through Suppliers . . . . . 120
The Trade Association in Management Guidance . . . . . 123
Labor-Management Cooperation . . . . . 125
Credit Associations . . . . . 128
Management Guidance by Educational Institutions . . . . . 129
Government Agencies . . . . . 129
Raising the Social Performance of Small Business . . . . . 132
Small-business Manuals Issued by the U.S. Department of Commerce . . . . . 133
State of New York Department of Commerce Small-business Series . 134

VII. MEETING FINANCIAL REQUIREMENTS . . . . . 135

From the Enterpriser's Standpoint . . . . . 135
From the Standpoint of the Credit Institutions . . . . . 136
Types of Financing Requirements . . . . . 138
Short-term Credit . . . . . 138
Term Loans . . . . . 139
Equity Capital . . . . . 140
Availability of Bank Credit . . . . . 140
Expansion of Term Loans . . . . . 145
Wartime Financing to Small Business . . . . . 147
Meeting Postwar Credit Needs . . . . . 148
The Bank Credit Prospect . . . . . 149
Unsatisfied Capital Requirements . . . . . 150
Proposals for New Facilities . . . . . 156
Community Industrial Development . . . . . 156
Investment Company for Small Business . . . . . 160
Direct Government Financing . . . . . 162
Capital Financing through the Banking System . . . . . 168
Tax Policy for Small Business . . . . . 172
Summary . . . . . 175
Note on Britain's Capital Bank for Smaller Enterprises . . . . . 177

VIII. COMPETITION—MEANS AND ENDS . . . . . 182

Conflicting Trends and Objectives . . . . . 182
Control of Market Channels . . . . . 185
Mass Producer in Distribution . . . . . 185
Changed Position of Wholesaler . . . . . 186
Realignments of Manufacturers and Distributors . . . . . 187
Sublimation of Price Competition . . . . . 189
Competing with Business Integration . . . . . 191
Price Manipulation and Regulation . . . . . 198

Resale Price Maintenance . . . 199
Loopholes in Fair-trade Pricing . . . 200
Sale below Cost . . . 203
Defenses against Price Discrimination . . . 205
Legal Barriers to Free Market . . . 206
Interstate Barriers . . . 207
Other Restrictions on Business Entry . . . 208
Patent Controls, Pro and Con . . . 209
Labor as a Factor in Competition . . . 213
Fair Competition and Small-business Survival . . . 217

IX. EDUCATION AND PUBLIC POLICY . . . 220

Community Guidance for Newcomers . . . 220
Role of the Business Colleges . . . 222
Opportunities for Retraining . . . 223
Qualifying Business Educators . . . 225
Research for Small Business . . . 226
Concern of Government in Small Business . . . 228
Recapitulation . . . 232

X. SUMMARY AND CONCLUSIONS . . . 233

Stability and Survival . . . 234
Size and Efficiency . . . 235
Management and Guidance . . . 236
Financial Requirements and Problems . . . 239
Taxation of Small Business . . . 242
Competitive Position of Small Business . . . 243
Small Business and Labor . . . 246
Education and Public Policy . . . 247

APPENDIX . . . 249

A NOTE ON THE COMMITTEE FOR ECONOMIC DEVELOPMENT AND ITS RESEARCH PROGRAM . . . 259
RESEARCH AND POLICY COMMITTEE . . . 270
RESEARCH ADVISORY BOARD . . . 271
MEMBERS OF THE SUBCOMMITTEE ON THE SPECIAL PROBLEMS OF SMALL BUSINESS 272

INDEX . . . 273

# I. WHY THE CONCERN FOR SMALL BUSINESS?

Discourse on small business was not rationed in the Second World War, and no postwar shortage is noticeable. No well-appointed trade association has been without its special project for small business; no respectable business convention closes without affirming that small business is the backbone of our democracy. In the midst of war, Congress found the small-business issue one of its most dependable outlets for self-expression; in the postwar period, as well, each end of the Capitol maintains its special committee on small business. The economic scene continues rife with proposals to ensure the survival and expansion of small business.

This study is intended to assist in focusing the diffuse discussion of small business on two questions. What is the role of small business in the economy? How can small business be helped to contribute its full share to postwar employment and prosperity?

The concern to keep economic power distributed among many independent proprietors is one that goes back to the nation's beginnings. It was a favorite theme with Franklin and Jefferson, who feared that industrialization might lead to a propertyless labor proletariat. It has been exemplified in our antitrust laws and fair-trade acts, designed to check the sublimation of small business. The last prewar wave of interest in the problems of small business (associated with the hearings and reports of the Temporary National Economic Committee) stemmed from the depression of the 1930's and its disastrous effects on many small enterprises. The wartime public interest in small business was concentrated on checking losses in members and ensuring its equitable treatment under military requirements and wartime controls. The postwar concern for small business looks beyond its present appearance of prosperity to the more fundamental issue of whether or not small business can hold its place in the swift current of our economic destiny.

## WAR IMPACT ON SMALL ENTERPRISE

Small enterprises were among the early casualties in the change to an economy geared for total warfare. To attain maximum concentration on the war effort it was necessary to commandeer critical commodities for production of combat weapons, to withhold nonessential goods and services from the market, to establish priorities and allocations for producers' goods, to draft into military service many proprietors of small businesses, to ration some consumers' goods and services, and even to prohibit general purchase and sale of others.

These wartime measures meant the curtailment or elimination of many thousands of small firms dependent upon a continuous flow to consumers of the very items that had to be commandeered for war. The marks of wartime control were visible in abandoned filling stations, neighborhood stores, and shops of self-employed craftsmen, contractors, and agents. Although small manufacturers eventually got their chance to share in war contracts and make a telling contribution to the war effort, the total number of enterprises—including retail and service lines—was reduced by one-sixth between Pearl Harbor and the end of 1943. But while small proprietors were closing down for lack of materials, employees, and replacements of equipment, the war effort required additional facilities in modern plant and equipment to be placed mainly at the disposal of large enterprise. Big business attained new heights of productive activity with fresh incentives to develop superior know-how in mass-production methods. Wartime progress in the division of complex skills cut into the very trades in which the versatility of the small establishment had been a major factor in its success. The American public could grasp the reason for these developments, but their reasonableness did not eliminate uneasiness over a trend fraught with grave implications for the traditional American background.

Small business appears to have weathered its wartime difficulties. Many smaller firms had attained new high levels in volume of business and profits at the war's end. From a low of 2.8 million at the end of 1943 the number of business units climbed, in the estimates of the Department of Commerce, to the unprecedented total of 3.5 million by the midyear of 1946.

The picture at the moment looks rosy. There is slight evidence of financial stringency such as clouded the history of small enterprise in the 1930's. But the position of the small firm over the long pull is far from secure.

## TRADITIONAL SYMBOL OF INDEPENDENCE

Today, as in the earlier periods of agitation on behalf of small enterprise, the public issue goes beyond any measures needed to alleviate current difficulties. It involves a reexamination of the place of small business in our economy and the possibility of creating an economic climate in which small business may be virile and significant.

The last few generations have witnessed progressive concentration of economic control. The development of big business has had its counterpart in the development of big government. Under widening government regulation big corporations tend to take on the character of quasi-public utilities. In the wake of big business has emerged big labor, commanding nation-wide powers in collective bargaining. Farming, until recently regarded as the epitome of independent individual enterprise and the free market, has been brought under a system of production controls, subsidies, price supports, and integrated marketing, all of which add agriculture to the other nationally managed areas of our society. Small business is thus left as the only relatively "unadministered" sector of the economy.

Of all economic elements, small business enterprises have been the least amenable to centralized control, hence a nuisance in a government-managed economy. This fact has been significant to Americans who are aware that elimination of independent small business featured the modification of the economic pattern in every country where totalitarian government waxed strong. It is hard to contemplate a vigorous middle class or a strong nucleus of independent voters without the small-business element. In serving its own interest small business serves as a social and political stabilizer, its very numbers acting as safeguard against concentration of power in any one group.

Small business enterprise is for a large part of the public the symbol of a society in which the hired man can look forward to becoming his own boss. In speaking of free enterprise one does not think first of railroads, public utilities, General Electric or General Motors, although they, too, may have written epics of success in competition that tested their mettle. Free enterprise suggests more readily the multitude of small stores and craft shops that line the streets of all our cities. Implicit in the American's conception of free enterprise is opportunity for individuals to try their luck in new ventures, with enough flexibility in the business system for many small tries, some succeeding, some failing, and making of American business a more flexible going concern.

The future of small business is not of concern only to small businessmen. Big business knows that its chances to continue under private auspices rest heavily upon the presence of many virile, healthy small businesses, bent on retaining the opportunities and liberties that go with private enterprise. For the wage earner, in turn, the alternative of self-employment in small business is an important morale factor. To many an employee it means a sense of independence that might otherwise be lost. Small business is, moreover, a customer and distributor of the products that mean the pay checks for laborers in big industrial units.

### *Self-employment Opportunity*

In a population as large and varied as that of the United States, there is a marked difference in the opportunities for employment. Entrepreneurship is a chosen adventure for some; for others, it is, in a sense, imposed.

At its best, small-business ownership is chosen by men of superior ability and adequate financial resources as the most satisfying outlet for their talents and initiative. But small business has also proved a satisfying alternative to people who do not find employment opportunities with established companies because of peculiarities of personality, education, or background. War experiences have undoubtedly added to the number of those who find themselves unable to fit into the discipline of employment in a large organization, even if the opportunity to obtain a job offers itself. For such people an answer is found in self-employment. The successes in the history of American business include many who could not or would not work for others but found their initial economic niche as peddlers, junkmen, storekeepers, truckers, self-employed craftsmen, and small contractors. Denied that opportunity of self-support, a not insignificant fraction of the 3 million owners of small business enterprises might have to be counted among the dependents and among the disgruntled elements in the body politic. So the essential democracy of the world of small business asserts itself in the varied talents and background from which it may draw its new blood.

Small business, then, has social as well as economic values. To preserve them, however, may entail some debatable public costs. What price is worth paying to preserve small business? In the answers to that question lie niceties of distinction between measures that help small business to play a more virile role in our economic life and those which would merely postpone a reckoning with the causes of small business failure.

## THE WASTE OF SMALL BUSINESS?

It is easy, of course, to grow too idyllic about small business, just as it is easy to shed unnecessary tears for it. The failures in small business ventures have not been so articulate as the successes, and they have been much more numerous. The freedom of small businessmen to run their own shows only to lose their savings or to sell out to the larger competitors has in one sense meant the freedom to widen the gap between losers and winners.

Even so, the right to enter the lists is widely cherished, although it may mean joining the ranks of the vanquished. How expensive a luxury that may be to the American economy is an unanswered question. In fact, back of our other anxieties about small business is our irksome ignorance of just what does take place in the succession of births and deaths in small business.

Basic information on the cost of the turnover in small enterprise is lacking to such an extent that few conclusions can be drawn. Business firms are counted and classified at census time, and rough estimates are made of entries into and exits from the business population during the intervening years. But this is simply a count. We know next to nothing about the character of these individual entries and discontinuances of small enterprises—how much has been invested in the new enterprises or how much has been lost in their individual operations.

We cannot tell if the small enterpriser who drops out would have been better off had he never ventured into a business of his own. The individual cases have not been studied in sufficient numbers or detail to see if, in his apparent failure, the would-be enterpriser still came out ahead. We do know that at least in some cases, while the little grocer or clothier was in the process of becoming a "failure," his family was getting bread and milk from the store into the kitchen, that shirts and shoes were likewise available from the stock, that these contributed toward a total living which compared favorably with what might otherwise have been done at the time. Especially when matched against the alternative of unemployment, the venture might well be worth the few hundred dollars of savings. Out of such experiences have evolved new starts and occasional final successes. The restless individual who has had such a lesson in the responsibilities and tribulations of being his own boss is likely to reenter employment for others with a new tolerance and a new willingness to cooperate as an employee.

Meanwhile, the flow of new enterprisers offers a salutary threat to the perpetuation of monopoly. The best of the newcomers activate industry with new investment and new ideas, needling established companies into competitive alertness and increased efficiency. Small enterprisers help keep the advantages of a competitive market open to the consumer. There is less chance for a "public-be-damned" policy as long as little enterprises, with their individualized catering to customers, are around to woo customers away. As to employment, the small, independent firm provides its managers and employees with outlets for their versatility that form a valuable leaven in a mass-production economy.

Partly for such reasons as these the conservation of small business must be considered an important objective—even while we derive benefit from mass production—in the fashioning of a balanced, virile economy.

### *A Trend to Be Reversed*

The widespread fear that small business is being crowded out in an unequal struggle for survival has one source antedating the war, in the popular identification of size with know-how and stability. Over the past generation savings have gravitated toward investment in companies listed on the Stock Exchange rather than in small companies. The prestige that attaches to the large firm has come to have an appeal for the young man seeking a career, even though the chances are that his place therein would be a minor one. It is big business that catches the public eye with the advertisement of its achievements.

Technological resources and the miracles of modern research are associated with big business. Business schools and engineering schools have been largely concerned with developing the professional skills for which big companies offer the obvious market. In spite of the traditional blessing of independent enterprise, little has been done to dignify business ownership as worthy of professional or educational attention.

Those who are concerned with the future of small business are anxious to see this psychology reversed. They would like to see the best talent of the next generation go into self-employment and business ownership, thus to give full play to the capacities of people with courage, versatility, and imagination. It is partly for this reason that legislation is evolving to make small-business entry more attractive, to liberalize credit and to make taxation less burdensome on small business, and to encourage public and private services for the guidance of small enterprises.

## THE NEED FOR NEW SMALL BUSINESS

In the total of 45 million persons gainfully employed as of 1939, business firms outside of agriculture accounted for 28 million; of that business total about two-fifths, or roughly 11 million, gained their livelihood from the 3.3 million firms with 0 to 50 employees. Using those bench marks, we may say that if productive civilian employment is to continue for 55 million of the 60 million currently in the postwar labor force, without further concentration of our economy in big business, then small business must be organized to furnish a livelihood for not less than 14 million persons in 4 million small enterprises.

What are the chances of small business retaining such a major role in the postwar economy?

From 1941 to 1943 the number of operating business enterprises in industry and trade was reduced by about one-sixth; the net loss was roughly from 3.3 to 2.8 million. This wartime reduction in the number of small business units was not accompanied by a net loss in the nation's business activity, for the obvious reason that the personnel removed from small business was not idle; it was employed in the business of war—not only in the armed forces but also in the production of war materials and in wartime services on the home front.

With the end of the war the trend in numbers was reversed. The self-employed who had been drawn into the home-front army as munitions workers, truckmen, and other wartime help went back to their automobile agencies and filling stations, their specialty shops, and their sales routes. Servicemen formerly in small business also returned to proprietorships that they had abandoned with the onset of war. To their numbers have been added thousands of other workers opening their own establishments with the accumulated savings of four years of high wartime wages. Many a man in the armed forces has eagerly turned his back on the discipline of military organization to reenter civilian life as his own chief. Others are still preparing for or in search of the right opening; at least 30 per cent of the men in the service had planned to assume business ownership, according to the sample polls taken while they were in uniform.

The fact that so many want to enter the ranks of small business and that we actually have witnessed a mushrooming of small business to a new peak is itself no assurance that postwar small business will thrive. The very number of new or enlarged ventures is another matter of concern in visualizing the future of small business. A large fraction of those who have opened new businesses have little or no experience in the field. Unquestionably, many have underestimated the capital and the knowledge needed to compete successfully with established business, especially since the level of management and quality of equipment required to hang on in the postwar business world is bound to be higher than it was before the war.

These considerations make it in the public interest to scrutinize existing economic and legal policy and practice that affect small business to assure that all comers have a reasonable chance of success in the postwar competition.

Recognition of this responsibility is reflected in current voluntary efforts of private civic groups and, more extensively, in legislative proposals for educating, assisting financially, and otherwise guiding the small businessman. The guidance of newcomers to the field at this particular time has political and social implications that should be generally recognized; disillusionment on a large scale must be anticipated if entrants have been oversold on the values of proprietorship and not sufficiently cautioned as to the necessary financial and personal resources. It would, however, be a mistake to throw a wet blanket over the ambitions of those who with reason seek to enter business. It is better to err on the side of constructive encouragement, implemented by assistance in clearing away handicaps, thereby promoting productive small enterprises. Unless this is done, the expansion in postwar employment is less likely to be held.

Small business is a field in which anyone may consider himself an expert, and no one can have an adequate grasp of the whole field. It encompasses enterprises too small to have any use for a bank as well as corporations that are just not big enough to float their securities on the Stock Exchange. In the present small enterprise of authorship, the author has no illusions that he has sensed all the noteworthy problems confronting small business. He can only trust that his selection of subject matter will be significant and that his analysis will reflect less heat and somewhat more light than some of the ebullient disputation to which the airing of small business problems usually gives rise.

The amenities having been served with an introductory chapter on the *why* of small business and the to-do about it, we are ready for the overdue question, "What *is* small business?" Definition of the term is the business of the next chapter and a necessary first step in the analysis of the problems confronting small business.

## II. WHAT IS SMALL BUSINESS?

THE TERM "small business" is so commonly used that its meaning is usually taken for granted. Yet it has markedly different connotations for different people. The dividing line between "large" business and "small" business is, for instance, higher for manufacturers than for distributors, higher for wholesalers than for retailers, higher for dealers in commodities than for dealers in services. It is not possible to draw any mathematical boundary to take in all firms that could reasonably be classed as smaller business for some purposes, without including a number that could, just as reasonably, be classed as "medium" or even "big." We have to fall back on an assortment of criteria that provides elastic limits for small business. If the obviously small units are put in one sector and the giants in another, we can also recognize a middle-size group that shares the headaches of small business for some purposes and of big business for others.

### DEFINITION BY SIZE

How small must a firm be to be regarded officially as small business? Let us start with the statistics of the business population furnished by the Census Bureau and used by other divisions of the Department of Commerce.

#### *Department of Commerce Classification*

*Manufacturers* are within the Census classification of small business if they employ less than 100 people. That could place the dividing line, dollarwise, at from half a million to a million in annual sales, depending on the percentage of total value added by labor; with total assets averaging in the neighborhood of $250,000 and net worth around $100,000.

For *wholesalers*, Commerce shifts its yardstick to volume of sales rather than number of employees. It excludes from the ranks of small business any wholesaler with sales exceeding $200,000–a volume that may readily be reached, in wholesaling, with less than a dozen employees.

*Retail and service* enterprises, along with construction, hotels, and amusements, are classified on the basis of sales or receipts. Retail and service businesses are classed as "small" if annual sales or receipts are within $50,000. That volume is obtainable with less than half a dozen employees in retailing but may require up to 20 employees in some personal-service lines.

Application of these arbitrary upper limits established by the Commerce Department classification would give to small business roughly 92 per cent of all business establishments other than farms and professional offices, 45 per cent of the total personnel in business, and 34 per cent of the total value of output or sales. A percentage distribution derived by the Bureau of Foreign and Domestic Commerce from the last census of business is as follows:

TABLE 1

PERCENTAGE OF SMALL BUSINESS IN U.S., TOTAL*

| *Industry or trade* | *Establishments* | *Personnel* | *Value of output, sales, or receipts* |
|---|---|---|---|
| Manufacturing† | 91.6 | 29.9 | 30.6 |
| Wholesaling | 77.2 | 39.0 | 21.1 |
| Retailing | 91.2 | 56.2 | 42.4 |
| Service establishments | 98.7 | 73.8 | 65.5 |
| Hotels | 90.1 | 30.7 | 26.5 |
| Construction | 93.1 | 47.0 | 34.2 |
| Places of amusement | 89.8 | 56.6 | 33.3 |
| All industry | 92.5 | 44.8 | 34.1 |

* SOURCE: *Census of Business, 1939.*

† Proprietors and employees are included except for manufacturing, under which the Census tabulated only manufacturing *employees*. The total of output, sales, and receipts for the small businesses represented in the table was $43.6 billion, of which retailing and manufacturing each accounted for about 40 per cent.

## *Bureau of Labor Statistics (BLS) Definition*

We shall comment further on the Commerce definition of small business after looking at another widely-used measure for small business by size—that of the Bureau of Labor Statistics. The BLS has determined what small business is by establishing an "average size" in volume of employment for a number of industries and classing as "small" those establishments which fall below the average.

For *manufacturing*, the BLS finds that the average number of employees per establishment in the *Census of Business, 1939*, was 43. Hence, any plant with less than 43 employees is "small business" to the BLS, as against the 100-employee limit in the Department of Commerce.

For *wholesaling*, the BLS gets an average of $209,000 in sales; there it comes very close to coinciding with the ceiling for small business in the Commerce Department data.

In *retailing*, use of the average sets the BLS limit for small business at annual sales of $20,000, as against the $50,000 set by the Commerce Department. Even this lower limit takes in four-fifths of the establishments and 43.6 per cent of the employees in independent retail trade. Since the majority of retail establishments are manned solely by the owner, with no employees, adding proprietors to the number of wage earners would bring prewar personnel of the independent retailers within the $20,000 sales limit close to 60 per cent of the total.

For *service businesses*, the average of annual receipts per establishment puts the BLS dividing line at approximately $5,000—one-tenth of the dollar volume in the Commerce definition. Even this reduced ceiling still covers 87.7 per cent of service firms. If we include working proprietors with employees, 65 per cent of the personnel engaged in the service industries were, in prewar establishments, below the $5,000 limit as to annual receipts.

The use of the BLS averages provides marked contrasts from one industry category to another, notably in manufacturing. Thus, in rubber manufactures a plant of 203 workers would be under the average and, hence, small business. In printing and publishing, on the other hand, a firm in the small-business class would employ 13 or less.

A division of establishments and employees into small businesses and larger units, according to the BLS categories, is shown in the accompanying chart.[1]

[1] The distribution given in the BLS chart is by *wage earners*, hence understates the number of persons engaged in small business. More than 1.5 million firms, mainly in retail trade and the service businesses, hire no employees. In the case of manufacturers the chart (following the *Census of Business*) shows only the employees engaged directly in manufacturing. This omits approximately three million salaried and executive employees in manufacturing companies (see Chap. III).

## *What is Small Business?*

In analyzing financial problems of small corporations engaged in manufacturing, it has been common practice to set the dividing line between small and medium-size business notably higher, count-

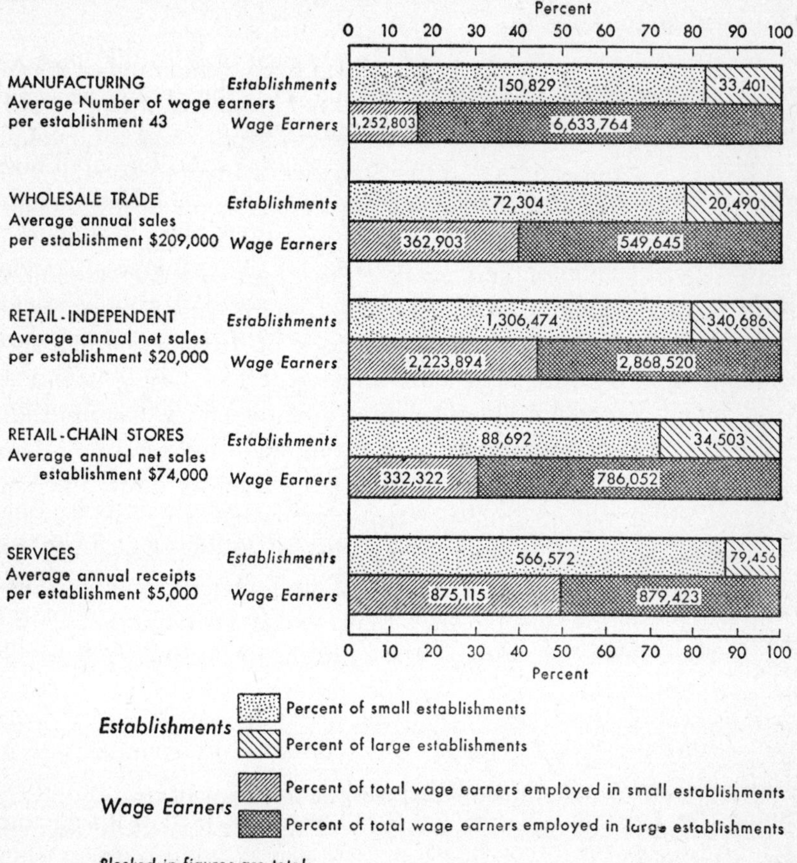


CHART 1. Proportions of large and small establishments and distribution of wage earners in 1939. (*Data from Census of Manufactures, Census of Business, 1939, and compiled by the U.S. Bureau of Labor Statistics. See Hearings before the Senate Small Business Committee, 77th Congress, 1st Session, Part* 12, *pp.* 1744–1745.)

ing as "small" plants with up to 250 wage earners. This was the demarcation used in the report of the TNEC and more recently by Congress for purposes of preferential treatment for small business in the sale of government surpluses.[1] On that basis, 97 per

[1] Reconversion Act of 1944, approved Oct. 3, 1944.

cent of all manufacturing establishments, employing 48 per cent of the factory wage earners, could be classed as small business in 1939.

*Size by Assets and Income*

Thus far we have measured business size by the number of persons engaged and the amount of annual business. Other yardsticks for business size include assets—net or gross—and net income.

From the Census data and the Statistics of Income issued by the Bureau of Internal Revenue, we can derive a rule of thumb that puts the average plant of 100 employees in the same class as a plant with $250,000 of total assets. The figure of $250,000 of total assets has the convenience of being a standard classification in the Bureau of Internal Revenue's Statistics of Income, a valuable source frequently utilized in separating small from larger businesses in financial studies.[1] The Securities and Exchange Commission, the TNEC, the National Bureau of Economic Research, and others have used the $250,000 of gross assets figure to mark the line between small and medium-size manufacturers.

Obviously, total assets do not give a precise yardstick. A broker's office may turn over several million dollars of business with little tangible assets other than the office furniture. In a highly mechanized glass plant, by contrast, gross assets may match annual sales. But within a given industry, particularly in one that runs to a fairly uniform pattern, comparison by size of assets is valid.

*Net income* has also been employed as a means of distinguishing small business from medium or large. The TNEC used the income limit of $25,000 for small business, $50,000 for medium-size business, and any income above $50,000 as large business. Here again, wide variations must be kept in mind. Obviously, even large firms may not make a net profit of $25,000 in poor years, and little

[1] The Bureau of Internal Revenue also classifies by net capital assets, which consists of "(1) depreciable tangible assets such as buildings, fixed mechanical equipment, manufacturing facilities, transportation facilities, and furniture and fixtures, (2) depletable tangible assets—natural resources, (3) intangible assets such as patents, franchises, formulas, copyrights, leaseholds, good will, and trademarks, and (4) land." *Statistics of Income for 1941*, Part 2, p. 236. Capital assets run, on the average, between 35 and 40 per cent of gross assets.

ones may exceed it in favorable years. Thus in 1939 a net annual operating profit of $25,000 was generally associated with manufacturers in the bracket above a million dollars of total assets. But in 1941 that income was often reached by corporations having less than a quarter million in total assets.[1]

The following table is a rough composite of the limits of size commonly employed in official data to identify firms that are taken to be unquestionably within the classification of small business:

TABLE 2

| *Criterion* | *Manufacturing* | *Wholesale* | *Retail and service* |
|---|---|---|---|
| Number of employees | 100 | 10 | 10 |
| Sales or receipts | $500,000 | $200,000 | $50,000 |
| Total assets | 250,000 | 50,000 | 15,000 |
| Net worth | 150,000 | 25,000 | 10,000 |
| Net profits | 12,500 | 10,000* | 3,500* |

* Includes owners' compensation.

## *Limitations of the Size Classification*

Classification of small business in terms of physical volume is useful and convenient for tabulation of over-all statistics, but it is not expected to cover all firms that have small-business problems. When the Department of Commerce defines a small retail business as one with sales under $50,000, it is merely indicating that a retail store doing more than $50,000 a year of sales is relatively not small, considering the common run of small retail stores. And when the BLS divides service establishments at $5,000 of receipts, it is merely reflecting the fact that the majority of service shops have been under that figure. Neither of these categories has any bearing on what is considered small among manufacturers. Moreover, a retail shop with sales volume several times $50,000 may have financial growing pains or financial handicaps akin to those of the manufacturer with 99 employees, whose establishment is officially classified as small business.

*Intraclass Variations.* Even moderate assumptions about the accuracy of size classifications, as applicable within major areas

[1] Bureau of Internal Revenue, *Statistics of Income for 1939, Part 2* and *Statistics of Income for 1941, Part 2.*

of business, need reservations in a comparison between specific and apparently related lines. For example, there are two main types of wholesale drug business: One is the so-called "service" or regular pharmacy wholesaler; the other deals mainly in cosmetics and sundry specialties carried in drugstores. The contrast in their respective size distributions is shown in Table 3.

TABLE 3

| *Sales-volume class* | *Number of establishments* | *Sales* | *Personnel* |
|---|---|---|---|
| Service wholesalers (without liquor) | | | |
| (= 100%) | (214) | ($251,534,000) | (11,796) |
| Under $100,000 | 2.8% | 0.1% | 0.2% |
| 100,000–199,999 | 3.3 | 0.4 | 0.5 |
| 200,000–299,999 | 9.3 | 2.1 | 2.8 |
| 300,000–499,999 | 14.5 | 5.2 | 5.4 |
| 500,000–999,999 | 25.7 | 16.9 | 17.2 |
| 1,000,000 and over | 44.4 | 75.3 | 73.9 |
| Specialties and sundries (= 100%) | (484) | ($60,385,000) | (3,139) |
| Under $10,000 | 17.3% | 0.8% | 4.1% |
| 10,000–49,999 | 43.2 | 8.7 | 21.1 |
| 50,000–99,999 | 19.4 | 10.9 | 16.3 |
| 100,000–199,999 | 12.6 | 14.1 | 18.7 |
| 200,000–299,999 | 2.3 | 4.5 | 6.8 |
| 300,000 and over | 5.2 | 61.0 | 33.0 |

Here we have two related lines catering to the same retail druggists. In the first group, 214 establishments do an aggregate business of a quarter billion dollars. Only 6 per cent of the drug wholesalers in this group would qualify as small business by the Commerce Department's test. In the second (drug specialties), 484 wholesale firms do an aggregate business of only $60 million, and over 92 per cent come inside the small business ceiling of $200,000 in sales volume. Clearly, our conclusion as to smallness or bigness of business must be conditioned by the character of the particular field in which it operates.

## POSITION IN THE INDUSTRY

The operators of a business themselves usually measure its smallness or bigness by the position it occupies in its own industry. In the classic case of the automobile industry, Hudson, Packard, and Studebaker are thought of as small manufacturers as compared with Chrysler, Ford, or General Motors, although no one would pretend that they are small in the absolute sense. Any one of them, with more than $50 million of annual sales in prewar years and with its securities well established on the Stock Exchange, would rate as the giant in many another industry.

More debatable is the question as to whether a refrigerator firm or a tire firm doing a business up to $5 million could in any circumstances be regarded as small business. From testimony at Congressional hearings of the Senate and House Small Business Committees, it is evident that such firms have had very serious and sympathetic consideration given to their handicap of "smallness" in competition with the big-name firms of their respective industries, particularly on war contracts. When it came to obtaining working capital for a big job or for general expansion, the wartime definition of a small business was elastic enough to allow the inclusion, for financing by the Smaller War Plants Corporation, of $5-million firms competing with larger companies.

## ORGANIZATION AND OPERATION

In studying the problems that go with smallness, we must take account of characteristics other than those of size, whether physical or financial. Small business means, typically, an identity of management and ownership, an absence of specialized staff for separate functions and of facilities designed specifically for research and analysis, inability to finance itself by floating securities or to secure its funds through sources such as investment bankers, a personal relationship between owners and employees and customers, the affiliation of the firm with a local community, and chief dependence for its market on the local area. These factors, when present in combination, make a small business recognizable as such even when its volume of business is substantial.

*Type of Management.* Simplicity of organization is a well-recognized criterion for small business. The small business establishment is popularly referred to as an "independent." That is to say, its management is not controlled from a central office that determines policy for subsidiary units. This singleness or independence is a distinction that runs through voluminous hearings of the Federal Trade Commission and various Congressional committees, in which independent dealers contrast their position to that of the chains or the factory-owned outlets of the large manufacturer.[1]

The simplicity of organization that marks an enterprise as small business is reflected in the identity of ownership and management. The small business is most typically the business of a single proprietor or a partnership. It means a job as well as an investment to its owner. Less than 10 per cent of small business is incorporated; when the corporate form is used, the ownership is usually confined to a small group, perhaps a close-knit trio or quartet who own all the stock and share the management of the enterprise, dividing their talents among production, purchases and sales, and finance or office control. To preserve owner-management, the small business often deliberately limits its growth to a rate that can be supported by the profits of the enterprise, rather than reaching out for capital that may bring in outsiders and weaken the control of the original group.

In general, not only is small business owner-managed, but the management maintains direct contact with the labor force. As far as possible, the owner himself selects his employees; the owner, working along with his employees, strives for and expects a relationship of mutual loyalty.[2] An introduction of intermediate steps between owner and workers, with department heads given differing functions of management, is symptomatic of the transition from small to medium-size and large business. When a firm acquires diffused absentee ownership, stockholders who are strangers to the establishment, and specialized management divorced from ownership, it has acquired some of the chief characteristics of big business.

*Market Limitations.* The small business—typically, though with notable exceptions—finds its chief market in and around its own community. One argument for the establishment of the SWPC was that small business did not get its share of war contracts because

[1] *Cf.* Di Venuti, *Small Business Problem Discussions*, Senate Small Business Committee, March, 1941.

[2] The emphasis on personal loyalty cropped up frequently in the small-business survey made for the Committee for Economic Development by the National Opinion Research Center, small proprietors complaining of "union interference" with the mutuality of interest which they claimed they had formerly enjoyed with their workers.

the thousands of small businessmen could not afford to maintain their own pipe lines to the procurement offices in Washington.

By this test, a physically large plant may be rated as small business as long as it remains tied to its own community. This was illustrated in an appearance before the Senate Small Business Committee by a labor leader seeking war business for a refrigerator plant with 3,000 employees. "Now you would not consider a company employing 3,000 men a small business, would you?" a Senator asked him. The reply was, "Yes, sir, that is small business in my thinking." The union man then explained that the company in question was an "independent" and was very small alongside a competitor like General Electric. He added, "I say they are small business because they are part of that local community and haven't any way of maneuvering their manufactures around or moving their plant to other towns and shoving their people around." The acquiescence of the committee was expressed in the response of its chairman, Senator Murray: "I have always considered a concern small if it is free and independent and does not spread over a number of states, with branches throughout the country."[1]

## YARDSTICKS OF PUBLIC SPOKESMEN

A palpable fact is that really small-size business units—the establishments of less than eight employees, which make up 90 per cent of all business firms and about 23 per cent of the earners (including proprietors)—are not the ones that account for the bulk of the public discussion of small business and its problems. Almost invariably, the business representatives who appear to plead the case of small business before the FTC or the Antitrust Division or the Small Business Committees of Congress are themselves within the top 10 per cent of business enterprises.

It is true that aid to veterans seeking to open very small businesses received attention in reconversion legislation. But except for this gesture, federal legislation attempting to meet the special problems of small business has its direct practical application mainly within the group of some 24,000 manufacturers in the employment range of 50 to 500 workers per establishment.

[1] Senate Small Business Committee, 77th Congress, 1st Session Hearings, Dec. 16, 1941, Part I, pp. 80–81.

The Reconversion Act of 1944 supplies one of the rare instances in which Congress offers a definition of small business. In connection with the proviso to give special consideration to small plants in the allocation of surplus war materials, it states:[1]

For the purpose of this title, a small plant means any small business concern engaged primarily in production or manufacturing either employing 250 wage earners or less or coming within such other categories as may be established by the head of such executive agency in consultation with the chairman of the Board of Directors of the Smaller War Plants Corporation. Such other categories should be defined by taking into consideration the comparative sizes of establishments in a particular industry as reflected by sales volumes, quantities of materials consumed, capital investments or by other criteria which are reasonably attributable to small plants rather than medium- or large-size plants.

The views of Congress on what constitutes small business are of interest as a reflection of the more articulate public opinion on the postwar requirements of small business. In a reconversion bill introduced on behalf of the Senate Small Business Committee, the stated purpose was, "To stimulate and encourage small business enterprise," and it defined a small business as

Any enterprise for profit which,

If engaged primarily in production or manufacturing, shall have employed 500 persons or less for the calendar year next preceding . . . or

If primarily a wholesale establishment, whose net sales shall aggregate not more than a million dollars for such calendar year; or

If primarily a retail, amusement, service, or construction establishment, whose net sales or receipts for such calendar year shall aggregate not more than $250,000.

Provided that [the business] shall not include any business concern which [is] a dominating unit in its trade or industry or otherwise under the management or control of such dominating unit.

In making such determination . . . shall consider the comparative size of establishments in the particular trade or industry involved.[2]

In this reflection of Congressional thinking, three factors stand out as entitling a firm to consideration as small business—limited

[1] Public Law 458, passed by 78th Congress, 2d Session, Oct. 3, 1944. War Mobilization and Reconversion Act of 1944, Title II, Sec. 204.

[2] *S.* 1913, introduced in 78th Congress, 1st Session.

size, comparatively low position in the industry, and the necessity of facing its competition independently. Under this definition by the Senate Small Business Committee, all but 0.12 per cent of the business establishments of the nation would come under the blanket of small business. In other words, if the goal is a healthy growth of independent business, all but the acknowledged giants of American business—all but 3,600 companies at the top of the heap of 3 million—may in some connections be treated as small business.

## THE COMPOSITE DEFINITION

With this review of the problems of classifying small business and the number of definitions, valid or otherwise, that exist, it is not surprising that the term "small business" is sometimes called a slogan and not a description of an area of enterprise.

It is clear, however, that any approach to a common denominator for small business must consider the following:

*Size.* Arbitrary limits of $1 million for volume of business, $500,000 for total assets, and 250 employees for personnel would not be too high, especially if we think of small business as the kind of business intended to strengthen independent individual enterprise and vigorous competition to cope with the growth of monopoly.

*Management.* On the score of management, the term "small business" should be reserved for the type of firm that consists of a single independent organization directly under the supervision of its owners, who are also its managers—whether incorporated or not. Where there is a divorce of management from ownership and intervening authority between owner and employees or between owner and customers, the concern is not conducted as a small business.

*Financing.* The equity capital of small business is held within the inner circle of owner-managers. Small business does not ordinarily go into the open market to sell securities or credit paper but depends on commercial credit, bank credit, and plowed-in profits to meet its financial requirements.

*Area of Operations.* Typically, small business is local in character, although there are exceptions as obvious as importing and exporting. Integration with the home locality is found in ownership, product, workers, and customers, so that small enterprise ordinarily has a direct tie with the growth and well-being of the community in which it resides.

These limits put more than 95 per cent of the businesses of the nation within our definition and about half of the persons employed in nonagricultural enterprise. What small business needs in the way of special help, therefore, is not one program, but a number of programs tailored to its successive levels—to the million establishments of the self-employed with net worth under a thousand dollars, as well as to the small department store or the independent factory whose pay roll may be the main support of the home town. Later chapters will specify these needs.

It is not to be expected that available data, upon which we shall have to depend for the analysis of the small-business area, will fit perfectly into the composite definition at which we have here arrived. Interpolating will often be required, on the part of the reader as well as the author, so that available figures may afford a truer perspective on the problem under discussion.

An analysis of the prewar position of small business in different lines of industry is the subject of the next chapter.

## III. PREWAR AND POSTWAR PATTERN

NOT ALL ASPECTS of the importance we attach to small business can be determined quantitatively. Figures will not accurately measure the convenience to residents of having small enterprises in their neighborhood or the contribution of the sawmill, foundry, or repair shop that takes orders too small for a large firm or the value to the community of the drugstores and delicatessen shops that remain open for the late worker. Values hidden in the sense of community well-being and confidence in our form of society, which the average American derives from the presence of millions of small independent proprietors adding body to the so-called American "middle class," likewise escape measurement.

We can, however, get some idea of the quantitative significance of small business in the economy through the number of firms and the number of people they support; the volume of sales, receipts or output; and the numbers on the pay rolls of small business. We can also learn something of the structure of small business and its many variations by noting the relative position of small enterprises in specific industrial groups.

The statistics of the business population given here are derived largely from the Census of Business. Although some changes in the totals have taken place since the last business census in 1939, more recent estimates by the Department of Commerce do not show that the prewar pattern has been disturbed appreciably.[1]

### BUSINESS POPULATION BY SIZE

*Number of Firms*

For a first perspective on the business pattern, we may break down the business population of 3.3 million firms into a few groups based on the number of employees per firm (see Table 4).

The housewife may be less surprised than the industry executive

[1] See "The Business Population in Wartime," *Survey of Current Business*, May, 1944; "The Post-war Business Population," *Survey of Current Business*, January, 1947.

to find that the most numerous type of business firm by far is the one-man enterprise—the self-employed individual operating his retail store, repair shop, filling station, etc. This is the small business which rarely knows a banker, is seldom listed by Dun & Bradstreet, and is not accounted for in the Statistics of Income by the Bureau of Internal Revenue. Its prewar annual sales or receipts were less than $3,000. If its proprietor were to come across this volume and turn to the chapter on financing, he would probably regard the subject matter as utterly alien to what he calls small business. The million and a half of these one-man firms constitute more than 45 per cent of all nonfarm enterprises. Almost as numerous are business units employing from one to three people. The million and a quarter businesses of this size represent nearly three-eighths of the total number of firms.

These enterprises amount to 82 per cent of the total number of business firms. If firms employing from 4 to 100 people are added to their total, all but 27,000 of the nation's 3,300,000 business firms outside farming are accounted for. Thus, in the prewar pattern less than 1 per cent of the nation's business enterprises consisted of companies with 100 or more employees.

If we hold to the ceiling of 250 employees used for our composite definition of small business in the previous chapter, we should include nearly 16,000 firms that had more than 100 but less than 250 employees. That would leave only about 11,000 firms to represent the intermediate and big business classifications.[1]

### *Number of Employees*

The pattern changes sharply, however, if, instead of comparing the number of firms, we compare the number of persons who get their livelihood from small and big business. Table 4 shows that approximately 28.7 million persons earned their livelihood in business establishments in 1939. The tiny shops whose proprietors

[1] For detailed breakdown by industry and size, see Appendix Table 1. The estimates of number of firms made by the Department of Commerce run about 50 per cent higher than those given in the standard series of Dun & Bradstreet. The difference is accounted for by about a million very small businesses, for which Dun & Bradstreet obtains no credit ratings. The Dun & Bradstreet totals exclude many of the common service establishments like barber shops, beauty parlors, cleaners and dyers, etc., as well as the very small retailers.

TABLE 4

ESTIMATED NUMBER OF BUSINESS FIRMS AND PERSONS ENGAGED BY SIZE OF BUSINESS*
(1939)

| *Size class, by number of employees per firm* | *A* | | *B* | |
|---|---|---|---|---|
| | *Number of firms* | *Per cent* | *Number of persons engaged* | *Per cent* |
| Total | 3,316,700 | 100.0 | 28,707,500 | 100.0 |
| No employees, total | 1,503,200 | 45.3 | 1,844,400 | 6.4 |
| 1–100, total | 1,786,600 | 53.9 | 10,907,400 | 38.0 |
| 1–3 | 1,221,200 | 36.8 | 3,165,400 | 11.0 |
| 4–7 | 304,600 | 9.2 | 1,805,800 | 6.3 |
| 8–19 | 165,700 | 5.0 | 2,018,300 | 7.0 |
| 20–49 | 69,600 | 2.1 | 2,103,300 | 7.4 |
| 50–99 | 25,500 | 0.8 | 1,814,600 | 6.3 |
| 100 and over | 26,900 | 0.8 | 15,955,700 | 56.6 |
| 100–249 | 15,700 | 0.5 | 2,394,800 | 8.4 |
| 250–499 | 6,300 | 0.2 | 2,071,900 | 7.2 |
| 500 or more | 4,900 | 0.1 | 11,489,000 | 40.0 |

* SOURCE: Bureau of Foreign and Domestic Commerce, Business Structure Unit. Estimates include paid employees, enterprisers, and family workers. Because of rounding, the totals in this and succeeding tables do not necessarily equal the sum of the components.

hire no help accounted for roughly 6 per cent of that total. Enterprises employing from 1 to 100 employees accounted for another

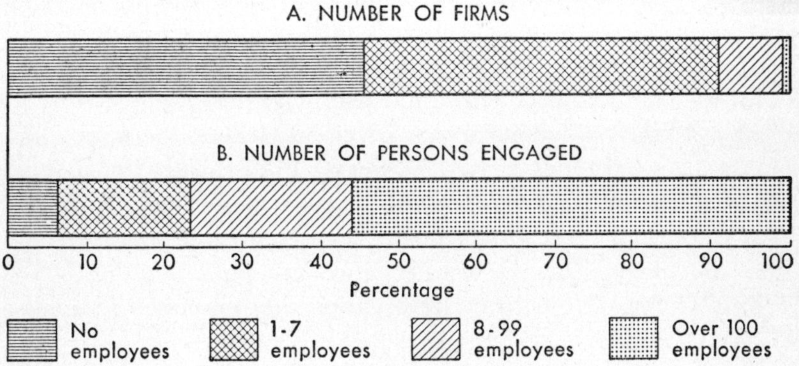

A. NUMBER OF FIRMS

B. NUMBER OF PERSONS ENGAGED

0 10 20 30 40 50 60 70 80 90 100

Percentage

No employees | 1-7 employees | 8-99 employees | Over 100 employees

CHART 2.

Source: Adapted from Table 4, above.

38 per cent. Companies employing 100 persons or more, though less than 1 per cent of all firms, provided jobs for 16 million earners,

or 56 per cent of all business personnel. If we set the dividing line between medium-size and big business at 500 employees, then we see that there were 11.5 million employees in the 4,900 largest enterprises, or 40 per cent of the total employed in business.

*Business Population by Industry and Size*

The relative importance of big and little firms in major industrial categories may be seen from Tables 5 and 6. As Table 5 shows, about three-fourths of all the little enterprises are in the retail trade and the common service industries. Medium-size and big firms are chiefly in manufacturing. The parallel Table 6 shows that more than half of the employment provided by small business is in distribution and services and that manufacturing provides the bulk of the employment in large establishments.

It would be a mistake, however, to discount the cumulative effect on the total economic picture of the factory, mine, or construction unit employing less than 100 workers. These smaller industrial enterprises taken together employ 3.5 million people. (The importance of such firms is analyzed in later sections on the separate industries.)

*Volume of Business*

Unfortunately, the tables showing number of employees do not have exact counterparts for the dollar amount of business done. In the Census data, distribution and services lines are classified by amount of sales or receipts, and manufacturers are sorted by the number of their wage earners. Using $50,000 as the upper limit for small retail and service business, that dollar classification excludes from the ranks of small business many firms with from 15 to 100 employees. Nevertheless, it will serve our present general purpose to draw upon the Census figures as adapted by the Department of Commerce, with the reservation that the limits set tend to understate the business done by small enterprise.

In amount of business done, the units classified by Commerce as small business accounted for about 34 per cent of the total value of the sales or output. Here, as in the matter of employment, there is a wide variation among the different areas of business (see Table 7). Although wholesalers in the small-business classification had

TABLE 5

ESTIMATED NUMBER OF OPERATING BUSINESS FIRMS, BY INDUSTRY AND SIZE, 1939*
(In thousands)

| *Industry* | *Total all size classes* | *0–99 employees* | *Per cent* | *100 employees and over* | *Per cent* |
|---|---|---|---|---|---|
| Total, all industries | 3,316.7 | 3,289.7 | 100.0 | 27.0 | 100.0 |
| Mining | 21.4 | 20.3 | 0.6 | 1.2 | 4.4 |
| Contract construction | 202.1 | 200.6 | 6.1 | 1.5 | 5.6 |
| Manufacturing | 214.2 | 199.9 | 6.1 | 14.3 | 53.0 |
| Transportation, communication, and public utilities | 207.7 | 205.4 | 6.2 | 2.3 | 8.5 |
| Wholesale trade | 144.8 | 143.2 | 4.3 | 1.7 | 6.3 |
| Retail trade | 1,601.4 | 1,598.5 | 48.6 | 3.0 | 11.1 |
| Service industries | 638.7 | 636.9 | 19.4 | 1.8 | 6.7 |
| Finance, insurance, and real estate | 286.4 | 285.2 | 8.7 | 1.2 | 4.4 |

TABLE 6

ESTIMATED EMPLOYMENT INCLUDING PAID EMPLOYEES, ENTREPRENEURS, AND UNPAID FAMILY WORKERS BY INDUSTRY AND SIZE OF FIRM, 1939*
(In thousands)

| *Industry* | *Total all size classes* | *0–99 employees* | *Per cent* | *100 employees and over* | *Per cent* |
|---|---|---|---|---|---|
| Total, all industries | 28,707.5 | 12,751.8 | 100.0 | 15,955.7 | 100.0 |
| Mining | 790.1 | 237.4 | 1.9 | 552.7 | 3.5 |
| Contract construction | 1,457.8 | 912.0 | 7.1 | 545.8 | 3.4 |
| Manufacturing | 11,270.6 | 2,417.6 | 19.0 | 8,853.0 | 55.5 |
| Transportation, communication, and public utilities | 2,968.0 | 638.8 | 5.0 | 2,329.2 | 14.6 |
| Wholesale trade | 1,572.2 | 952.7 | 7.5 | 619.5 | 3.9 |
| Retail trade | 6,663.4 | 4,909.2 | 38.5 | 1,754.2 | 11.0 |
| Service industries | 2,645.4 | 1,788.7 | 14.0 | 856.7 | 5.4 |
| Finance, insurance, and real estate | 1,340.0 | 895.4 | 7.0 | 444.6 | 2.7 |

* *Survey of Current Business*, May, 1944, pp. 12–13, revised.

only about 21 per cent of the total volume of sales, small retailers did better than 42 per cent of all the retail business in the country. Service establishments[1] classed as small—meaning under $50,000

[1] Exclusive of transportation and other public utilities, which were not taken in the Census of Business.

of annual receipts—accounted for more than 65 per cent of all receipts.

TABLE 7

Dollar Volume of Small Business in Specified Lines

| *Industry or trade* | *Value of output* | *Percentage of small business in United States total* |
|---|---|---|
| Manufacturing, establishments with less than 100 employees | $17,366,697 | 30.6 |
| Wholesaling, under $200,000 in annual sales | 4,100,404 | 21.1 |
| Under $50,000, annual sales or receipts: | | |
| Retailing | 17,836,171 | 42.4 |
| Service establishments | 2,241,709 | 65.5 |
| Construction | 1,546,891 | 34.2 |
| Places of amusement | 332,837 | 33.3 |
| Hotels | 229,163 | 26.5 |
| Composite small business | 43,653,872 | 34.1 |

Source: *Census of Business, 1939.* Data adapted by C. C. Fichtner, U.S. Bureau of Foreign and Domestic Commerce, 1941, from hearings, Senate Small Business Committee, 77th Congress, 1st Session, Part 1, p. 292.

## THE AREAS OF SMALL BUSINESS

The over-all data presented so far have furnished a rough idea of what part small business is of the nation's total business. A brief look at the major groupings, or kinds, of businesses will tell more specifically where small business dominates and where it is only a frill on the edge of an industry, where it runs to tiny units and where it takes on greater size, where it is apparently slipping and where it is holding its own. Let us begin with distribution businesses.

### *Distribution*

#### *Retail Trade*

Retail stores, operated by 1.6 million firms, are about half the nation's separate business enterprises. Retail trade also accounts for half of the self-employed proprietors with no employees, and half of all independent businesses employing three persons or less.

We have to go far below the official dividing line of $50,000 in annual sales to reach the level of the average retailer. More than 900,000 retailers (54 per cent of the total) had annual sales under $10,000 in 1939. More than 600,000 had annual sales below $5,000, while 300,000 of those had annual sales of less than $2,000. Food shops, including eating and drinking places, were most numerous among these little retailers; behind them were the filling stations and a host of miscellaneous lines, general stores, apparel, accessories, and drugs.

*Chain Stores.* In the retail field much attention has been given by the independent dealers to the spread of chain stores. Whatever threat the chain store may constitute for the independent retailer does not lie in increased numbers. From 1929 to 1939 the number of independent retail stores increased (by 252,000) while the number of chain-store units decreased (from 148,000 to 123,000). In 1929 chain-store units were 9.6 per cent of all retail stores. By 1939 they had dropped to 7 per cent.

It is true that the reduction in the number of chain stores was accompanied by an increase in sales per chain store while sales per independent store declined. The net effect, however, does not represent a drastic change in their relative position. During the decade the relation of chain sales to independent sales moved within a range of 3 per cent as follows:

TABLE 8

| *Year* | *Percentage of retail sales** | |
|---|---|---|
| | *Independent stores* | *Chain and mail order* |
| 1939 | 77.2 | 22.8 |
| 1935 | 75.8 | 24.2 |
| 1929 | 79.1 | 20.9 |

* *Census of Business, 1939*, Vol. 1, Retail Trade, Part 1, pp. 48, 49.

*Department Stores.* The growing popularity of department stores has been a potent factor in competition with the specialized retail store. The 4,000 department stores of the country did a total business of just under $4 billion in 1939. This was 9.5 per cent of all retail sales in that year and 39.3 per cent of the total sales in the nine related kinds of business with which department stores mainly compete.[1] The gain that this represents over the

[1] *Census of Business, 1939*, Vol. 1, Retail Trade, Part 1, p. 14. The nine related kinds of business include general stores (with food), dry goods and general merchan-

previous decade may be seen in the following tabular comparison (Table 9):

TABLE 9
DEPARTMENT STORE SALES

| *Year* | *Sales, millions* | *Per cent of all retail sales* | *Per cent of sales in nine related lines* |
|---|---|---|---|
| 1939 | $3,975 | 9.5 | 39.3 |
| 1935 | 3,311 | 10.1 | 39.6 |
| 1929 | 4,350 | 9.0 | 29.5 |

Although the retail field has to reckon with the great department stores, mail-order houses, and chains in its midst, it remains essentially small business, both in number of firms and in number of employees. As we can see from Table 10, retailers with zero to three employees provide a livelihood for 2.7 million earners, representing 40 per cent of the 6.7 million persons engaged in retail trade. Retailers with 4 to 99 employees add another 2.2 million, leaving only 1.75 million employees with the 2,600 retail firms (chains and independents) in the class of 100 or more employees. The top group included 1,530 stores reporting annual sales of a million dollars or more.

*Wholesale Trade*

Like the retail trade, the great majority of wholesale firms are small establishments. More than one-fifth of the firms consist of the self-employed proprietor, with no employees. Another two-fifths consist of firms with 3 employees or less. Wholesale houses with 100 or more employees make up less than 2 per cent of the total number of wholesalers.

In terms of employment, about half of the persons engaged in wholesaling in 1939 were in firms with less than 50 employees.

Taking the figure of $200,000 annual sales as the limit for small business at wholesale, the Census data show 65 per cent of the units below that figure in 1929 and 75 per cent in 1939. Whole-

dise, variety stores, apparel group, furniture-household-radio group, hardware stores, drugstores, jewelry stores, news dealers.

salers doing less than $200,000 got 12 per cent of the total sales in 1929, but their share rose to 21.2 per cent in 1939.

TABLE 10

DISTRIBUTION OF RETAILERS BY SIZE AND LINE, 1939

| *Retail lines* | *Total all sizes** | *0–3 employees* | *4–99 employees* | *100 employees and over* |
|---|---|---|---|---|
| *A. Number of firms, thousands* | | | | |
| Food stores | 516.7 | 483.5 | 32.9 | 0.4 |
| Eating and drinking places | 295.4 | 239.1 | 56.1 | 0.2 |
| Filling stations | 226.7 | 215.6 | 10.8 | 0.1 |
| Apparel, shoes, accessories | 86.1 | 69.4 | 16.4 | 0.4 |
| General merchandise | 74.5 | 61.8 | 11.4 | 1.1 |
| Hardware, lumber | 69.2 | 51.9 | 17.1 | 0.1 |
| Automotive lines | 53.5 | 30.0 | 23.6 | 0.1 |
| Drugs | 52.2 | 39.6 | 12.6 | 0.1 |
| Home furnishings and appliances | 44.5 | 33.5 | 11.0 | † |
| Other retail | 182.7 | 160.0 | 22.5 | 0.1 |
| Total retail* | 1,601.5 | 1,384.4 | 214.4 | 2.6 |
| *B. Number of employees, thousands* | | | | |
| Food stores | 1,474.4 | 862.0 | 309.4 | 303.0 |
| Eating and drinking places | 1,181.1 | 529.5 | 551.3 | 100.3 |
| Filling stations | 534.9 | 388.7 | 82.7 | 63.5 |
| Apparel, shoes, accessories | 532.3 | 146.2 | 178.2 | 207.9 |
| General merchandise | 1,068.4 | 120.7 | 150.6 | 797.1 |
| Hardware, lumber | 385.8 | 113.1 | 173.0 | 99.7 |
| Automotive lines | 447.9 | 70.0 | 323.1 | 54.8 |
| Drugs | 247.7 | 100.0 | 98.1 | 49.6 |
| Home furnishings and appliances | 218.7 | 71.3 | 123.9 | 23.5 |
| Other retail | 572.2 | 295.0 | 222.4 | 54.8 |
| Total retail | 6,663.4 | 2,696.5 | 2,212.7 | 1,754.2 |

* Owing to rounding, figures do not equal the sum of components.

† Less than 50 firms.

There was a decline in the aggregate value of sales through wholesalers of 17.5 per cent during the 1929–1939 decade. Yet wholesale trade showed a gain of more than 18 per cent in the number of establishments during the same period, suggesting an influx of small wholesalers. The figures for establishments and sales given in the Census are shown in Table 11:[1]

[1] *Census of Business, 1939*, Vol. 2, Table D, p. 8. The field of wholesale trade, as defined for census purposes, is somewhat broader than the usual conception of "whole-

TABLE 11

| *Year* | *Number* | *Net sales* |
|---|---|---|
| 1929 | 168,820 | $66,983,024,000 |
| 1935 | 176,756 | 42,802,913,000 |
| 1939 | 200,573 | 55,265,649,000 |

To some extent, the shift in size classification may reflect the lower prices in 1939 compared with 1929, which would reduce the dollar volumes involved. It seems more likely, however, that some areas of large-scale wholesaling have been reduced by the tendency to by-pass wholesalers, as in the purchase of industrial equipment, and also by the development of large retail enterprises, both independent and chain, that purchase directly from the manufacturer.

The gain in total business done by small wholesalers during the war period was striking, although there was a drop of approximately 20 per cent in the number of wholesale establishments between 1941 and the end of 1943. The shutdowns and suspensions reflected wartime difficulty in getting merchandise, as well as better employment opportunities elsewhere.

### *Services*

Next to retail trade, the service lines—the beauty shops, the cleaners, the repair shops, etc.—provide the widest gateway for the entry of small enterprisers with very limited capital. If we may speak of distribution as typically "small" business, then we may speak of the services as being typically "tiny" business. Entry is easy, and the turnover of population is correspondingly high. In the service industries, the majority of employment was contributed by firms with 0 to 19 employees. In 1939, of the total of 639,000 service firms, 55 per cent hired no help. Another 35 per cent had from 1 to 3 employees. Only one-tenth of the service enterprises, therefore, was big enough to take on 4 or more employees. The more familiar of the service lines, accounting for

saler"; it includes manufacturer-owned sales outlets, petroleum bulk stations, agents, brokers, and assemblers of farm products, as well as the more conventional type of wholesalers. This explains why the number of "wholesale *establishments*," as indicated above, is greater than the number of *firms* indicated in the Appendix.

more than 60 per cent of all service establishments, included the following:[1]

TABLE 12

| | *Number* | *Total annual receipts, (000)* | *Average* |
|---|---|---|---|
| Barber shops | 117,998 | $230,983 | $1,958 |
| Beauty parlors | 83,071 | 231,670 | 2,789 |
| Cleaning and pressing establishments | 52,516 | 140,578 | 2,677 |
| Automobile repair shops | 51,827 | 228,214 | 4,403 |
| Shoe repair shops | 50,115 | 106,737 | 2,130 |
| Hand laundries | 15,245 | 45,783 | 3,003 |
| Blacksmith shops | 16,797 | 22,567 | 1,344 |
| Watch and jewelry repairs | 12,485 | 29,902 | 2,395 |
| Radio repair shops | 10,732 | 21,687 | 2,021 |
| Shoeshine parlors | 7,968 | 8,210 | 1,030 |

The gross receipts of most service firms left little for wages. The great majority did less than $3,000 per annum; only 8,443 service establishments did a business exceeding $50,000 per year. When these at the top are excluded, the remaining 638,000 establishments, taking in 1,295,000 earners (including proprietors), shared, in aggregate, annual receipts of $2,242 million.

It is in the personal-service and repair-service enterprises that the really little businesses are found. The larger service enterprises are mainly hotels, amusements, and the business services (advertising, including billboards and sign painting; credit bureaus; business research; mailing and duplicating; commercial laboratories; etc.). But even in hotels and amusements, close to half of the employment was in enterprises with less than 100 employees.

*Year-to-year Change.* Considering the high turnover and the meager returns available in most cases, there is remarkably little net change, year to year, in the total number of service enterprises. From the boom year 1929 to depression year of 1933 the net decline in number of service establishments was barely 2 per cent, as compared with 32 per cent for manufacturing and 18 per cent for

[1] *Ibid.*, Vol. 3, p. 2. See also Appendix Table 1.

contract construction during the same period.[1] This is true despite the fact that there had been a substantial increase of numbers in the service industries during the decade following the First World War (repair shops had sprung up to match the increase in automobiles, radios, and other mechanical devices). After 1933 the number increased steadily to a new high in 1941. Then new opportunities in war work lured thousands of proprietors of service shops into high wage jobs on war production. The decline in numbers from 1941 to 1943 was about 15 per cent, but the rebound between the end of 1943 and the end of 1946 was at least 20 per cent. Postwar improvements in living standards are reflected in additional service occupations associated with cultural advancement, health, and recreation—areas of elastic demand associated with better living.[2] The business service lines, likewise numerically reduced during the war, have given even more definite indications of revival as peacetime business expands its requirements.

*Transportation, Communication, and Public Utilities*

"Transportation, Communication, and Public Utilities" is the title used in the tabulations made by the Department of Commerce for statistics covering a widely varied range of services in these categories, from self-employed truckers to huge public utilities. Of the 200,000 firms included in this grouping, nearly three-fourths have no employees. They consist mainly of truckers and taxicab drivers who own their own vehicles. Less than 1.5 per cent of the concerns have more than 100 employees, and these larger companies include the railroads, the light and power companies, and other public utilities. Hence, more than two-thirds of the employment in this general field is with companies of 500 or more employees.

As would be expected from the development of automotive transportation, the number of business firms in this field increased greatly in the decade between 1929 and 1939. According to the

[1] See E. F. Denison, "Service Industries—Trends and Prospects," *Survey of Current Business*, January, 1945. Also *Survey of Current Business*, May, 1944, p. 10.

[2] A few familiar examples would be home modernization and services on electrical appliances, beauty parlors and health clubs, restaurants and night clubs, commercial sports and amusements, expanded tourist activities, concert and lecture bureaus, "confidential" business letters.

Commerce Department estimates, it rose from 167,000 in 1929 to 207,000 in 1939 and even stepped somewhat higher in the fall of 1941.[1] There was a decline during the war, although it was less marked than in most other distribution and service lines. The total employment in small transportation business alone includes more than half a million persons, and ease of entry may be expected to keep that figure up.

*Finance, Insurance, and Real Estate*

If we go a little beyond the narrow use of the term, finance, insurance, and real estate may be included with "service" industries.

Finance is popularly associated with big names and with large sums. Most of the business volume is, in fact, in the hands of a few large financial institutions. Yet the number of concerns in the field of finance that come under the head of small business is extremely high.

For the general field of finance, insurance, and real estate, the Department of Commerce estimates for 1939 give 286,000 firms, of which 112,000, or roughly 40 per cent, were no-employee concerns and an additional 128,000, or 45 per cent, had 1 to 3 employees. Hence, 85 per cent of all such firms had 3 employees or less.

Approximately 85 per cent of the insured commercial banks of the country in 1940 had deposits of less than $5 million; the deposits of 43.5 per cent were less than $1 million.[2]

Banks and trust companies employ about 100,000 persons, and brokers and investment bankers employ close to 65,000. The rest of the employment in finance, insurance, and real estate runs largely to real estate dealers and agents (275,000 monthly average in 1939) as well as the primary insurance carriers (341,000 workers monthly average in 1939).[3]

The number of concerns in the general field of finance, insurance, and real estate dropped 10 per cent in the depression of the early 1930's. After 1935, however, the number of concerns held

[1] *Survey of Current Business*, May, 1944.

[2] Research Council, American Bankers Association, "Bank Lending Activity," February, 1940.

[3] *Cf. Social Security Yearbook 1940*, p. 214.

fairly even at around 280,000, until the war sharply reduced the one-man concerns in real estate and insurance. Many of those called to service or war work have reopened their offices.

In 1939 about 1.3 million employees found their livelihood in finance, insurance, and real estate. Of these, 340,000 were employed by the insurance carriers, which are the big concerns, whereas the great number of small firms is made up chiefly of insurance agents and brokers. Despite the large volume of business done by the one per cent of financial institutions with 50 or more employees, the majority of executives and employees in the combined fields of finance, insurance, and real estate are in firms with less than 50 employees.

### *Production—Manufacturing, Construction, Mining*

#### *Manufacturing*

Information is more plentiful for manufacturing, over a longer period of time, than for other activities. Compared with the distribution and service lines, manufacturing usually requires larger capital for entry, has more of its units incorporated, and needs more complete accounting and operating records.[1] It is in this area that public interest in the problems of small business was, for the most part, concentrated during the war.

There is ample reason for the emphasis on manufactures in small business. The 200,000 firms engaged in manufactures are only about 6 per cent of the nation's business enterprises, but they accounted for 11 million out of the 28 million persons engaged in business in 1939.

The distribution of employment by size of firm is markedly different from that in retail trade and the services, as is evident from Table 13. If we make use of the conventional dividing line between small and medium-size manufacturing at 100 employees, then about 92 per cent of the firms and 21 per cent of the persons engaged in manufacturing are definitely in small business. The intermediate firm, operating with 100 to 500 workers, accounts

[1] It will be recalled that whereas a majority of firms in the service industries had annual receipts of $5,000, the Census of Manufactures has excluded firms with less than $5,000 output from the manufacturing category and has listed most of them with repair shops in the service industries.

TABLE 13

DISTRIBUTION OF MANUFACTURERS BY SIZE AND LINE, 1939

| *Manufacturing lines* | *Total* all sizes* | *0–99 employees* | *100–499 employees* | *500 employees and over* |
|---|---|---|---|---|
| *A. Number of firms, thousands* | | | | |
| Foods and kindred products, including tobacco | 53.1 | 51.4 | 1.1 | 0.3 |
| Printing, publishing, etc. | 37.5 | 36.8 | 0.6 | 0.1 |
| Lumber and timber basic products | 22.7 | 22.1 | 0.6 | 0.1 |
| Apparel, etc. | 20.4 | 18.9 | 1.4 | 0.1 |
| Chemicals and allied products | 14.4 | 13.2 | 1.2 | 0.3 |
| Iron, steel, and nonferrous metals | 13.7 | 11.8 | 1.7 | 0.3 |
| Furniture and finished lumber | 10.3 | 9.5 | 0.7 | 0.1 |
| Machinery (except electrical) | 8.4 | 7.2 | 1.0 | 0.2 |
| Textile mill, leather and leather products | 7.9 | 5.1 | 2.2 | 0.6 |
| Paper and allied products | 2.5 | 2.1 | 0.4 | 0.1 |
| Automobiles, equipment, and transportation equipment | 2.2 | 1.7 | 0.2 | 0.2 |
| Electrical machinery | 1.7 | 1.3 | 0.3 | 0.1 |
| Miscellaneous manufacturing | 19.4 | 18.9 | 0.4 | † |
| Total manufacturing | 214.2 | 199.9 | 11.9 | 2.4 |
| *B. Number of employees, thousands* | | | | |
| Foods and kindred products, including tobacco | 1,657.8 | 379.7 | 254.6 | 1,023.5 |
| Printing, publishing, etc. | 618.7 | 254.1 | 121.9 | 242.7 |
| Lumber and timber basic products | 460.6 | 219.2 | 125.0 | 116.4 |
| Apparel, etc. | 939.8 | 395.1 | 279.7 | 265.0 |
| Chemical and allied products | 1,437.5 | 224.7 | 250.6 | 962.2 |
| Iron, steel, and nonferrous metals | 1,549.9 | 213.1 | 332.1 | 1,004.7 |
| Furniture and finished lumber | 421.6 | 140.1 | 136.0 | 145.5 |
| Machinery (except electrical) | 708.3 | 123.4 | 257.1 | 327.8 |
| Textile mill, leather and leather products | 1,695.8 | 162.3 | 364.2 | 1,169.3 |
| Paper and allied products | 290.3 | 73.9 | 84.5 | 131.9 |
| Automobiles, equipment, and transportation equipment | 742.8 | 40.0 | 56.7 | 646.1 |
| Electrical machinery | 436.2 | 35.7 | 63.9 | 336.6 |
| Miscellaneous manufacturing | 311.3 | 156.3 | 89.1 | 65.9 |
| Total manufacturing | 11,270.6 | 2,417.6 | 2,415.4 | 6,437.6 |

* Owing to rounding, figures do not equal the sum of components.

† Less than 50 firms.

for nearly 2½ million workers—almost as many as in all the service industries. Though not small, this important segment of manufacturers is confronted with many of the competitive problems of small business, since its competition may come from organizations with 3,000 or more employees.

From the point of view of employment, the relative importance of small and large manufacturers varies widely from industry to industry. Cigarette manufacture may be cited at one extreme. The eight largest cigarette manufacturing companies have 99.4 per cent of all employees in the industry. In electrical machinery and automobiles, also, the predominance of a few large companies in the total employment of the industry is a familiar fact. At the other extreme is printing and publishing, with 40 per cent of total employment in firms of less than 100 employees. In women's apparel, too, the majority of workers are in shops of less than 100 employees.

Both small and large manufacturers have shown progressive increase in value added by manufacture. Establishments employing up to 100 wage earners increased the aggregate value added in their product about 2.5 times during the three decades before the war—from about $3 billion in 1909 to $7.8 billion in 1939. In the same period, manufacturers employing more than 100 wage earners per establishment increased the value added by their production about threefold, from $5.5 billion in 1909 to $16.9 billion in 1939.

### *Industrial Concentration*

Census data bear out the popular belief that the movement in manufactures is to large industrial units. Between 1929 and 1939, the following changes toward concentration of manufacturing took place:[1]

| | *Per Cent* |
|---|---|
| *A.* Number of establishments *decreased* | 10.9 |
| Wage earners *decreased* | 5.8 |
| *B.* Central administrative offices *gained:* | |
| In numbers | 45.8 |
| In wage earners | 14.8 |
| In value of product | 1.6 |
| In value added by manufacturing | 1.0 |

[1] *Census of Manufactures, 1939,* Vol. I, p. 229.

| | *Per Cent* |
|---|---|
| Independent manufacturers *lost:* | |
| In numbers | 18.1 |
| In wage earners | 23.3 |
| In value of product | 37.0 |
| In value added by manufacturing | 38.2 |

*C.* Corporations decreased 2.9 per cent in number, to 95,187
Noncorporate enterprisers decreased 18.1 per cent, to 89,043
Corporations decreased dollar value of products 15.8 per cent to $52.6 billion
Noncorporate enterprises decreased dollar value of products 23.6 per cent to $4.2 billion

A hopeful aspect of the record, from the viewpoint of small-business survival, is in the signs that the law of diminishing returns may be catching up with the more extreme examples of swollen size and progressive absorption. Comparing 1929 Census figures on employment with those of 1939, we find that the smallest firms—those with 5 employees or less—dropped in aggregate employment from 3.2 per cent of all wage earners in 1929 to 2.6 per cent of the wage earners in the later census. At the other extreme, also, firms with 1,000 or more employees, which had had 24.5 per cent of all manufacturing wage earners in 1929, came down to 22.4 per cent in 1939. But, to the contrary, gains in relative percentages were registered in all the middle classifications, from 6 to 500 employees.[1]

A similar tendency favoring middle-size firms may be noted in the relative value of products. Comparison of the two census years indicates that the size groups from $5,000 to $5 million of total assets made gains in their percentage of the total during the decade. The share of the total declined for manufacturers in the class above $5 million.[2] Many of the largest plants undoubtedly were used well below their capacity in the 1930's and moved to lower size brackets. Nevertheless, the evidence gives us some basis for drawing the hopeful inference that the independent, medium-size manufacturing concern is at least holding its own and can maintain its position under peacetime conditions.

## *Construction*

In contract construction, the large percentage of small enterprises is comparable to that in retailing and the service industries.[3]

[1] See *Census of Manufactures, 1939*, Vol. I, Chap. IV, p. 119.

[2] *Ibid.*

[3] Contract construction includes only those firms in the construction business which

In general, the small business of construction is done on one- and two-family houses, while big business concentrates on commercial and industrial construction and on apartment houses. The BLS finds that

> Except in cities of a half million population or more, over one-fourth of the new one-family homes were put up by one-house builders, and over half of the new homes were constructed by builders of fewer than 5 houses per year each. Even in the 13 biggest cities, less than half of the one-family homes were erected by builders who constructed as many as 15 such houses in the year 1938.[1]

As of 1939 more than half (53.1 per cent) of the 215,000 establishments in contract construction had annual receipts of less than $5,000. The establishments that did less than $50,000 of annual volume were 93.1 per cent of the total; they engaged 47 per cent of the workers and accounted for 34 per cent of the receipts in the industry.[2]

More than one-third of the prewar construction firms consisted of self-employed artisans with no employees, and roughly another third had 1 to 3 employees. Of the approximately 1,400,000 directly employed in contract construction, about 65 per cent were connected with firms having under 100 employees.

Estimates by the Department of Commerce indicate that the number of firms in construction dropped from 236,000 in 1929 to 181,000 in 1935. From then on there was a consistent recovery until a high of 248,000 firms was reached early in 1942. The decline in small-scale construction in the war years then shows up in the statistics, with many of the self-employed taking jobs in the war effort, which engaged the large firms for the most part. Their

---

work on a contract basis for others. Two types of contractors are included: general contractors who ordinarily assume responsibility for the entire construction project and may subcontract portions of the job requiring special skills or equipment and special trade contractors specializing in such activities as plumbing, painting, electrical work, carpentering, etc., who may not only work under a subcontract for a general contractor but may also work directly for the owner. Builders engaged in building structures on their own account for rental or sale are classified in the Finance, Insurance and Real Estate Division, in the Social Security data upon which the Federal statistics are based.

[1] BLS Serial No. R 1151, September, 1940.

[2] *Census of Business, 1939*, Vol. IV, Construction, p. 17.

return to self-employment has accompanied the resumption of housebuilding, in which supply seems destined to lag behind demand far into the postwar period. There is some doubt, however, if the shoestring small operator, doing a single house at a time, will be as prevalent as he was in the prewar period.

*Mining and Quarrying*

This classification includes the mining of coal, fluid fuels, metallic ores, stone, and other products. About 50 per cent of its 800,000 wage earners are in coal mining. There were about 20,000 firms in 1939 almost equally divided between corporations and proprietorships in operation. There are very few no-employee concerns, but 7,200 of the 16,000 proprietors and firm members performed manual work, indicating scattered small-scale operations. About 40 per cent of the total number of firms have 3 or fewer employees, and another 40 per cent have 4 to 20 employees. Only about 20 per cent have more than 20 employees per establishment. However, the 5 per cent of firms at the top give employment to about two-thirds of all persons engaged in mining. The 80 per cent of small firms, with up to 20 employees per establishment, employ about one-eighth of the persons engaged in mining. Although mining has many small establishments, it is not regarded as a fertile field for newcomers in the postwar industry.[1]

## PREWAR TREND OF THE BUSINESS POPULATION

Are small enterprises gradually slipping out of the business structure? The spectacular development of large-scale production during the war seemed to fortify the widely held opinion that the ranks of small business have been consistently thinning over the years. Although this pessimism may be justified by relative volume of business done by small and large establishments, the *number* of small enterprises can be shown to have been notably steady, at least since the turn of the century.

Business censuses have not long classified the business population by size of enterprise. But because more than 90 per cent of all business establishments are in small business, and since the bulk

[1] *Sixteenth Census of the U.S., 1940*, Vol. I, Mineral Industries 1939, pp. 17, 18, 19, 112, 113; see *Survey of Current Business*, May, 1944, pp. 10, 12, and 13.

TABLE 14

NUMBER OF BUSINESS FIRMS PER 1,000 POPULATION 1900–1943

| *Year* | *Number of business establishments** | *Estimated population†* | *Number of establishments per 1,000 population* |
|---|---|---|---|
| 1900 | 1,174,300 | 76,094,134 | 15.43 |
| 1905 | 1,357,455 | 83,819,666 | 16.19 |
| 1906 | 1,392,949 | 85,436,556 | 16.30 |
| 1907 | 1,418,075 | 87,000,271 | 16.30 |
| 1908 | 1,447,554 | 88,708,976 | 16.31 |
| 1909 | 1,486,389 | 90,491,525 | 16.42 |
| 1910 | 1,515,143 | 92,406,536 | 16.39 |
| 1911 | 1,525,024 | 93,867,814 | 16.24 |
| 1912 | 1,564,279 | 95,331,300 | 16.40 |
| 1913 | 1,616,517 | 97,226,814 | 16.62 |
| 1914 | 1,655,496 | 99,117,567 | 16.70 |
| 1915 | 1,674,788 | 100,549,013 | 16.65 |
| 1916 | 1,707,639 | 101,965,984 | 16.74 |
| 1917 | 1,733,225 | 103,265,913 | 16.78 |
| 1918 | 1,708,061 | 103,202,801 | 16.55 |
| 1919 | 1,710,909 | 104,512,110 | 16.37 |
| 1920 | 1,821,409 | 106,466,420 | 17.10 |
| 1921 | 1,927,304 | 108,541,489 | 17.75 |
| 1922 | 1,983,106 | 110,054,778 | 18.01 |
| 1923 | 1,996,004 | 111,949,945 | 17.82 |
| 1924 | 2,047,302 | 114,113,463 | 17.94 |
| 1925 | 2,113,312 | 115,831,963 | 18.24 |
| 1926 | 2,158,457 | 117,399,225 | 18.38 |
| 1927 | 2,171,688 | 119,038,062 | 18.24 |
| 1928 | 2,199,049 | 120,501,115 | 18.24 |
| 1929 | 2,212,779 | 121,769,939 | 18.17 |
| 1930 | 2,183,008 | 123,076,741 | 17.73 |
| 1931 | 2,125,288 | 124,039,648 | 17.13 |
| 1932 | 2,076,580 | 124,840,471 | 16.63 |
| 1933 | 1,960,701 | 125,578,763 | 15.61 |
| 1934 | 1,973,900 | 126,373,773 | 15.61 |
| 1935 | 1,982,905 | 127,250,232 | 15.58 |
| 1936 | 2,009,935 | 128,053,180 | 15.69 |
| 1937 | 2,056,598 | 128,824,829 | 15.96 |
| 1938 | 2,101,933 | 129,824,939 | 16.19 |
| 1939 | 2,116,008 | 130,879,718 | 16.16 |
| 1940 | 2,156,450 | 131,954,144 | 16.34 |
| 1941 | 2,170,615 | 133,060,045 | 16.31 |
| 1942 | 2,151,549 | 133,770,500 | 16.08 |
| 1943 | 2,023,007 | 133,942,410 | 15.10 |

* *Statistical Abstract of the United States, 1943,* Table 414, p. 378 (Dun & Bradstreet data as of midyear).

† *Ibid.,* Table 5, p. 3. Does not include troops abroad. Estimated population as of July 1.

of the turnover is in small enterprises, we may take the year-to-year record of the business population as being, in effect, the year-to-year record of the number of small firms.

The annual estimates of Dun & Bradstreet (Table 14) indicate that the net change in the number of businesses since the beginning of the century has kept pace with general population trends. Dun & Bradstreet figures show that there were 1,174,300 establishments in 1900 in a population of 76 million; this was equivalent to 15.4 business units for every thousand people. From then until 1929 the number of business units steadily increased until it reached about 2.2 million in 1929, an increase to 18 establishments per 1,000 of population.

There was a drop in the early 1930's, but a recovery was made during the latter half of the decade. By 1940 the number of business establishments was about 16.3 per 1,000. While the latter figure is still below the 18 per 1,000 attained in the late 1920's, it is nevertheless substantially higher than the 15.4 rate in the smaller population of 1900.

The more recent estimates by the Department of Commerce, which include little firms with no credit rating, show a net increase from 2.9 million firms in the boom year 1929 to 3.4 million firms in 1941.[1]

While a balanced business expansion should mean an increase in successful small enterprises as well as in big businesses, the correlation between total business population and prosperity is far from perfect. The yearly figures of the accompanying table reveal a sharp increase in the number of firms in the depression year of 1921, whereas the number of businesses per 1,000 of population declined from 1926 to 1929, despite the business boom. In a depression period many jobless persons go into self-employment to tide themselves over until new job opportunities develop. A few stay in business and ride along successfully as business conditions improve. Others take new jobs as employment picks up. Certainly not all business "deaths" mean business failure. Not uncommonly, when business is brisk, the small businessman takes advantage of the chance to sell out at a profit to a chain or to a big company. He is equally prone to sell out at a loss when he cannot ride out the depression by himself.

[1] *Survey of Current Business,* May, 1944, p. 10.

It is clear, therefore, that changes in the total of business "births" and "deaths" can have paradoxical causes, depending on what kinds of small business are started and what kinds of enterprise or self-employment pass out of the picture.

*Population Shifts in Industry*

In a dynamic economy, progress means obsolescence of some types of business as well as increase in others. Village retail stores and blacksmith shops may close, and farm hands may go to the cities; at the same time, filling stations mushroom, and radio shops spring up everywhere. Different forces that have operated toward increases or declines in different sectors of our economy are reflected in the following table of changes between 1929 and 1939:

TABLE 15

CHANGE IN NUMBER OF OPERATING FIRMS, 1929–1939 BY BROAD INDUSTRIAL GROUPS*

| | *Increase or decrease in number of firms, 1929–1939* | *Percentage change* |
|---|---|---|
| All groups, total | +270,972 | +9.2 |
| Industrial groups showing *decrease* in number of firms | −82,235 | |
| Finance, insurance, real estate | −16,971 | −9.3 |
| Mining, quarrying | −3,000 | −11.1 |
| Manufacturing | −25,061 | −13.5 |
| Construction | −37,203 | −14.7 |
| Industrial groups showing *increase* in number of firms | +353,207 | |
| Transportation and public utilities | +32,100 | +27.2 |
| Wholesale trade | +25,504 | +24.0 |
| Retail trade | +250,792 | +18.0 |
| Service, amusements, hotels, and tourist courts | +44,811 | +6.5 |

* SOURCE: *Domestic Commerce*, May, 1944, p. 8.

## WAR IMPACT ON SMALL BUSINESS

With the foregoing review of the prewar position of small business let us consider what the war meant to small business and its position in the early postwar period.

*Wartime Business Population.* Although the number of small businesses declined during the war, their total amount of business rose. Because small business was mainly in civilian lines, its share of the total wartime volume was less than proportionate to the wartime increase of large-scale concerns. During the two years from December, 1941, to December, 1943, nearly a million enterprises (mainly in distribution lines) closed shop. Only about half a million new firms were started during the same period, so there was a net drop of half a million enterprises in the business population.

The number of business discontinuances is normally high. In 1940, for example, nearly 400,000 businesses closed down, exclusive of transfers. In 1942 and 1943 combined there were about 300,000 more discontinuances than would normally have been expected in peace years. It might be argued that this was a remarkably small increase in business deaths for a war period. More significant, as a matter of fact, in the net loss of a half million business enterprises during the first year and a half of the war, was the abnormally low number of new business entries. New entries for the first three months of 1943 dropped to a low of 32,000.[1]

The rate of business failures also reached a new low during this period. For the decade immediately preceding the war, Dun & Bradstreet reported a yearly average of 17,361; for the three years 1941–1943 inclusive, the average was only 8,158. The number of failures with liabilities above $100,000 dropped—from 652 a year during 1930–1940 to 117 for 1941–1943.[2]

Along with shortages of civilian merchandise and the drafting of men into the armed forces, lucrative war jobs were a potent reason for business discontinuances. Full employment and high wages gave the little fellow small incentive to move from a well-paying job to the risky venture of opening a business while labor and materials were scarce.

Small retail, service, and construction enterprises were mainly represented in the net decline of a half million firms in 1942 and 1943. One-man concerns and firms with less than four employees accounted for more than 95 per cent of the exits from business.

[1] Manufacturers furnished an exception to the downward trend, because new as well as established firms were needed to fill war contracts. The number of manufacturing firms showed a net increase of nearly 15,000 between 1939 and 1943. (See "The Business Population in Wartime," *Survey of Current Business*, May, 1944, p. 10.)

[2] *Dun's Statistical Review*, *passim*.

There was a slight drop in the number of food-producing enterprises, but that loss was more than offset by new manufacturing enterprises producing machinery, ships, aircraft parts, and transportation equipment.

In the service lines the number of discontinuances in early 1943 was three times as great as the number of new businesses, but the volume of employment did not fall off. Only domestic service dropped sharply as servants went into other service lines like restaurants and laundries. New recruits for the service industries, where demand was accelerated by wartime conditions, were brought in from the ranks of those not formerly employed.

*Wartime Share of Small Business.* In 1939, firms with from 1 to 100 employees employed 42.5 per cent of the total employees in business, but in 1943 the same firms employed only 31.5 per cent. In terms of taxable wages paid, the share of firms with less than 100 employees decreased during the four years from 37.5 to 25.5 per cent of the total taxable payroll.[1] Although the drop in employment by manufacturing concerns with less than 50 employees was significant, employment in the smaller retail and wholesale establishments held up well despite the decline in number of firms. Percentage changes between 1939 and 1943, in relative numbers and share of employment, are shown on page 47.

*Recovery in Business Population.* In November, 1943, the Dun & Bradstreet reference list of rated firms carried the lowest number of business enterprises in nine years. Since then, the list has consistently picked up.

In spite of the difficulties of opening new business during the war, signs of recovery in the business population became evident as early as the middle of 1943. By that time the number of discontinuances turned downward while the number of new entries began to rise. Approximately 330,000 new businesses opened during the year and a half from the middle of 1942 to the end of 1943, while the rate of discontinuances dropped by the middle of 1943 to one-half of what it had been a year earlier. By the spring of 1944 new businesses were coming in twice as fast as businesses were discontinuing.

[1] D. W. Paden, "Industrial Concentration of Employment," *Survey of Current Business*, April, 1945, p. 13.

## *Prewar and Postwar Pattern*

During the year following the end of the war, business population recorded an increase in numbers that was even more marked than the decline during the first war year. The distribution of that increase in major branches of industry to the end of 1946 is revealed in the table on page 48.

TABLE 16

PERCENTAGE OF NUMBER OF EMPLOYING ORGANIZATIONS AND EMPLOYMENT IN LARGE AND SMALL CONCERNS, BY INDUSTRY, 1939 AND 1943*

| *Industry and size of firm* | *Per cent of firms* | | *Per cent of employment* | |
|---|---|---|---|---|
| | *1939* | *1943* | *1939* | *1943* |
| All industries, total | 100.0 | 100.0 | 100.0 | 100.0 |
| 1–49 employees | 96.5 | 96.3 | 34.1 | 25.3 |
| 50 or more employees | 3.5 | 3.7 | 65.9 | 74.7 |
| Mining, total | 100.0 | 100.0 | 100.0 | 100.0 |
| 1–49 employees | 87.9 | 89.5 | 19.0 | 16.6 |
| 50 or more employees | 12.1 | 10.5 | 81.0 | 83.4 |
| Contract construction, total | 100.0 | 100.0 | 100.0 | 100.0 |
| 1–49 employees | 97.1 | 95.2 | 42.3 | 54.1 |
| 50 or more employees | 2.9 | 4.8 | 57.7 | 45.9 |
| Manufacturing, total | 100.0 | 100.0 | 100.0 | 100.0 |
| 1–49 employees | 82.2 | 80.0 | 17.1 | 8.3 |
| 50 or more employees | 17.8 | 20.0 | 82.9 | 91.7 |
| Transportation, communication, and public utilities, total† | 100.0 | 100.0 | 100.0 | 100.0 |
| 1–49 employees | 93.0 | 94.0 | 21.4 | 17.5 |
| 50 or more employees | 7.0 | 6.0 | 78.6 | 82.5 |
| Retail and wholesale trade, total | 100.0 | 100.0 | 100.0 | 100.0 |
| 1–49 employees | 98.5 | 98.4 | 58.8 | 52.6 |
| 50 or more employees | 1.5 | 1.6 | 41.2 | 47.4 |
| Finance and service, total | 100.0 | 100.0 | 100.0 | 100.0 |
| 1–49 employees | 98.0 | 97.9 | 66.4 | 53.7 |
| 50 or more employees | 2.0 | 2.1 | 33.6 | 46.3 |

* SOURCE: Basic data from Bureau of Old-Age and Survivors Insurance (*Survey of Current Business*, April, 1945, p. 14).

† Does not include railroads.

## POSTWAR PROSPECTS FOR SMALL BUSINESS

Even for those who expected the worst for small business as they saw war production concentrated in the hands of the giants of American business, the outcome of the wartime experience is not disheartening. Many small businesses scored substantial gains in

TABLE 17

NUMBER OF FIRMS IN OPERATION AND RATES OF CHANGE*

| Industry | Number of firms, thousands | | | | | Average annual rate of change, per cent | | | |
|---|---|---|---|---|---|---|---|---|---|
| | *Sept., 1941* | *Dec., 1943* | *Dec., 1945* | *June, 1946* | *Dec., 1946* | *Sept., 1941– Dec., 1943* | *Dec., 1943– Dec., 1945* | *Dec., 1945– June, 1946* | *June, 1946– Dec., 1946* |
| Total, all industries | 3,398.0 | 2,835.6 | 3,224.1 | 3,494.7 | 3,644.6 | −7.7 | +6.6 | +17.5 | +8.7 |
| Mining and quarrying | 23.4 | 26.0 | 26.3 | 27.2 | 28.0 | +4.8 | +.6 | +7.0 | +6.0 |
| Contract construction | 243.8 | 147.1 | 189.2 | 232.2 | 247.9 | −20.1 | +13.5 | +50.6 | +14.0 |
| Manufacturing | 225.8 | 227.6 | 262.5 | 287.8 | 307.8 | +.4 | +7.4 | +20.2 | +14.4 |
| Transportation, communication, and other public utilities | 209.2 | 187.9 | 206.1 | 216.8 | 222.6 | −4.7 | +4.7 | +10.7 | +5.3 |
| Wholesale trade | 146.2 | 114.0 | 143.2 | 160.1 | 169.0 | −10.5 | +12.1 | +25.2 | +11.4 |
| Retail trade | 1,620.8 | 1,318.0 | 1,493.5 | 1,614.5 | 1,674.1 | −8.8 | +6.5 | +16.9 | +7.5 |
| Finance, insurance, and real estate | 285.0 | 267.5 | 286.0 | 294.8 | 298.5 | −2.8 | +3.4 | +6.2 | +2.5 |
| Service industries | 643.8 | 547.5 | 617.3 | 661.2 | 696.6 | −7.0 | +6.2 | +14.7 | +11.0 |

* SOURCE: *Survey of Current Business*, July, 1947, p. 16.

civilian production and distribution. For the time being, small business as a whole appears prosperous.[1] As to the wartime advantages yielded to big business, there is no certainty that a pattern created by special war requirements and by the retirement of small enterprises for the duration will apply to the peace era.

To maintain its place in the economy after the war, small business has quantitative and qualitative objectives to attain. The first, filling the vacuum created by the curtailment of business births during the war, has been taken; the ground lost in numerical strength has been regained. The second step is for small business to find its place in providing new goods and services stimulated by the war so that there will be productive investment in small enterprises comparable to the expected growth in national output.

In evaluating the general prospect of increased small-business activity, the carry-over of the war experience should be remembered. Granting the dominance of big business in the total of wartime contracts, it is notable that 30 per cent of the number of contracts of $10,000 or better let during the war were let to small business. It could be argued that they represented a mere filling in of the spaces among the big-business contracts. Nevertheless, in the aggregate they have meant additional funds and a fruitful education for the small businessman in new postwar possibilities. The war work of small manufacturers included many new lines of business endeavor, involving new materials and services. Small business successfully carried out these assignments. A residue of that experience with light metals, plastics, new machinery, and new processes is now available for peacetime application.

In view of technological improvements and improvements in manufacturing equipment, the probability is that in postwar manufacturing, small business will consist of larger and better equipped units than in the prewar period. The burden of continuing a virile small manufacturers' sector appears to depend mostly on manufacturers with 100 to 500 employees. At this level, the independent firm not only seems able to maintain its competitive position against big business but can often count on large organizations to be its most valuable customers.

The long-term trend, of course, has been one of decline in the

[1] See in Chap. V, section on The Rate of Profits.

number of manufacturing firms. In the prewar decade the number appeared to settle at about 40,000 less than in the late 1920's. Even the wartime emphasis on manufacturing produced less than 20,000 new concerns. In view of the wartime expansion of the big manufacturers and the potential peacetime uses of their technological gains, it would be too optimistic to expect a spectacular net increase in the number of manufacturing concerns over the prewar period. There seems greater likelihood that products will be diversified and that those who have already acquired the know-how will extend their lines. This general statement does not, however, rule out the possibility of a rash of postwar innovations, notably in the light metals and plastics, which may give rise to new small craft shops. If, as is expected, electric power becomes more widely available, small manufacturers will probably find it easier to take advantage of favorable local conditions.

In construction, the self-employed artisans of the prewar period are resuming their role as independent small-time contractors. The shortage in housing at all income levels promises to provide work for every type of contractor during the immediate postwar years. Industries concerned with prefabrication of construction units will probably merchandise them through local lumber yards and have them set up by independent small crews. New construction techniques offer a good illustration of developments that, while spelling mass production in the first instance, offer opportunities for creation of new activities in small business.

A substantial part of the increase in small business after the war must come in retailing. After due allowance is made for the large chains and the large department stores, retailing remains the broadest area in which employment is provided by the small, independent business units. The relatively small capital required will continue to make retailing the favorite field of the small enterpriser who has only his own savings on which to get started. According to the Information and Education Division of the Army Service Forces, 45 out of 100 of the servicemen with definite plans to operate particular types of business intended to go into retailing.[1]

A large number of new retailers makes prospects brighter for the wholesalers as well. Ambitious postwar plans for new and

[1] See "Postwar New Business Plans of GI's," *Domestic Commerce*, January, 1945, p. 11.

improved products also point in this direction. Recent quarterly surveys by Dun & Bradstreet indicate that more than one-third of all manufacturers plan to manufacture new products and at least 40 per cent of them have plans to expand their sales territories. In these efforts to locate new outlets and new distributors, high activity for wholesalers has been in evidence.[1]

In the service industries, as in retailing, rapid recovery is likely because of the small funds required to get started. Moreover, if high production and employment and good incomes continue, consumers will want more of the services already in common use as well as more cultural and recreational services. There should be new demands for beauty parlors, decorators, and health centers; new forms of recreation and amusement; and calls for the services of independent truckers, taxi drivers, plane pilots, travel agents, and insurance agents, in addition to an expansion of existing promotional and consultative services.[2]

*Balance between Big and Small Business.* There is no guarantee, of course, that all of these possibilities will allow small business to retain even its proportionate prewar share during the postwar period. There is logic in the paradox that the prosperity of small business will depend heavily on the efforts of big business to create a high level of employment and prosperity, so that small business may actually have greater *absolute* prosperity when it has a smaller *percentage* of the total product.

One cannot get around very far among the large business organizations without being impressed with the progress that they have already made in preparing the way for new products and the improvement of old ones. The giants of industry have taken the

[1] Postwar Plans of Manufacturers and Wholesalers, Chart, by Dun & Bradstreet, 1945. See also, CED Marketing Committee's survey of manufacturers' plans, *American Industry Looks Ahead.*

[2] According to an estimate by the Department of Commerce, the personal services may give livelihood to 115,000 more people in 1948 than they did in 1941—provided high employment can be maintained. Barber shops, beauty parlors, cleaning, pressing, and alteration shops, and shoe repair offer the best chances for one- or two-man firms, whereas laundry and cleaning establishments have a much higher percentage of wage earners. Business services, such as advertising agencies, accounting and bookkeeping, adjustment and credit bureaus, are next in line as an expanding field for small business. Hotels and lodging places are surpassed only by the recreational, and amusement services in the list of service industries that have potentialities for expansion. (See Denison, *op. cit.*)

initiative in opening up consumer demand. They are entrenched; they have the know-how for promotion as well as production of lines; they have the research facilities to keep out in front of their competition. Only an extreme optimist would suppose that really small enterprisers may affect big business's superior position even slightly through direct competition. It is more likely that small enterprise will develop as auxiliary to its larger competitors.

The rise in living standards made possible by mass production in the 1920's created new wealth that demanded custom-made, individualized production in apparel, home furnishings, jewelry, and other crafts and services. At the same time, the automobile, paved highways, business machines, radios, and phonographs all helped build demand for new services for the upkeep of the products made possible to a wider public by mass production. There is no reason to fear a dearth of new wares and services for small-business activity.

*Urge to Business Entry.* Prevailing forces point in the direction of current expansion of small business that will hold its numbers well above prewar peaks. Among the factors contributing to the momentum are these:

1. Morc individuals have the accumulated savings to go into business for themselves or to back others in enterprise than ever before.

2. Wartime employment, both civilian and military, developed new skills and self-confidence in people who hoped to go into business someday but had felt unready.

3. Many members of the armed forces, psychologically or physically unsuited to working closely with others, are seeking an economic outlet in self-employment.

4. Government pressure for easier financing, both for veterans and for small businessmen, enables some to go into business who could not have done so from their own resources alone. Private financing agencies have likewise inaugurated a policy for more liberal loans. Availability of capital is stimulating new enterprise in areas requiring substantial stock and equipment, thus broadening the field of entry.

5. The accumulated backlog of demand for remodeling, minor installations, maintenance, and repairs to homes and buildings will

last a good while. Such operations will continue to attract small enterprisers.

6. New products partially developed during the war offer a variety of novel applications and opportunities for partnerships between technicians and financial backers. The new patents owned and made available by the government provide an added stimulus.

7. The growth in population and especially in new families calls for additional servicing by small enterprise.

The cumulative effect of these factors can mean only a substantial increase in business entries and expansion of established small firms.

The larger funds held by many new small enterprisers today will help reduce the number of early business deaths usually associated with a high business birth rate. The critical problem is that of equipping the newcomers with sufficient managerial know-how to hold down a debacle that might ensue because many overeager and unqualified venturers have been led by favorable conditions to go out on their own.

It has been observed that over the years the small business population exhibits remarkable stamina and will to survive in the presence of big-business competition. Small business has also been ingenious in taking advantage of the opportunities that flow to it from the activity of large-scale enterprise. The record justifies the assumption that those who would engage in small business furnish a core of essentially good material for survival and success. To capitalize on the potentialities requires, however, a nation-wide effort to raise the general level of efficiency of small business and to ensure a fair field for fair play in the tough competition that the postwar period will undoubtedly present.

The succeeding section deals with the competitive problems of small business and the direction that efforts to meet the problem may have to take.

# IV. VITAL STATISTICS OF SMALL ENTERPRISE

UP TO THIS point we have been discussing the anatomy of small business, its contours and dimensions. From here on we shall consider how small enterprises perform: how well they survive, how profitable they are, how efficiently they operate, how successfully they cope with existing trade practices or legislative controls. We shall also try to get some idea of how small business adapts itself to current economic developments, as in labor relations, technology, and public policy.

To help gauge the stamina of small enterprises, the vital statistics of business should be looked at first.

The information reviewed in the previous chapter, on year-to-year changes in the total business population, told little of the life span of small enterprises in particular lines of business or of the reasons for their failure, if they failed. It told us merely that there are usually enough new businesses to take the place of those discontinued. If we could register every new enterprise, whether incorporated or not, with the record of its starting position—initial investment, number of owners and their former connections, number of employees, and other relevant data on its size and character—and if we had a similar registration for every business that closed, then we might draw some dependable conclusions on the relation between size and survival capacity. To date there has been no systematic analysis of business entries and exits from which to determine how much investment or experience it takes to give the average enterpriser a better than even chance of survival beyond the first year in a given line of business—or, indeed, how important the size of initial investment may be alongside other factors in success or failure.

Evidence from which to draw some conclusions about the survival factors in small business is not entirely lacking, however. Listings of bankrupt firms have from time to time been classified by the amount of liabilities. We have some sample studies of business mortality analyzed by the apparent causes of failure. In a few communities, business history has been traced over a series of years to see how many firms dropped out in the successive years following their organization. More recently, the Old-Age and Survivors Insurance files have yielded a record of discontinuances by size for firms with one or more employees. From such sample studies, checked against the experience of bankers, industry executives, government agencies, and others, a composite impression, which is probably not far from a true general picture, may be obtained.

## CHARACTERISTICS OF SMALL-BUSINESS MORTALITY

The statistics of business population discussed in the previous chapter showed that a large annual turnover is normal to small business. We saw that it was not uncommon during the prewar years for as many as half a million firms per year, mostly very small, to drop out of the business roster and for about the same number of new firms to replace them. The annual number of births and deaths gave us a gross turnover equal to about one-third of all active firms in a given year. Should this high turnover be considered alarming? Should we try to curtail it?

*Discontinuance versus Failure.* Discontinuances in the war years were discounted as being of a special emergency character, affected by the draft, highly paid war jobs, and merchandise shortages. But in peacetime a less charitable view is taken of small-business discontinuances. "Going out of business" is often assumed loosely to be synonymous with liquidation and failure. Hence, statistics on discontinuances are interpreted to mean "nine out of ten small businesses fail." By the same token, the large annual number of business births and deaths has been offered as evidence that the small-business structure is frail, that only a very exceptional small enterpriser can stay in business, and that early failure is normal to small business. To test the validity of this impression, the grand totals of small-business mortality need to be analyzed.

Discontinuance may represent a true liquidation of the business, with or without insolvency, or a transfer of the business, either at a sacrifice or at a profit. A business may be discontinued because the proprietor retires and a successor is unavailable, or the firm may be absorbed, just because it is a sound business, by a chain or other large company. More than a third of the prewar business discontinuances were changes of ownership rather than liquidations of the enterprise. In 1940, for example, it is estimated that 570,000 business firms discontinued business under their existing ownerships. Of that number, 209,000 represented transfers of ownership, with the business continuing in operation. In 1941, when the war was sensed, there were approximately 690,000 withdrawals, but 281,000 of them were transfers rather than liquidations. Even among the liquidators, many undoubtedly used their experience to enter a related line that would be less cramped by wartime shortages. They showed up among the 448,000 new firms opened that very year.[1]

*Mortality among Self-employed.* Looming large in the total of business mortalities are the one-man firms with no employees. Although they account for less than 6 per cent of the total labor force in business, they make up more than 45 per cent of the total population of business firms. In 1940, 60 per cent of all the business discontinuances were in this no-employee class of proprietors. Yet if we are mainly concerned with that portion of small business which may provide outlets for investment funds stimulating additional postwar employment, the turnover in these one-man firms is not critical. Essentially they represent self-employed labor; the choice is made between working for others and self-employment, even as it might be made between one job or employer and another. The turnover of these one-man firms may be equivalent to an annual shifting of between 400,000 and 500,000 workers—which might mean one-third of the total number of one-man firms in the business population at a given time. That is a moderate shift when compared with the gross turnover of factory workers, where the annual separation rate averaged close to 45 per cent of the total employed, during the prewar decade.[2]

The firms with 1 to 3 employees, which ordinarily account for 35 to 40 per cent of the business population, have a discontinuance

[1] "Recent Trends in Business Population," *Survey of Current Business,* May, 1946, p. 21. Under *discontinuances,* Department of Commerce data include only true liquidations of the business; Dun & Bradstreet data include transfers and reorganizations.

[2] BLS, *Handbook of Labor Statistics,* 1941, Vol. 1, p. 533.

rate in line with their ratio to the total number of businesses. All firms from 0 to 3 employees made up 82.3 per cent of the business population in 1939; they accounted for 96 per cent of all discontinuances in 1940. In the remaining 4 per cent of discontinuances

TABLE 18
BIRTH RATES* AND DEATH RATES* IN THE UNITED STATES BUSINESS POPULATION, 1900–1941†

| *Year* | *Rate per 1,000 listed concerns* | | *Year* | *Rate per 1,000 listed concerns* | |
|---|---|---|---|---|---|
| | *Births* | *Deaths* | | *Births* | *Deaths* |
| 1900 | 231 | 212 | 1921 | 251 | 222 |
| 1901 | 235 | 203 | 1922 | 248 | 240 |
| 1902 | 243 | 211 | 1923 | 235 | 209 |
| 1903 | 238 | 212 | 1924 | 233 | 200 |
| 1904 | 233 | 203 | 1925 | 235 | 213 |
| 1905 | 242 | 211 | 1926 | 224 | 218 |
| 1906 | 240 | 215 | 1927 | 222 | 209 |
| 1907 | 239 | 213 | 1928 | 217 | 210 |
| 1908 | 242 | 225 | 1929 | 205 | 217 |
| 1909 | 242 | 222 | 1930 | 194 | 219 |
| 1910 | 236 | 230 | 1931 | 167 | 189 |
| 1911 | 239 | 214 | 1932 | 163 | 219 |
| 1912 | 236 | 202 | 1933 | 176 | 169 |
| 1913 | 239 | 215 | 1934 | 192 | 183 |
| 1914 | 235 | 222 | 1935 | 195 | 192 |
| 1915 | 227 | 207 | 1936 | 203 | 190 |
| 1916 | 216 | 202 | 1937 | 194 | 171 |
| 1917 | 208 | 222 | 1938 | 185 | 174 |
| 1918 | 180 | 178 | 1939 | 178 | 165 |
| 1919 | 180 | 115 | 1940 | 177 | 157 |
| 1920 | 252 | 193 | 1941 | 152 | 151 |

* Includes transfers of ownership or changes in legal organization.
† SOURCE: Dun & Bradstreet, Inc., *Vital Statistics of Industry and Commerce*, January, 1942.

are included small businesses with from 4 to 100 employees—a class that accounts for about one-sixth of the active business population and more than one-fourth of the personnel engaged in business enterprise.[1]

[1] No estimates of discontinuances by size of firm are available for years prior to 1940. Percentage distribution is shown in "New and Discontinued Business, 1940–43," *Survey of Current Business*, July, 1944, p. 13.

*Birth Rate Determines Mortality.* The rate of discontinuances is generally not far from the birth rate of new enterprise, whether the year is a good one or a bad one. On the business upswings, however, births exceed deaths, while in recession years entries are fewer than the exits. Thus, the year 1922, which showed the highest rate of discontinuances since the First World War, was likewise close to the top in the rate of business births. The year 1941, on the other hand, represented low points both in the rate of entry and the rate of discontinuance. The approximation of business birth and death rates for the prewar years is given in Table 18 (page 57).

Such studies as have been made of business mortalities, tend to bear out the conclusion that the determining factor in discontinuances of very small business enterprises is not the business cycle so much as it is the personality, experience, and ability of the enterpriser. The less successful he is in conducting his own business the more likely he is to accept a favorable opportunity in employment for others or to take advantage of a chance to sell out. But in a poor year of the business cycle the failure to make a profit may not move him; on the contrary, since he can get no buyer for his business and employment opportunities elsewhere are scarce, he is likely to do the best he can with his own enterprise. To that extent the mortality rate is kept from rising in a year of low business opportunities.[1] In any event, the process of sifting out the inept, the poorly located, the undercapitalized, and the otherwise unfortunate will deplete the ranks of every new batch of entrepreneurs whether business in general is poor or good.

## BUSINESS FAILURES

*The Trends.* The forced closings that show as business failures have averaged around 4 per cent of total discontinuances during the past decade. While the business exits, like the entries, may hit low points in poor years and highs in good years, the curve of failures behaves in a more orthodox way in relation to the business cycle. The year-to-year trend of business failures compared with that of discontinuances may be seen from Table 19 (page 59).

[1] The main importance of generally high business activity for small business is that in good times the profit ratio of small business makes a much sharper improvement than is the case with large business (see Chap. V, pp. 88*ff*).

Following the First World War, there was a sharp increase in failures during the postwar recession of 1920–1922. Failures continued relatively high while the war babies were being tested

TABLE 19

RELATIVE YEAR-TO-YEAR CHANGES IN BUSINESS DISCONTINUANCES AND FAILURES, 1914–1941 *

| *Year* | *Failures* | | *Discontinuances*† | |
|---|---|---|---|---|
| | *Number* | *Per cent change* | *Number (000)* | *Per cent change* |
| 1914 | 18,280 | ....... | 369 | |
| 1915 | 22,156 | +21.2 | 347 | −6.0 |
| 1916 | 16,993 | −23.3 | 344 | −8.6 |
| 1917 | 13,885 | −18.3 | 385 | +11.2 |
| 1918 | 9,982 | −28.1 | 305 | −20.8 |
| 1919 | 6,451 | −35.4 | 197 | −35.4 |
| 1920 | 8,881 | +37.7 | 353 | +79.2 |
| 1921 | 19,652 | +121.3 | 427 | +12.1 |
| 1922 | 23,676 | +20.5 | 478 | +11.9 |
| 1923 | 18,718 | −20.9 | 417 | −12.8 |
| 1924 | 20,615 | +11.0 | 411 | −1.4 |
| 1925 | 21,214 | +2.9 | 451 | +9.7 |
| 1926 | 21,773 | +2.6 | 471 | +4.4 |
| 1927 | 23,146 | +6.3 | 456 | −3.2 |
| 1928 | 23,842 | +3.0 | 463 | +1.5 |
| 1929 | 22,909 | −3.9 | 483 | +4.3 |
| 1930 | 26,355 | +15.0 | 481 | −0.4 |
| 1931 | 28,285 | +7.3 | 404 | −16.0 |
| 1932 | 31,822 | +11.3 | 454 | +12.4 |
| 1933 | 20,307 | −36.2 | 332 | −26.9 |
| 1934 | 12,185 | −40.0 | 361 | +8.7 |
| 1935 | 11,879 | −2.5 | 380 | +5.3 |
| 1936 | 9,185 | −22.7 | 382 | +0.5 |
| 1937 | 9,017 | −1.8 | 351 | −8.1 |
| 1938 | 12,836 | +42.4 | 365 | +4.0 |
| 1939 | 14,708 | +14.6 | 349 | −4.4 |
| 1940 | 13,619 | −7.4 | 337 | −3.4 |
| 1941 | 11,848 | −13.0 | 327 | −3.0 |

* SOURCE: "Small Retailers Face the War," Senate Committee Print No. 13, September, 1942 (adapted from Dun & Bradstreet, *Vital Statistics of Industry and Commerce*).

† Includes transfers of ownership or changes in legal organization.

out during the 1920's. From the boom of 1929 to the depression of 1932, the annual figure of business failures climbed from 22,909 to a peak of 31,822. Their corresponding current liabilities rose from $483 million to $928 million. After that purge, business failures dropped to a low point of 9,017 by 1937. Following a rise in 1938 and 1939, failures steadily receded, so that for 1942 the aggregate of current liabilities was only $100 million. The 9,405 failures for the year 1942 represented $\frac{43}{100}$ per cent of the total business concerns listed by Dun & Bradstreet. This was equivalent to about $\frac{3}{10}$ per cent of the business population if we include unrated as well as rated firms.

The declining trend of failures continued during the war. In May of 1944 the number was 47 per cent lower than in May, 1943. The record low of 810 failures was in 1945. The reduction in business failures applied to practically all branches of industry, but it was most striking in retailing, which accounted for only 40 per cent of business failures in 1944, compared with its usual share of 60 per cent or more in peacetime years.[1]

The war hurt a number of small manufacturers who were unable to obtain materials or workers. For these, the ratio of failures to total firms was more than double the average for industry as a whole. Yet even among them only 1 discontinuance in every 20 resulted in a loss to creditors in 1942, and only 1 in 65 among the manufacturers discontinuing in 1945 was reported as a failure. This record can hardly be maintained during the postwar period. By the middle of 1947 there was evidence, in the rising failure index, of some shakedown of weak firms no longer bolstered by a sellers' market.[2]

*Size and Business Failure.* Because small enterprises form the bulk of the business population, the bulk of business failures also are small businesses. We are interested, however, in knowing if the incidence of insolvencies among small enterprises is greater than its percentage of the total business population warrants.

An idea of the relative size of the bankrupt firms may be obtained from the available statistics of business failures through classification by the amount of current liabilities. For two prewar

[1] *Dun's Statistical Review*, August, 1944, p. 7, and succeeding issues.
[2] *Ibid.*, August, 1947, pp. 10–12.

years, 1939–1940, the distribution by size of liabilities is as follows:[1]

TABLE 20

| *1939 (Revised)* | *Number* | *Per cent* | *Current liabilities (000)* | *Per cent* | *Total liabilities (100)* | *Per cent* |
|---|---|---|---|---|---|---|
| United States total..... | 14,768 | 100.0 | $182,520 | 100.0 | $209,454 | 100.0 |
| Under $5,000.......... | 6,522 | 44.2 | 14,621 | 8.0 | 14,621 | 7.0 |
| $5,000–$25,000........ | 6,873 | 46.5 | 65,833 | 36.1 | 65,833 | 31.4 |
| 25,000–100,000........ | 1,146 | 7.8 | 52,409 | 28.7 | 52,409 | 25.0 |
| 100,000–1,000,000...... | 213 | 1.4 | 39,355 | 21.6 | 45,602 | 21.8 |
| 1,000,000 and over..... | 14 | 0.1 | 10,302 | 5.6 | 30,989 | 14.8 |

TABLE 21

| *1940* | *Number* | *Per cent* | *Current liabilities (000)* | *Per cent* | *Total liabilities (000)* | *Per cent* |
|---|---|---|---|---|---|---|
| United States total..... | 13,619 | 100.0 | $166,684 | 100.0 | $190,342 | 100.0 |
| Under $5,000.......... | 6,891 | 50.6 | 16,584 | 10.0 | 16,584 | 8.7 |
| $5,000–$25,000........ | 5,442 | 40.0 | 55,001 | 33.0 | 55,001 | 28.9 |
| 25,000–100,000........ | 1,067 | 7.8 | 48,419 | 29.0 | 48,419 | 25.4 |
| 100,000–1,000,000...... | 209 | 1.5 | 36,956 | 22.2 | 46,431 | 24.4 |
| 1,000,000 and over..... | 10 | 0.1 | 9,724 | 5.8 | 23,907 | 12.6 |

If the break at $100,000 of liabilities is assumed to take place somewhere in the size class of 50 to 99 employees, then the ratio of business failures to business population does not appear to put larger businesses in a more favorable light than small businesses. In both classes the annual failures are less than 1 per cent of the business population in that class. It is evident that the total liabilities involved in the group under $5,000 constitute a small fraction of the aggregate of liabilities for all classes. The fact that the cases with liabilities under $5,000 are only as numerous as those in the next higher group, when we know that actually the very small businesses are by far the most numerous, indicates that many of the unsuccessful little fellows liquidate with settlements that do not show up as listed failures.

If it is assumed that the group with liabilities between $25,000

[1] *Ibid.*, February, 1941, p. 9.

and $100,000 is in the area of small business which has from 4 to 99 employees, then this group accounts for considerably less than its share of business failures compared with the ratio for larger firms.

*Cyclical Factor*. If the trend of business failures by size of firm is followed through the cyclical changes, some difference in behavior of small and large firms may be noted. Failures among small firms evidently do not follow the rise and fall of the business cycle so closely as those among large firms. This is brought out by comparison of the number of failures with more than $100,000 of liabilities with those with less than that amount both before and after the depression of the early 1930's. The record appears in Table 22, which shows the rise and fall of the index of failures for small and large businesses in comparison with the Federal Reserve index of production.

The point that failures in bigger business show relatively a greater percentage of rise and fall with the business cycle can be overemphasized. The actual number of big-business failures is so small that it takes only a few more cases to affect the index materially. Moreover, many big-business bankruptcies are not eliminations of firms but reorganizations and absorptions. The comparison is of interest, nevertheless, as indirect confirmation of the previously noted characteristic of small-business discontinuances in general—that the number of deaths is a function of the number of births among small enterprises, apart from the cyclical factor.

A consideration that may contribute to the relative insensitivity to the business cycle of the bankruptcy record for smaller firms is that small firms deal mainly in consumers' goods, production of which does not fluctuate so violently as that of producers' goods.[1] A second factor may be the relatively smaller fixed charges carried by a small firm and its resulting ability, by cutting corners and reducing owners' salaries, to avoid bankruptcies when a corresponding deficit position in a large firm would make a receivership inevitable. Finally, the chances are that the largest element in the

[1] On the other hand, a credit man familiar with the problems of small retailers has called the author's attention to cases where small merchants have been crowded into bankruptcy by rising prices in presumably good times. Carrying inventory and credit accounts when prices have risen sharply may completely drain the small firm with meager capital and credit resources.

apparent insensitivity of small-business bankruptcies to the business cycle is the fact that the small firm eliminates itself from the records by having its investment wiped out with as good an informal settle-

TABLE 22

NUMBER OF FAILURES AND BUSINESS ACTIVITY*

(For the indexes, 1935–1939 = 100)

| *Year* | *Failures with liabilities of $100,000 and over* | *Index* | *Failures with liabilities of less than $100,000* | *Index* | *Federal Reserve index of industrial production* |
|---|---|---|---|---|---|
| 1921 | 873 | 347.8 | 18,779 | 176.6 | 58 |
| 1922 | 868 | 345.8 | 22,808 | 214.5 | 73 |
| 1923 | 743 | 296.0 | 17,975 | 169.0 | 88 |
| 1924 | 650 | 259.0 | 19,965 | 187.7 | 82 |
| 1925 | 591 | 235.4 | 20,623 | 193.9 | 90 |
| 1926 | 610 | 243.0 | 21,163 | 199.0 | 96 |
| 1927 | 708 | 282.0 | 22,438 | 211.0 | 95 |
| 1928 | 689 | 274.5 | 23,153 | 217.7 | 99 |
| 1929 | 744 | 296.4 | 22,165 | 208.4 | 110 |
| 1930 | 947 | 377.3 | 25,408 | 238.9 | 91 |
| 1931 | 1,055 | 420.3 | 27,230 | 256.0 | 75 |
| 1932 | 1,625 | 647.4 | 30,197 | 283.9 | 58 |
| 1933 | 830 | 330.7 | 19,029 | 178.9 | 69 |
| 1934 | 469 | 186.8 | 11,255 | 105.8 | 75 |
| 1935 | 280 | 111.6 | 11,230 | 105.6 | 87 |
| 1936 | 178 | 70.9 | 9,007 | 84.7 | 103 |
| 1937 | 287 | 114.3 | 9,203 | 86.5 | 113 |
| 1938 | 283 | 112.7 | 12,553 | 118.0 | 89 |
| 1939 | 227 | 90.4 | 11,181 | 105.1 | 109 |
| 1939 † | 227 | 90.4 | 14,541 | 136.7 | 109 |
| 1940 | 219 | 87.2 | 13,400 | 126.0 | 125 |
| 1941 | 163 | 64.9 | 11,685 | 109.9 | 162 |
| 1942 | 123 | 49.0 | 9,282 | 87.3 | 199 |
| 1943 | 66 | 26.3 | 3,155 | 29.7 | 239 |

* SOURCES: R. A. Foulke, *Behind the Scenes of Business*, Dun & Bradstreet, 1937, p. 210; *Dun's Review*, February 1940, pp. 40, 42; *ibid.*, February 1941, pp. 42, 44; *ibid.*, February, 1943; *ibid.*, February, 1944; *Federal Reserve Bulletin.*

† New series including failures without official bankruptcy procedures, provided loss to creditors was involved.

ment as the situation permits. In other words, the little fellows hurt themselves and their families when they fail, without doing much damage to the economic structure. Furthermore, the extent of that damage must be related to the alternative of unemployment if they did not have their businesses. Undoubtedly, there is a social waste in excessive discontinuances, and it should be reduced by large-scale public effort to assure better prepared new enterprisers. The record of small-business failures, nevertheless, does not suggest the curtailment of freedom of entry as a remedy.

### REASONS FOR BUSINESS FAILURE

Evaluating the reasons for business failure is still a subjective exercise. The bankrupt and his creditors often disagree on the principal underlying causes; the former tends to stress external factors, and the latter finds the reasons for failure primarily in the individual's own shortcomings.

With bankruptcies decreasing notably in the late 1930's and into the war period, there was little pressure to stimulate recent studies of their causes. The few systematic analyses that are available deal with the depression years immediately after 1929; at that time considerable weight was given to the general economic letdown and the diminished values of inventories, real estate, and securities, as well as to the impact of failures of other firms. The fact is, however, that boom years as well as depression years may be high in failures—as witness the 22,909 bankruptcies in 1929 compared with 19,652 in 1921.[1] The variety of available field studies provides no clear consensus on the weights to be given to the various causes of failure; nevertheless, this section is an attempt to arrive at a summary.

Bradstreet's *Business Year Review* for 1932 dealt gently with the failure cases in that depression year, lumping 51 per cent under "external causes" or unfavorable circumstances. As for the failures due to internal causes, 30 per cent were attributed to lack of capital, less than 17 per cent to incompetence and inexperience, and a scattered few were classified under fraud, extravagance, or neglect. Few other analyses, however, have been so charitable.[2]

[1] See Table 19, above.

[2] See Emmett E. Barbee, "Reasons for Failure," *Credit and Financial Management*, November, 1941; John A. Cover, "Business and Personal Failure and Adjustment in

In a joint study made by the Department of Commerce and the Yale Institute of Human Relations, covering 500 failures in New Jersey during 1930, "external conditions" were allowed as the principal cause in only a small fraction of the cases, most being attributed to the shortcomings of the enterpriser. An analysis by Emmett E. Barbee supports this position. He conclndes that 80 to 90 per cent of failures are directly traceable to the man who fails.[1]

The factor most frequently cited as the cause of business failure is lack of capital, which is inevitable, since bankruptcy itself represents the inability to muster the current assets with which to meet current obligations. But the New Jersey study, probing the frequency with which this reason is given, arrives at the following conclusions:

> Lack of capital was not an important cause of failure in the cases studied. In most of those cases where failure was attributed to lack of capital, something else was the cause. These individuals had control over all the capital they could efficiently administer; in fact, in a few instances, the figures seemed to indicate that too much capital, rather than too little, contributed to the downfall. The owners of the businesses had received more credit than their business ability seemed to warrant. They had received generous extensions of credit, the proceeds from which had been used up gradually, through lack of proper management. They then lacked capital, it is true, but this condition was a result of failure rather than a cause of it. Undoubtedly at times competent businessmen launch themselves on enterprises with possibilities for success and are forced into failure because, for some reason or other, they are unable to secure credit to carry on the business, but these cases are rare and were inconspicuous in the New Jersey study.[2]

The New Jersey study found that 23.5 per cent of the proprietors kept no books and 39 per cent never took inventory. The study found, furthermore, that of those who did a credit business and were able to furnish figures, the bad-debt loss was 7.2 per cent, while the average loss on installment credit was 17.1 per cent.

---

Chicago," *Journal of Business of the University of Chicago*, July, 1933, Part 2; U.S. Department of Commerce, *Business Failures in New Jersey*, Domestic Commerce Series No. 54, November, 1931.

[1] Barbee, *op. cit.*, p. 20.

[2] U.S. Department of Commerce Bulletin, Domestic Commerce Series No. 54, 1931, p. 20.

Perhaps the nearest approach to a balanced evaluation of the principal factors responsible for failures in small business is afforded in the accompanying table. It is reproduced from a study by John A. Cover of 1,600 failures, including 397 proprietors in retail business in Chicago, covering the period between January, 1931, and April, 1932 (see Table 23, page 67). In this breakdown, Cover properly groups the financial difficulties under weaknesses in management to account for more than 50 per cent of the causes of failure. Another quarter of the cases are included under environmental factors, such as changes in the neighborhood and changes in the character of the competition. The remainder includes personal and family situations that impinged unfavorably upon the business.

*Informal Failures.* There is virtually no literature on the more numerous cases of small-business failure not recorded as bankruptcies. Those who quietly slip out of the business picture after informal settlements take their reason for failure with them. Some inkling of the causes has been sought, for our present purpose, through the experience of credit men who have dealt widely with liquidations that did not warrant bankruptcy procedure. Commonly involved in these cooperative settlements are new enterprises that can be halted before they get too deeply involved or cases of misfortune that enlist a sympathetic working out of the problem on the part of the creditors.[1] The pattern of causes they reveal, however, differs only slightly from that which appears in the bankruptcy cases.

The following ideas on the "why" of small business failures have been culled from formal studies and from oral comments:

1. Deficiencies in management supply the underlying cause of failure in the majority of cases, usually with unfavorable external conditions to make the failure decisive.

2. Most failures are in the very young enterprises, reflecting a

[1] Many a business failure is the obverse side of what might, with a better combination of breaks, have turned out a success. There is little point in dwelling here on the foibles of Lady Luck. We must assume that in the aggregate a relative balance is struck between the cases in which the enterpriser makes his own breaks and those in which he is swept along by them. Policy must necessarily be based on situations that can be improved, through better preparation, technical guidance, and financial support.

TABLE 23

PRINCIPAL FACTORS IN FAILURE OF INDIVIDUAL PROPRIETORS IN RETAIL BUSINESS*

| Factors | Number of cases | | | Percentage of cases | | |
|---|---|---|---|---|---|---|
| Management | 199 | .. | .. | 50.1 | | |
| Capital | ... | 26 | .. | ..... | 6.5 | |
| Inadequate at organization | ... | .. | 12 | ..... | .... | 3.0 |
| Mortgage | ... | .. | 2 | ..... | .... | 0.5 |
| Fixtures and equipment | ... | .. | 12 | ..... | .... | 3.0 |
| Overhead | ... | 48 | .. | ..... | 12.1 | |
| Credit extension | ... | 18 | .. | ..... | 4.5 | |
| Expansion | ... | 15 | .. | ..... | 3.8 | |
| Location | ... | 22 | .. | ..... | 5.6 | |
| Experience | ... | 28 | .. | ..... | 7.0 | |
| Negligence | ... | 11 | .. | ..... | 2.8 | |
| Indorsing notes | ... | 6 | .. | ..... | 1.5 | |
| General incompetence | ... | 25 | .. | ..... | 6.3 | |
| Environmental conditions | 109 | .. | .. | 27.4 | | |
| Competition | ... | 70 | .. | ..... | 17.6 | |
| Price | ... | .. | 15 | ..... | .... | 3.8 |
| Chain | ... | .. | 37 | ..... | .... | 9.3 |
| Other | ... | .. | 18 | ..... | .... | 4.5 |
| Neighborhood changes | ... | 20 | .. | ..... | 5.0 | |
| Highway obstruction | ... | .. | 2 | ..... | .... | 0.5 |
| Migration | ... | .. | 2 | ..... | .... | 0.5 |
| Closed factories | ... | .. | 12 | ..... | .... | 3.0 |
| Closed banks | ... | .. | 4 | ..... | .... | 1.0 |
| Inventory deflation | ... | 10 | .. | ..... | 2.5 | |
| Burglary or fire | ... | 9 | .. | ..... | 2.3 | |
| Family affairs | 39 | .. | .. | 9.8 | | |
| Medical expenses | ... | 13 | .. | ..... | 3.2 | |
| Illness of bankrupt | ... | 9 | .. | ..... | 2.3 | |
| Extravagance | ... | 9 | .. | ..... | 2.3 | |
| Dependents | ... | 8 | .. | ..... | 2.0 | |
| Personal characteristics | 8 | .. | .. | 2.0 | | |
| Speculation | 29 | .. | .. | 7.3 | | |
| Real estate | ... | 24 | .. | ..... | 6.0 | |
| Stock | ... | 5 | .. | ..... | 1.3 | |
| Miscellaneous | 13 | .. | .. | 3.3 | | |
| Total | 397 | | | 100.0 | | |

* *Journal of Business*, Vol. VI (July, 1933), Part 2, p. 18 (study directed by John A. Cover).

lack of preparation. As important as the business inexperience of the enterpriser is his failure to lay the groundwork for determining the scope of the enterprise, the character of its market, and the kind of equipment—personal and physical—it requires.

3. The prevailing weaknesses of management fall within the area of *financial* management. They range from a complete absence of record-keeping and loose credit-granting to a lack of regard for the necessary relationship between available funds and their appropriate uses.

4. The small enterpriser tends to be tied up in the immediate operations of purchase, sales; or craftsmanship without taking time for analysis of his position either by himself or by outside counsel. Insolvency thus often comes as a shock to the enterpriser.

5. Personality difficulties that doom small proprietorships include a lack of alertness to meet changing situations, inability to maintain friendly relations with help and customers, and, to a lesser extent, shiftlessness, neglect, and personal involvements in questionable outside activities.

6. The advent of severe competition often marks the turning point in the life of the business, determining whether it will meet the challenge with a reexamination of the enterprise and a fresh grip on its problems or go under for lack of inherent strength.

7. External factors, like economic changes, unfavorable legislation, and "acts of God," occasionally wipe out a well-managed business, but these are of comparatively minor importance in the total.

## LIFE SPAN OF SMALL BUSINESS

The competitive problem of small business is sometimes expressed in a question as to the survival chances of a new business. What percentage of new business will not outlast the first year? What percentage will keep going 5 years, 10 years, or longer? Does a business with a small investment have as good a chance of survival as the one with a larger investment? For answers we have to depend, at this date, upon the few interesting and suggestive investigations of specific communities that have been made.

For the purposes of this discussion, the results of five such studies will be considered—three in retailing, one in manufactures, and one covering all lines.

### *Retail Survival*

*Indiana Stores.* The observations that follow are based on a study of 207 Indiana communities representing 40 per cent of the state's population, covering the period 1930–1937. The magnitude of the turnover is thus described:

> Out of a total of 10,430 stores in business at the end of 1929 and 13,585 starting during the first eight years, disappearances aggregated 14,509, or 139 per cent of the number of stores operating at the end of 1929. Since the actual number of closings exceeded openings by 924, there were 9 per cent fewer retail outlets in 1937 than in 1929.[1]

Of the stores entering business in 1930, approximately 27 per cent were still in business 7 years later. Almost exactly one-fourth of the retail stores started in 1930 were out of business by 1931; another 18.5 per cent of the original number went out by the end of the second year, and another 10 per cent by the end of the third year. So within 3 years after the given date more than half of the stores were out of business. From then on the loss was progressively smaller each year.

As can be seen from Table 24 (p. 70) the percentage of businesses remaining at the end of 7 years differed markedly from one line to the next. In the drug business better than 50 per cent survived, but less than 16 per cent of the restaurants remained. A relatively high degree of longevity was achieved by the hardware business. Other lines with a notably high percentage of exits were the garage and the retail automobile sales businesses. Grocery and apparel businesses did somewhat better than average.

It was possible to break down the discontinuances in the 207 Indiana towns according to their capital rating in the Dun & Bradstreet reference book. Roughly one-fifth of the discontinuances had no rating whatever. About 53 per cent of the discontinued businesses had a capital rating under $2,000. Of the grocery stores, which accounted for about 40 per cent of the firms in the original sample, nearly 80 per cent of the discontinuances had a capital rating of less than $2,000 or no rating at all.

*Buffalo Study.* When the study of towns in Indiana is compared with other studies along the same lines, variations are found, which may reflect differences in size of community. In a study of retail trade in Buffalo, covering the 10-year period 1918–1927, the num-

[1] See G. W. Starr and G. A. Steiner, "The Births and Deaths of Retail Stores in Indiana, 1929–1937," *Dun's Review*, January, 1940, p. 24.

ber surviving the first year was only 40 per cent of those entering the grocery business; 56 per cent for shoe stores; 65 per cent for hardware; 73 per cent for drugs. The findings of the Buffalo study seem to bear out the point that the chance for survival is progressively improved after the initial year; each year thereafter there was a decline in the percentage dropping out. At the end of the seventh year the surviving groups ranged from 10 per cent of the starting number for the grocers to 42 per cent for the druggists.[1]

TABLE 24

LIFE SPAN OF RETAIL STORES IN 207 INDIANA TOWNS, 1930–1937*

| Retail trades | Per cent entering business 1930 | Per cent of stores which started in 1930 discontinuing in | | | | | | | Per cent still in business 1937 |
|---|---|---|---|---|---|---|---|---|---|
| | | 1st year | 2d year | 3d year | 4th year | 5th year | 6th year | 7th year | |
| Groceries | 100 | 22.5 | 16.4 | 10.3 | 8.1 | 5.4 | 4.5 | 2.7 | 30.1 |
| Shoes | 100 | 23.9 | 21.7 | 13.0 | 4.3 | ... | 2.2 | ... | 34.9 |
| Hardware | 100 | 11.5 | 16.4 | 9.8 | 3.3 | 1.6 | 6.6 | 4.9 | 45.9 |
| Garage and automobile sales | 100 | 30.5 | 19.9 | 11.9 | 6.3 | 5.7 | 5.7 | 3.4 | 17.4 |
| Department stores | 100 | 30.3 | 27.3 | 9.1 | 6.1 | 3.0 | .... | ... | 24.2 |
| General stores | 100 | 24.3 | 18.9 | 14.9 | 6.8 | 2.7 | 4.1 | 4.1 | 24.2 |
| Drugs | 100 | 14.0 | 14.0 | 6.5 | 5.4 | 2.2 | 5.3 | 2.2 | 50.4 |
| Restaurants | 100 | 33.1 | 20.4 | 8.4 | 11.3 | 5.1 | 4.4 | 1.8 | 15.5 |
| Men's clothing | 100 | 17.3 | 16.0 | 11.1 | 12.3 | 6.2 | 1.2 | 1.2 | 34.7 |
| Women's clothing | 100 | 21.9 | 21.9 | 6.1 | 5.3 | 6.1 | 4.4 | 2.6 | 31.7 |
| Furniture | 100 | 20.0 | 18.2 | 5.5 | 3.6 | 5.5 | 12.7 | 5.5 | 29.0 |
| Total | 100 | 24.9 | 18.4 | 9.9 | 7.6 | 4.9 | 4.8 | 2.7 | 26.8 |

* SOURCE: G. W. Starr and G. A. Steiner, "Births and Deaths of Retail Stores in Indiana, 1929–1937," *Dun's Review*, January, 1940, p. 27.

The Buffalo study emphasizes the fact that many withdrawals after the first two or three years are made by ambitious retailers who, having established a successful business, sell out and move on to other areas or larger opportunities. Of those who answered questions regarding the rise or fall in volume of business, importance was attached to the changing character of the neighborhood or the

[1] *Mortality in Retail Trade*, University of Buffalo Studies in Business, No. 4, 1930, p. 51.

community. This factor vied with chain-store competition as an alleged determinant in sales decline.[1]

*Illinois Study.* A study of mortality in 255 Illinois towns bears out the relationship between the growth and decline of neighborhood populations and the mortality of retail stores. It also shows that automobiles have moved trade from rural areas to nearby cities, but at the same time it points up the fact that many rural stores persist in the face of declining population.[2]

### *Manufacturing Discontinuances*

*Minnesota Study.* The relation of capital size to the length of business survival was brought out in a study by the University of Minnesota of manufacturing concerns in three Minnesota towns covering the years 1926–1930. In this case, the percentage of discontinuances by net worth groupings was as follows:[3]

TABLE 25

| *Net Worth* | *Discontinuances of 1926–1930 as a Per Cent of Total Enterprises in Existence, 1930* |
|---|---|
| $500,000 and over | 16.5 |
| 75,000–500,000 | 15.0 |
| 10,000– 75,000 | 35.8 |
| 2,000– 10,000 | 66.3 |
| Less than $2,000 or unclassified | 87.4 |
| All enterprises | 62.0 |

This short study of the Minnesota manufacturers is more eloquent as to the relation between size and longevity than is the Indiana study of retail discontinuances. That more than 70 per cent of the retail withdrawals (in Indiana) had capital ratings under $2,000 or no rating at all is not surprising if it is remembered that the majority of retail firms go into business on a shoestring. In the case of manufacturers, however, the average initial investment is considerably higher. Therefore, the fact that seven-eighths of all

[1] Among the grocers who reported declines in business, 57 per cent continued operating their stores in spite of a decline in sales over a 5-year period. See *ibid.*, p. 93.

[2] Paul D. Converse, "Business Mortality of Illinois Retail Stores," University of Illinois, *Business Research Bulletin* 41, p. 34.

[3] Senate Committee Print No. 13, September, 1942, p. 45.

the discontinuances among the Minnesota manufacturers had capital ratings under $2,000 would indicate that the low-capital group is responsible for a disproportionately high percentage of discontinuances among manufacturers.

### *Long-term Mortality Trend*

*Poughkeepsie Study.*[1] The longest period for which the mortality record of business enterprises has been followed is in a study made of business enterprises in Poughkeepsie, N.Y., covering nearly a century. It includes all businesses, excepting finance and utilities, listed in the city directories between 1844 and 1926. Nearly all were small enterprises. The study enables us to make at least two comparisons of direct interest: one on the difference in longevity of different types of enterprise, the second on how the mortality of recent years compares with that of the nineteenth century.

Taking the firms for the whole period (and counting any change in proprietorship as a new enterprise), 19 per cent of the proprietors still owned their businesses after 10 years. The highest percentage of survival was in wholesaling and manufacturing, in which 25.1 and 21.4 per cent, respectively, of the establishments continued for more than 10 years. The lowest survival rate was in small craft and service lines, where 18.1 and 16.6 per cent, respectively, remained under the same ownership for more than 10 years.[2]

A little more than 30 per cent of the enterprises dropped out within one year, averaging the entire period. The mortality in retail and service lines was somewhat higher than the average, while for wholesaling and manufacturing it was considerably less. By the end of the third year, a little more than half of the establishments had withdrawn.

Among the retail stores, confectioners, cigar stores, and saloons

[1] R. G. Hutchinson, A. R. Hutchinson, and Mabel Newcomer, "A Study in Business Mortality—Length of Life of Business Enterprises in Poughkeepsie, N.Y. 1843–1936," *American Economic Review*, September, 1938, pp. 497–514; also, by same authors, "Business Life and Death in a Hudson River Town," *Dun's Review*, June, 1939, pp. 12–18.

[2] Enterprises lasting more than 20 years—not counting change of proprietorship as a new business—made up 9.7 per cent of the firms established in Poughkeepsie from 1844 to 1916. Hutchinson, Hutchinson, and Newcomer, *op. cit.*, p. 500.

had the highest mortality; barbers and grocers did better than average.

TABLE 26

LENGTH OF LIFE OF ENTERPRISES ESTABLISHED BETWEEN 1844 AND 1926*
(Counting change in proprietorship as a new enterprise)

| *Years of life* | *Type and number of enterprises* | | | | | |
|---|---|---|---|---|---|---|
| | *Wholesaling, 183* | *Manufacturing, 1,194* | *Retailing, 5,567* | *Craft, 1,423* | *Service, 2,855* | *Total, 11,222* |
| | *Per cent* | | | | | |
| 1 or less.... | 22.4 | 24.0 | 32.5 | 31.9 | 32.9 | 31.5 |
| 2 or less.... | 32.2 | 37.1 | 45.8 | 46.7 | 47.2 | 45.2 |
| 3 or less.... | 43.7 | 49.8 | 55.0 | 56.5 | 56.8 | 55.0 |
| 5 or less.... | 57.9 | 63.2 | 66.2 | 68.1 | 69.0 | 66.7 |
| 10 or less... | 74.9 | 78.6 | 80.7 | 81.9 | 83.4 | 81.3 |
| Over 10.... | 25.1 | 21.4 | 19.3 | 18.1 | 16.6 | 18.7 |

* SOURCE: *Dun's Review*, June, 1939, p. 13.

A comparison of the life span of the corporations with non-incorporated enterprises indicates, as would be expected, that the former tended to outlive the latter. But considering that corporations are generally larger businesses and that their charters are for an unlimited period, it is significant that the corporations did not show an even greater difference in survival.

TABLE 27

LENGTH OF LIFE OF CORPORATIONS COMPARED WITH ALL ENTERPRISES, 1844–1926*

| *Years of life* | *All enterprises, per cent* | *Corporations, per cent* |
|---|---|---|
| Over 10.......................... | 21.4 | 29.3 |
| Over 5.......................... | 35.5 | 46.2 |
| Over 3.......................... | 46.9 | 59.0 |
| Over 2.......................... | 56.6 | 70.7 |
| Over 1.......................... | 70.2 | 83.9 |

* SOURCE: *Dun's Review*, June, 1939, p. 16.

*Stability of Survival Rate.* One of the most interesting features of the Poughkeepsie study is its evidence that high mortality in small business is no recent development. There is little to choose among the three 30-year periods between 1844 and 1933. Despite the arrival of chain stores, fewer grocers dropped out in the first year during the generation 1904–1933 than in the period 1844–1873. A larger percentage also survived the initial 3-year period, in the more recent three decades, than during the first 30 years. To judge from this one study, most lines of retailing lived somewhat longer during the last quarter of the nineteenth century than they did prior to that or during the first third of the twentieth century. But the difference is by no means significant, and some examples of recent improvement in longevity of independent establishments are in the very retail lines that have had chain-store competition.

TABLE 28
LENGTH OF LIFE OF 10 KINDS OF RETAIL ENTERPRISES IN THREE 30-YEAR PERIODS, 1844–1933, PER CENT*

| *Kind of business* | *Living 1 year or less* | | | *Living over 3 years* | | |
|---|---|---|---|---|---|---|
| | *1844–1873* | *1874–1903* | *1904–1933* | *1844–1873* | *1874–1903* | *1904–1933* |
| Confectionery stores | 47 | 50 | 44 | 20 | 29 | 24 |
| Cigar stores | 37 | 31 | 38 | 44 | 45 | 35 |
| Grocery stores | 39 | 20 | 29 | 35 | 57 | 46 |
| Meat markets | 43 | 40 | 29 | 43 | 36 | 51 |
| Saloons | 49 | 30 | 43 | 28 | 48 | 30 |
| Restaurants | 60 | 31 | 32 | 21 | 41 | 44 |
| Express service | 43 | 16 | 24 | 39 | 64 | 56 |
| Shoemakers | 34 | 28 | 28 | 38 | 52 | 51 |
| Tailors | 46 | 29 | 35 | 25 | 51 | 51 |
| Barbers | 35 | 25 | 25 | 49 | 56 | 55 |

* SOURCE: *Dun's Review*, June, 1939, p. 16.

## SUMMARY

Under a system of private enterprise, where entry into business is a matter for individual decision, the process of trial and error is bound to loom large in the comings and goings of individual ventures. It is also logical that those lines of business which require the smallest amounts of capital should account for the largest number of business births and also for the largest percentage of discontinuances.

A distinction should be made, however, between discontinuance and failure. Before the war more than one-third of all withdrawals from business represented not a net loss in the business population but rather a transfer—a change in organization or the form of ownership. Even with those which liquidate, failure cannot be assumed. Frequently, it is the successful business that is sold because of a good offer or a better opportunity elsewhere.

The degree to which other opportunities are available is a determining factor in continuance or withdrawal, particularly among one-man businesses. In this sector there is little capital at stake. The small contractor can readily take down his shingle and work as a carpenter or mason if there is a lull in residential building or if large-scale construction offers a better income.

The number of withdrawals in any year depends largely on the number of births in that year. Thus, we find a large number of discontinuances in good business years when business births are high and fewer discontinuances in the depression years when births are low.

Bankruptcies are not an important portion of discontinuances; usually they run less than 4 per cent. In the prewar years, bankruptcies in small business were found in less than ½ per cent of the corresponding population of business enterprises.

The life of the nation is continually undergoing changes to which small business must adapt. Some cities become larger, and some communities smaller. Neighborhoods run down. Suburbs grow as families move away from declining urban areas. Since small business is usually local in character, it is to be expected that small business especially will change and shift, die and be reborn as the local market undergoes such changes.

Also to be expected is that only a minority of the small-business venturers can be farseeing enough to know how to select the locality with the greatest promise or how to anticipate a changing market. When we recall how often Wall Street has been wrong in guesses about what will happen to the securities of large enterprises, it is not to be wondered at that the small businessman, with his comparative lack of background as well as information, does not do much better.

What cannot be measured from statistics of business mortality is the social cost that may result from the loss of savings by those who fail in business. If half a million firms change hands and drop out in a given year, they unquestionably include several thousand proprietors who were inadequately equipped for their undertakings, and this must involve some economic waste and social deterioration.

Gains from the experience of entrepreneurship for those who withdraw are as difficult to measure as is the possible demoralizing effect of failure. Private enterprise needs the dynamic element of new, independent ventures to keep alive the competition that is essential to the system. Many enterprises now classed as "middle-size" started as one-man concerns. There should be no disposition, therefore, to try to prevent excessive mortality in small business by obstructing freedom of entry. The emphasis should be, rather, on providing—through public agencies or private civic efforts—the guidance that would give the newcomers a better start and the incumbents better opportunity for improvement.

Despite the growth of large-scale enterprise, the mortality rate of small business has apparently not risen in recent years. Lines that have had to meet chain-store and mail-order competition have, on the whole, met that challenge and become more stable rather than less so. The trend of failures in small business generally has been downward since 1932. On balance, small business exhibits a high degree of stamina in a world where big business has made the spectacular gains. There is little in the record to indicate that the ability of the enterpriser has ceased to be the determining factor in success for the majority of small-business ventures.

# V. RELATIVE EFFICIENCY OF SMALL BUSINESS

THE COMMANDING position of big business in American industry does not prevent several hundred thousand venturesome souls from investing their talents and savings in small new enterprises each year. For these individuals the mortality record of small business seems to hold no terrors. It is enough that they have seen money made by similar small enterprises and that they have seen some of the little fellows grow to larger stature in the shadow of big business. If others can, they reason, why not they, too?

When one goes beyond the level of the self-employed to the independent business ventures of moderate size, the problem of attracting new investment capital arises. Enlargement of investment in small business must rest on a justified assumption that small business can carry its own weight as a contributor to the national income. There would be little point in embarking upon a national policy of promoting the growth of small business or granting it special privileges were that to mean wholesale subsidizing of economic inefficiency and wasteful employment of resources. If, on the other hand, there are segments of business in which the small enterprise has proved an efficient operating unit—comparing favorably with the efficiency of its large competitors but suffering from outside handicaps that retard its natural growth—then we are justified in fostering private and public measures that will give small enterprise a fair field in the competitive system.

For the prospective investor, confidence in the ability of small enterprise to operate profitably by the side of big business is, of course, requisite.

The miracles of mass production have been impressed upon us so much that the American flair for large-scale enterprise has become a national pride. "Bigger" means "better" to many Americans. Fewer questions are asked today than a generation ago about reasons other than efficient production that prompted the formation of the great corporate agglomerations now dominating wide areas of American business. In general, the public has been sold on the idea that corporate integration, mass production, superior management, and high efficiency all live together. Investment funds have followed the same trend. Even the smallest investor wants his funds in the blue chips of American industry. All this respect for bigness has tended to put small-scale enterprisers on the defensive; the burden of proof is on them to show that they, too, can win.

*Measuring Efficiency.* Measurement of the relative efficiency of small business by comparison with large-scale enterprise has serious shortcomings. Business efficiency is commonly gauged by the ability to hold down costs and earn a satisfactory profit. Cost records of a small business seldom permit accurate comparison with those of a larger unit. The tangible assets of the small business are usually small relative to the business done, and the ownership equity presents a different kind of base for calculating earnings than is applicable to big business. There are differences in the treatment of depreciation, inventory, and good will. In the small business it is not easy to separate owners' salaries and profits, and this makes for a variety of interpretations as to the rate of return that the business is earning.

The cases in which the end products of small and large businesses are strictly comparable are very few as compared with the total number of business enterprises. Even when the line is apparently the same, there are variations in quality, in kinds of customer, and in other aspects of the market.

Small and big business differ deliberately in their methods and objectives; the difference is often a factor in their joint prosperity. The custom tailor, for instance, is not interested in matching the timetable of the garment factory. His efficiency must be appraised in terms of his ability to profit through differentiation of his end product and service from that of the ready-to-wear trade. In distribution, the independent neighborhood shop may admittedly be unable to buy some standard items as cheaply as its rival chain store, but it may catch up on final cost by eliminating the intervening administrative controls that are essential to the larger organization. The small retailer may be in a position to take on wanted items for special customers in quantities profitable enough for him to carry that are too small for the chain store to consider in its buying program. These add up to the familiar and justifiable argument that opportunities for flexibility and informality in operation, when intelligently exploited by small enterprise, often result in a highly satisfactory relationship between cost and selling price.

It is common knowledge that there are many thousands of one-man enterprises in which the initial investment was so far below the minimum for efficient operation that even under favorable conditions no reasonable basis exists for expecting a stable or profitable operation. Businesses of this sort come and go with little attention paid to their comings and goings. At the other extreme are industrial combinations that have grown in complexity to the point where, according to the testimony of their own executives,[1] well-coordinated management is difficult to attain. Unprofitable operations within such corporate giants may be buried in the over-all showing because of the cumulative advantages of financial power, price domination, and market control, which offset weaknesses in specific areas of the total operation. The possibility that such corporations are taking in territory which should be left to much smaller businesses is suggested by studies of costs and profits, to be discussed later, in which the small units make a decidedly better showing than do the giants.

## SUMMARY OF EFFICIENCY COMPARISONS

From such tests of efficiency by size as it has been possible to review,[2] the following generalizations may tentatively be put down:

[1] See TNEC Monograph No. 13, pp. 130–31 quoting, among others, General Motors chairman (July, 1925): "In practically all our activities we seem to suffer from our great size. . . . There are so many people involved and it requires such a tremendous effort to put something new into effect that a new idea is likely to be considered insignificant in comparison with the effort that it takes to put it across. . . . Sometimes I am almost forced to the conclusion that General Motors is so large and its inertia so great that it is impossible for us to really be leaders."

[2] See, for general treatment of efficiency factors, J. M. Blair, "The Relation between Size and Efficiency of Business," *Review of Economic Statistics*, August, 1942; "Relative Efficiency of Large, Medium-sized and Small Business," TNEC Monograph No. 13; G. Rotholz, "A Critique of Tests of Efficiency," Graduate Thesis, University of Alberta, Winnipeg, 1943.

For cost comparisons: W. L. Mitchell, "Benchmarks of Profitable Operations in

1. The differences in efficiency among the small enterprises themselves are more extreme than those between small and large firms. The spread in costs between the average of the small-firm sample in a given line and the average of the larger size firms is usually narrower than the spread between the extremes within a size class.

2. The middle-size firms of an industry commonly make a better average showing on costs and earnings than do either the giants or the smallest members.

3. The over-all tendency is for unit costs to diminish as size increases until the big-business category is reached. But the very largest member of an industry does not usually show the lowest cost or the best profit rate on invested capital. In most cases a firm in the middle range makes the best showing, and frequently a small firm leads the industry in this respect.

4. Beginning with the lowest bracket—under $50,000 of invested capital—there is a fairly consistent rise in the average rate of earnings as size increases. But the point at which the optimum of profitability is reached differs widely from industry to industry. Thus, in tobacco manufacturing or special machinery lines, the highest rate of profit was found to be near the top, at levels of $10 million or more of total investment. In the garment industry, by contrast, the big profit rates were attained at around $100,000 of invested capital.

---

50 Retail Trades," *Dun's Review*, October, 1940; Mitchell, "How Expenses and Profits Vary with Retail Credit Policies," *ibid.*, November, 1940; Mitchell, "How Retail Advertising Expenditures Vary with Sales Volume and Size of City," *ibid.*, January, 1941; Mitchell, "Occupancy Expense and the Extent of Tenancy in Retailing," *ibid.*, February, 1941; "How Wages and Salary Expense Varies in 50 Retail Trades," *ibid.*, April, 1941. *Report of the FTC* on *Distribution Methods and Costs*, Part 1, Important Food Products; Part III, Building Materials; Part IV, Petroleum Products, Automobiles, Rubber Tires and Tubes, Electrical Household Appliances, and Agricultural Implements, Washington, D.C., 1944.

Size comparison of profits: W. L. Crum, *The Effect of Size on Corporate Earnings and Condition*, Harvard Business Research Studies No. 8, 1934; Crum, "Corporate Earnings on Invested Capital," *Harvard Business Review*, Vol. XVI, No. 3 (Spring, 1938); Crum, "Earning Power with Respect to the Size of Corporations," *ibid.*, Vol. XVII, No. 1 (Autumn, 1938); Crum, *Corporate Size and Earning Power*, Harvard University Press, Cambridge, 1939; R. C. Epstein, *Industrial Profits in the United States*, National Bureau of Economic Research, New York, 1934; J. L. McConnell, "Corporate Earnings by Size of Firm," *Survey of Current Business*, May, 1945; *How Profitable is Big Business?* The Twentieth Century Fund, Inc., New York, 1937.

5. The relative profitability of small and large business changes markedly as the general level of business activity changes. The profits of small businesses tend to rise more sharply than those of big business when general conditions are improving. Conversely, in a recession the drop in profits and the increase in the percentage of deficit firms is much more abrupt for small than for large business.

6. The disparity between the most profitable and the least profitable firms is relatively much greater for small business than for big business. The percentage of deficit firms is notably greater in the small-business brackets than in big business. In "normal" years, when medium-size and large businesses were showing a good average rate of return and a few well-managed small units were profitable, the number of deficit corporations in the lowest size bracket was sufficient to create a net deficit for the small-business group as a whole.

The available evidence, in data and opinion, emphasizes the high degree of selectivity that must be exercised in the investment of funds with small business, in view of the wide range in the degree of success that is achieved by small business.

### THE EVIDENCE ON RELATIVE COSTS

Physical comparisons of costs between small and large businesses have necessarily been confined to a sample of situations in which a representative number of companies in all size classes deal with the same commodity. The lines of manufacture or service that meet this test are whittled down further when we rule out cases in which there are significant differences in location, working conditions, access to raw materials, rents, and product variations.

The most comprehensive examination of unit costs available is that made by the FTC for the TNEC. Data on costs and financial position were supplied for 18 industries covering a total product roughly "equal to about one-fourth of the total value of product shown for all industries in the *Census of Manufactures, 1937*."[1]

[1] The industries tested were the following: cement, blast furnaces, steel mills, farm machinery, petroleum production, petroleum refining, beet-sugar production, cane-sugar production, sugar refining, milk distribution, butter, canned milk, flour milling, baking, motor vehicles, chemicals, fertilizers, rayon. See "Relative Efficiency of Large, Medium-sized, and Small Business," TNEC Monograph No. 13, p. 8.

*Company Size.* The FTC, straining somewhat to draw comfort for small business from its findings, points out that the big company often failed to make the best score.

In but one of the 59 individual company tests did the largest company have the lowest costs. In 21 of the 59 tests a company classified as medium-sized had the lowest cost. In 37 of the 59 tests a company classified as small had the lowest cost. [It was true, however, that the largest company was generally within the most efficient (low-cost) third in each array.] In only one of the 11 tests derived from the tables showing average costs of companies does the group containing the largest companies have the lowest average cost shown for any group. In 10 of the 11 tests the group containing companies generally classified as medium-sized had the lowest average cost shown for any group.[1]

*Plant Size.* Comparison by size of plant does not necessarily have the same significance as comparison by size of company, since a single large plant may belong to a company smaller than a corporation that has a combination of smaller plants. In the tests made by the FTC on the basis of individual plant costs, the lowest cost was achieved by the largest plant or one of the largest in 6 out of 53 tests. A medium-size plant had the lowest cost in 21 of the 53 tests, while in 26 of the tests small plants had the lowest costs. When the plants were grouped, the lowest average cost was invariably shown by plants classified as medium-size.

*Sample Cases.* The total sample used by the FTC included some industries for which it was necessary to take firms with assets up to $5 million as small business. (That was true, for example, in the cases of beet-sugar refining and farm machinery.) Three industries are selected for more detailed examination here of the size-cost relationship in which really small as well as large firms were in competition: cement, wheat flour, and milk.

*Cement.* In the sample of cement producers the smallest firms show cost per barrel ranging all the way from 91 cents for the lowest cost producer to $2.17 for the highest (Table 29, page 84). The spread for the next size group is narrower: from a low of 99 cents to a high of $1.34. The spread from low to high inside the big-business class is decidedly narrower than for the small-business

[1] *Ibid.*, p. 12.

group; the three big-business operators were only 14 cents apart, against a spread of $1.26 in cost per barrel for the small producers.[1]

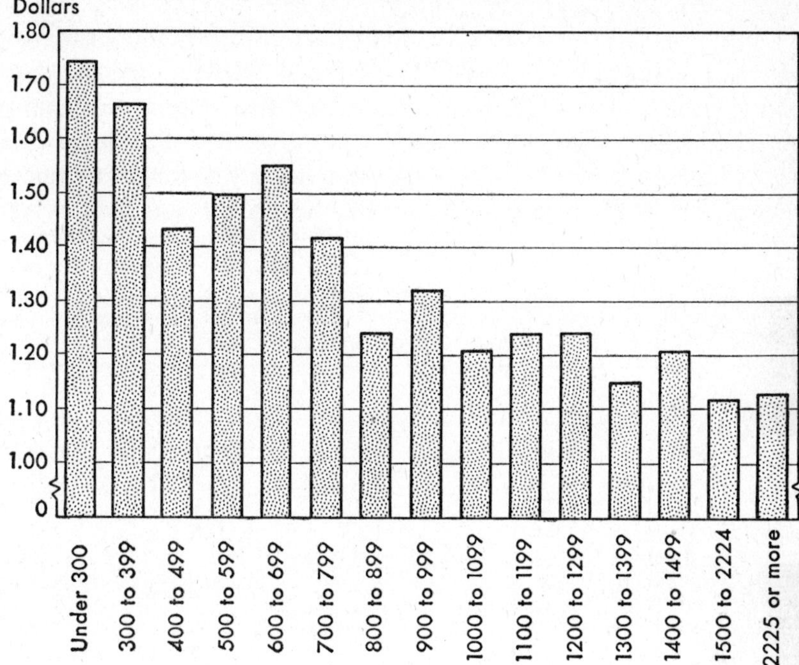


CHART 3. Unit production costs of cement. Production costs include plant cost, administrative costs applicable to production, and imputed interest. Vertical scale (note break between 0 and $1.00) = costs per barrel; horizontal scale = thousand barrels produced. Plants have been grouped according to annual production. Each class interval from 300,000 to 1,500,000 barrels of cement represents 100,000 barrels annually; but beyond the 1,500,000 class, because of the rapid increase in the size of plants, it was necessary to broaden the intervals to prevent individual disclosures. Sixteen large plants had to be grouped: Since the average number of plants in the 13 smaller class intervals was 7.5 per interval, the remaining 16 plants were divided into two groups of 8 plants each. (*Data from files of the U.S. Tariff Commission; graph by John M. Blair, Review of Economic Statistics, Vol. XXIV, p.* 129.)

Here we have both the lowest cost and the highest cost for the industry within the small-business group. The *lowest average* cost is scored by the firms in the intermediate-size class. The average

[1] It can be argued that since there are so many more cases in the small-firm sample than in the others, one would expect the greater dispersion that occurs in that sample. But then there are many more of the little fellows than of the business giants in "real life"; so that characteristic of the sample may be taken as a reflection of the actual situation.

cost for the smallest enterprises, taken as a group, is higher than for the others. Yet the difference between the group averages is not so striking as the spread within a given size.

What we fail to see from the above array in ascending order of cost is whether the most efficient of the small firms are the very small ones or those of more substantial size within the small-business class. Only when the firms are arranged in an ascending order of size do we discover that the tendency is for unit costs to go down as size increases—although the progression is not perfectly consistent (see Chart 3).[1]

TABLE 29

COSTS PER BARREL OF 45 CEMENT COMPANIES IN 1929 ARRANGED IN ORDER OF ASCENDING COSTS, BY SIZE CLASS*

| *Very small* † | | | *Small* ‡ | *Medium* § | *Large* ‖ |
|---|---|---|---|---|---|
| $0.91 | $1.23 | $1.50 | $0.99 | $1.14 | $1.18 |
| 1.02 | 1.26 | 1.51 | 1.15 | 1.18 | 1.19 |
| 1.05 | 1.27 | 1.53 | 1.19 | 1.19 | 1.32 |
| 1.13 | 1.28 | 1.54 | 1.28 | 1.41 | |
| 1.14 | 1.28 | 1.59 | 1.33 | | |
| 1.16 | 1.29 | 1.65 | 1.34 | | |
| 1.19 | 1.31 | 1.76 | | | |
| 1.19 | 1.31 | 1.90 | Avg. $1.21 | Avg. $1.23 | Avg. $1.23 |
| 1.20 | 1.33 | 2.00 | | | |
| 1.22 | 1.35 | 2.17 | | | |
| 1.23 | 1.38 | | | | |
| | | Avg. $1.37 | | | |

* SOURCE: Files of the U.S. Tariff Commission and TWEC Monograph No 13, p. 23.

† Companies with production under 2 million barrels.

‡ Production between 2 and 4 million barrels.

§ Penn-Dixie Cement Corp., Alpha Portland Cement Co., Ideal Cement Co., Medusa Portland Cement Co.

‖ Universal Atlas Cement, Lehigh Portland Cement, Lone Star Cement Corp.

*Flour.* For the processing of flour (Table 30, page 85), the cost studies of the FTC show an even greater variation among small firms than was found in the case of cement. The lowest cost small firm produced a barrel of wheat flour for about one-half of the average, while the small firm with the worst record showed

[1] John M. Blair, "Relation between Size and Efficiency of Business," *Review of Economic Statistics*, August, 1942, p. 129. Blair used the original data furnished to the FTC by the U.S. Tariff Commission to derive the trend of cost by size in the accompanying chart.

a cost nearly double the average of its class. In flour costs it is notable that nearly half of the small producers improved on the average performance of their large competitors.

TABLE 30

COST OF PRODUCING A BARREL OF WHEAT FLOUR (EXCLUDING COST OF WHEAT) IN 1922, BY COMPANIES OF DIFFERENT SIZE*

| *Small* | | | | *Medium* | *Large* |
|---|---|---|---|---|---|
| $0.59 | $0.85 | $1.05 | $1.31 | $0.71 | $0.69 |
| 0.63 | 0.86 | 1.08 | 1.31 | 0.74 | 0.78 |
| 0.63 | 0.86 | 1.09 | 1.33 | 0.80 | 0.94 |
| 0.70 | 0.86 | 1.09 | 1.40 | 0.85 | |
| 0.72 | 0.87 | 1.10 | 1.41 | 0.87 | Avg. $0.80 |
| 0.73 | 0.89 | 1.10 | 1.46 | 0.99 | |
| 0.73 | 0.89 | 1.10 | 1.46 | 1.13 | |
| 0.75 | 0.91 | 1.11 | 1.46 | 1.13 | |
| 0.75 | 0.91 | 1.11 | 1.47 | 1.15 | |
| 0.76 | 0.93 | 1.14 | 1.53 | 1.18 | |
| 0.77 | 0.93 | 1.15 | 1.55 | 1.21 | |
| 0.78 | 0.94 | 1.16 | 1.56 | 1.24 | |
| 0.78 | 0.96 | 1.17 | 1.57 | | |
| 0.79 | 0.97 | 1.18 | 1.63 | Avg. $1.00 | |
| 0.81 | 0.98 | 1.19 | 1.69 | | |
| 0.81 | 0.99 | 1.22 | 1.77 | | |
| 0.82 | 1.02 | 1.23 | 1.80 | | |
| 0.82 | 1.02 | 1.26 | 1.81 | | |
| 0.84 | 1.03 | 1.28 | 2.10 | | |
| 0.85 | 1.03 | 1.28 | | | |
| | | | Avg. $1.09 | | |

* SOURCE: TNEC Monograph No. 13, p. 67.

*Milk Distribution.* Shifting to an example in distribution—the distribution of milk—we find a cost pattern by size of distributor that is similar to the results in the manufacturing tests (Table 31, page 86).[1] Again, within the group classed as small are found both very low cost and highest cost firms. The average cost for the small-size group as a whole was higher than for the larger classes, but here, too, the averages from one class to the next are not so striking as the spread within a class.

The composite evidence seems to indicate that taken as a class, the smallest firms do not produce so cheaply as does their big-business competition. To offset that disadvantage in cost, the

[1] In this sample a small business is one that buys less than a million pounds of milk annually.

TABLE 31

COST OF DISTRIBUTING 100 POUNDS OF MILK BY 22 DEALERS IN WEST VIRGINIA FOR THE YEAR 1933

| | *Total distributing cost per 100 lb.* | *Delivery sales cost only per 100 lb.* |
|---|---|---|
| Small: | | |
| 1. | $1.51 | $0.40 |
| 2. | 1.93 | 0.70 |
| 3. | 2.24 | 1.21 |
| 4. | 2.45 | 0.77 |
| 5. | 2.48 | 0.91 |
| 6. | 2.91 | 1.07 |
| Average | $2.25 | $0.84 |
| Medium: | | |
| 1. | $1.72 | $0.72 |
| 2. | 1.78 | 0.57 |
| 3. | 1.86 | 0.73 |
| 4. | 1.96 | 0.69 |
| 5. | 2.05 | 0.62 |
| 6. | 2.24 | 0.85 |
| 7. | 2.28 | 1.16 |
| 8. | 2.49 | 0.88 |
| 9. | 2.78 | 1.04 |
| Average | $2.13 | $0.81 |
| Large: | | |
| 1. | $1.41 | $0.45 |
| 2. | 1.78 | 0.81 |
| 3. | 1.99 | 0.86 |
| 4. | 2.02 | 0.86 |
| 5. | 2.35 | 0.88 |
| 6. | 2.35 | 0.82 |
| 7. | 2.36 | 1.09 |
| Average | $2.04 | $0.82 |

* SOURCE: TNEC Monograph No. 13, p. 56.

small business must catch up by reduction of overhead, by giving a distinctive service, or by accepting a lower net profit. Yet the most efficient of the little fellows somehow manage to score better than the average of the larger firms, while the intermediate-size firms are well out in front in ability to hold down costs. The performance of the more efficient small and intermediate firms is often related to favorable factors of location, man power, or relative freedom from outside pressures or restrictions.

*Efficiency of Very Small Firms.* Obviously, the type of cost-efficiency analysis here presented has little if any direct bearing on the 2 million small retailer and service shops in which the proprietor is practically the whole works and in which his versatility is the key to efficiency. Many small operators achieve success, but their formula for doing so follows about the same degree of accuracy as a grandmother giving the recipe for her popular cake. Much remains to be done toward setting standards for the small enterprise on such operational factors as utilization of space, turnover of inventories, depreciation of equipment, and selling costs as a percentage of sales. So far, the allocation of costs to specific subsections of the operations of the tiny enterprise—at least any breakdown that would permit comparisons with the chains, mail-order houses, or department stores—has not yet been achieved.[1]

The only efficiency test on which the little firms are at all comparable to their bigger competitors is the general rate of profits.

## RATE OF PROFITS

Comparison of profits between small and large firms must be approached cautiously. We have to contend with lack of uniformity in accounting methods, in purposes of reports to stockholders, and in the relation between capital resources and volume of sales. Since the dividing line between salaries and profits is not so well defined in a small business as in a large, the real rate of profit in the small business is debatable. Some revealing patterns, nevertheless, emerge from the data available. (For general comparisons of business profits by size, the financial returns for corporations supplied the Bureau of Internal Revenue provide most of the data.)

*Dispersion of Small-business Profits.* The diversity in the rate of profit of small firms in the same line is even more striking than the

[1] Progress in this direction, limited but increasing, is being made by the Department of Commerce through its series of cost studies. See Charles H. Sevin, *Distribution Cost Analysis*, Economic Series 50, 1946. Averages based on regional or local experience would obviously be more useful to the very small business than national averages.

diversity in costs. If we consider all corporations in each size class, those with deficits as well as those with net incomes, we invariably find the lowest average rate of profits in the assets class under $50,000. In every year, good as well as bad, a large fraction of the income tax returns from the small firms reported deficits. In no year during the decade 1931–1940 did corporations with asset size below $50,000 show a net profit *in the aggregate*. In the next class—$50,000 to $100,000 of total assets—a net income for the whole group was not shown until 1936.

Taking by way of illustration the prewar years 1936, 1939, and 1941, we get the following showing for corporations with assets under $50,000:

TABLE 32

| | *1936* | *1939* | *1941* |
|---|---|---|---|
| Number of returns with balance sheets*..... | 227,343 | 226,877 | 213,086 |
| Number with no net income.............. | 145,627 | 147,822 | 108,033 |
| Number with income..................... | 81,716 | 79,055 | 105,053 |
| Per cent with no net income.............. | 64.1 | 65.2 | 50.7 |

* Breakdown by asset classes is available only for corporations that submitted balance sheets. Presumably the percentage with no net income would at least be as great among the firms that did not submit balance sheets.

Among the deficit corporations alone, the average ratio of deficit to equity is highest for the smallest size class; the average deficit rate goes down as size increases. On the other hand, the small businesses that are in the black average a higher rate of return than is scored by the upper size classes with net income. This result is found to hold for any recent year regardless of the general level of business (see Tables 33 and 34, page 90).

*Year-to-year Record.* In comparing the profitability of small business with that of larger business, the year for which the comparison is made is highly significant. From the year-to-year evidence of the income tax returns, it is apparent that the earnings of small business, in comparison with large-scale enterprise, suffered relatively more when general business activity was low and showed relatively greater improvement when general business conditions were good.

The accompanying Chart 4, showing profit returns by size

of corporate assets, bears out the point that a level of business substantially above that of 1940 is needed to keep small business out of the red. That is not the same as saying that an increase in small-business prosperity cannot come unless there is an increase in small business's share of the nation's total sales volume. Indeed, a puzzling feature of the marked improvement in small

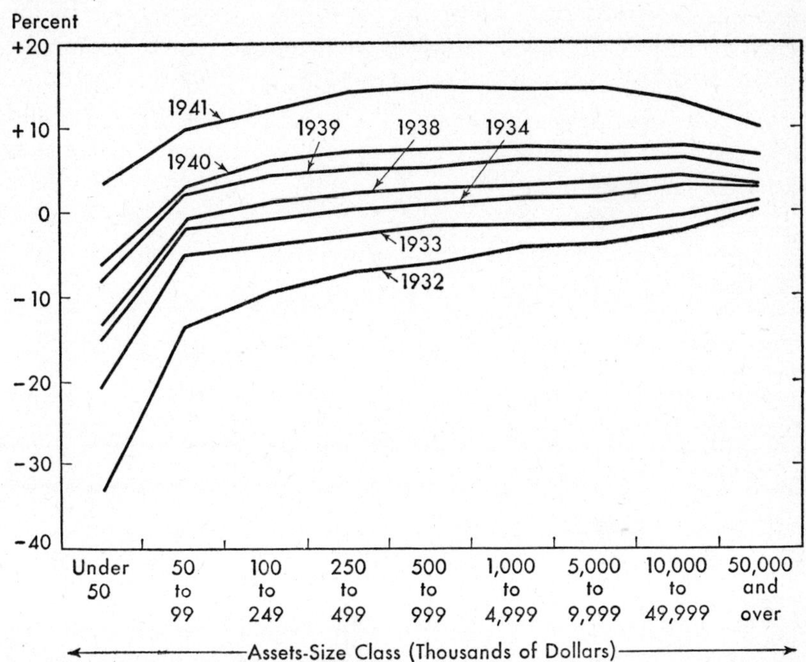


CHART 4. Ratio of net profits before taxes to equity, all corporations, by assets-size classes. (*U.S. Department of Commerce, based upon data of the U.S. Bureau of Internal Revenue.*)

business prosperity from 1939 to 1941 is this: While there was a sharp increase in general business activity over the two-year period, it was not accompanied by a proportionate increase in the volume of goods sold by small business.

According to the Statistics of Income compiled by the Bureau of Internal Revenue, the greatest percentage increase in sales during the period from 1939 to 1941 was registered by big business, not by little business. As we can see from Table 35 (page 91), the gross receipts from sales reported by *all* corporations that submitted balance sheets for 1941 ($176.7 billion) were about 45 per cent above the corresponding aggregate figure for 1939 ($121.6 billion). The *largest* firms (those with assets in excess of $10 million) registered increases of around 55 per cent. Meanwhile,

TABLE 33

RATE OF RETURN ON EQUITY IN 1934, FOR INCOME AND DEFICIT CORPORATIONS SEPARATELY AND BOTH COMBINED, BY SIZE CLASSES AND FOR ALL SIZES COMBINED*

| *Size class*† | *Income corporations* | *Deficit corporations* | *Both combined* |
|---|---|---|---|
| Under 50 | 10.06 | —37.4 | —14.40 |
| 50–100 | 8.38 | —13.0 | —2.68 |
| 100–250 | 8.10 | —10.3 | —1.22 |
| 250–500 | 8.02 | —8.25 | —0.09 |
| 500–1,000 | 7.88 | —7.50 | 0.32 |
| 1,000–5,000 | 7.30 | —5.07 | 1.11 |
| 5,000–10,000 | 7.07 | —4.62 | 1.42 |
| 10,000–50,000 | 6.87 | —2.48 | 2.51 |
| 50,000 and over | 5.69 | —0.022 | 2.74 |
| All sizes combined | 6.59 | —3.05 | 1.75 |

TABLE 34

RATE OF RETURN ON EQUITY, FOR INCOME CORPORATIONS, BY SPECIFIC SIZE CLASSES AND FOR ALL SIZES COMBINED*

| *Size class*† | *1931* | *1932* | *1933* | *1934* | *1935* |
|---|---|---|---|---|---|
| Under 50 | 10.80 | 8.06 | 7.99 | 10.06 | 10.11 |
| 50–100 | 7.53 | 6.03 | 6.64 | 8.38 | 8.41 |
| 100–250 | 6.65 | 5.84 | 6.63 | 8.10 | 8.27 |
| 250–500 | 6.73 | 6.00 | 6.95 | 8.02 | 8.29 |
| 500–1,000 | 6.49 | 5.98 | 6.99 | 7.88 | 8.41 |
| 1,000–5,000 | 6.48 | 5.67 | 6.84 | 7.30 | 8.23 |
| 5,000–10,000 | 7.22 | 6.03 | 6.68 | 7.07 | 7.50 |
| 10,000–50,000 | 7.11 | 6.29 | 7.13 | 6.87 | 8.17 |
| 50,000 and over | 7.04 | 5.50 | 4.76 | 5.69 | 6.70 |
| All sizes combined | 6.99 | 5.75 | 5.83 | 6.59 | 7.51 |

* SOURCE: W. L. Crum, *Harvard Business Review*, Vol. 17 (1938–1939), p. 21.

† Total assets, in thousands of dollars.

firms in the *lowest* assets class ($50,000 and under) showed an increase in aggregate commodity sales of not quite 2 per cent for 1941 over 1939; they showed a corresponding 8 per cent increase in other operating receipts. Their combined commodity sales and operating receipts exceeded those of 1939 by about 3 per cent. Those in the next larger group (assets $50,000 to $100,000) had a corresponding increase of less than 19 per cent from 1939 to 1941.

TABLE 35

REPORTED AGGREGATE SALES VOLUME BY SIZE OF CORPORATE ASSETS, 1939 AND 1941 *
(Thousands of dollars)

| *Asset classes* | *Cost of goods and service operations* | | *Receipts for sales and operations* | |
|---|---|---|---|---|
| | *1939* | *1941* | *1939* | *1941* |
| Total | 86,827,917 | 125,737,410 | 121,600,668 | 176,717,221 |
| Under 50 † | 6,926,737 | 7,100,103 | 9,425,037 | 9,706,189 |
| 50 under 100 | 5,059,920 | 6,033,420 | 6,669,638 | 7,952,198 |
| 100 under 250 | 8,445,448 | 11,070,162 | 11,088,132 | 14,543,177 |
| 250 under 500 | 6,710,294 | 9,508,689 | 8,896,730 | 12,695,471 |
| 500 under 1,000 | 6,673,473 | 9,716,490 | 8,902,432 | 13,117,796 |
| 1,000 under 5,000 | 14,416,234 | 21,861,114 | 19,843,580 | 30,136,872 |
| 5,000 under 10,000 | 5,170,306 | 8,311,047 | 7,493,111 | 12,064,168 |
| 10,000 under 50,000 | 12,228,196 | 19,239,205 | 18,033,055 | 27,911,004 |
| 50,000 under 100,000 | 4,514,707 | 6,964,341 | 7,082,399 | 11,027,605 |
| 100,000 and over | 16,682,601 | 25,932,839 | 24,166,555 | 37,562,741 |

* SOURCE: *Statistics of Income for 1939*, Part 2, pp. 140, 141; *Statistics of Income for 1941*, pp. 136, 137.

† The number of firms with assets under $50,000 submitting returns with balance sheets was, for 1939, 226,877; for 1941, 213,086. The average total assets for the firms in this class were, for 1939, $18,252; for 1941, $18,834. The costs of goods and service operations per firm, in the class under $50,000, was, for 1939, $30,530; for 1941, $33,320. The receipts for sales and operations per firm were, for 1939, $41,542, for 1941, $45,551.

That the small-business improvement immediately before the war came with a smaller share of the nation's sales is shown in Table 36 (page 92). Whereas the under-$50,000 class accounts for 7.8 per cent of all sales and operating receipts reported in the income tax returns of 1939, that group showed only 5.5 per cent of the aggregate for 1941.[1]

[1] The relatively small percentage of sales increase required by small business to improve its profit position holds throughout the decade of the 1930's. In the low year of 1932 the corporations with assets under $50,000 had an average net deficit of 32.8 per cent. During the succeeding years their general position improved until 1941, when for the first time in more than a decade the group of corporations in the lowest assets class showed an average net profit (3 per cent) rather than an average deficit. The change in profit position from year to year is shown in Chart 4. But over these years when the gross sales for all levels of business had more than doubled, the sales reported by the smallest corporations had increased by less than 50 per cent. Meanwhile, the share of the smallest corporations in total sales went down from 8.8 per cent

A truer impression of the improved position of the small firms from 1939 to 1941 may be had from the following figures on small-business sales. A good many firms that had been in the smallest business class—under $50,000 of total assets—in 1939 moved into the next higher class by 1941, many of those formerly in the next

TABLE 36

GROSS SALES AND RECEIPTS FROM OPERATIONS FOR SPECIFIED YEARS AS SHOWN IN RETURNS TO THE BUREAU OF INTERNAL REVENUE*

(Number of returns shown in parentheses; sales in thousands of dollars)

| *Year* | *Total, all asset classes* | *Firms with total assets* | | | |
|---|---|---|---|---|---|
| | | *Under $50,000* | | *$50,000–$100,000* | |
| | | *Aggregate sales and receipts from operations* | *Per cent of total* | *Aggregate sales and receipts from operations* | *Per cent of total* |
| 1933 | $74,951,334 (388,564) | $6,626,862 (211,586) | 8.8 | $4,143,018 (56,205) | 5.5 |
| 1935 | 102,883,997 (415,205) | 9,162,885 (227,545) | 8.9 | 5,916,697 (58,434) | 5.8 |
| 1937 | 130,003,679 (416,902) | 10,696,483 (228,721) | 8.2 | 7,412,166 (60,238) | 5.7 |
| 1939 | 121,600,668 (412,759) | 9,425,037 (226,877) | 7.8 | 6,669,638 (60,256) | 5.5 |
| 1941 | 176,717,222 (407,053) | 9,706,189 (213,086) | 5.5 | 7,952,198 (61,525) | 4.5 |

* SOURCE: *Statistics of Income for 1933*, Part 2, p. 166; *Statistics of Income for 1935*, Part 2, p. 60; *Statistics of Income for 1937*, Part 2, p. 80; *Statistics of Income for 1939*, Part 2, p. 140; *Statistics of Income for 1941*, Part 2, p. 136.

to the lowest class likewise stepped up into a higher class, etc. Part of this shift is reflected in the fact that although there were 226,877 returns to account for the 1939 aggregate in the under-$50,000 class, the corresponding returns numbered only 213,086 for 1941. On a per capita basis, therefore, the average sales per firm were $41,542 in 1939 against $45,551 in 1941. That makes an increase of better than 10 per cent in sales and operating receipts per firm in the smallest assets class.

---

in 1933 to 5.5 per cent in 1941. The data are given in Table 36 (above), which also shows that the next larger group of corporations fared better than those in the lowest size class but still did not step up sales at a rate equal to that of business as a whole.

There was no striking difference in the average assets per firm for the two years—$18,252 in 1939 compared with $18,834 in 1941—so that the additional 10 per cent in gross was done with practically no increase in size of firm. We are still left with the interesting result, however, that small business improved spectacularly in net income and climbed out of the red with a relatively small increase in gross sales.

How then can we account for the rise in small business profits? The following explanation suggests itself.

After several years of poor business, some of the least profitable small firms had dropped out, leaving a stronger group to survive into the better years. In a year of high business activity, small firms could be more independent about the kind of business they accepted and the margins at which they made sales. In other words, they shifted to more profitable types of business with fewer bad accounts. Moreover, small business could increase total sales without adding appreciably to operating cost—due in part, perhaps, to the ability to take cash discounts and reduce interest payments on debt, with better collections and fewer credit losses, and in part to a fuller use of equipment and personnel. On the strength of the Bureau of Internal Revenue data it may be said that for the smallest corporations there was roughly a $1 increase in total cost of sales for every $2 increase of gross sales. By contrast, for businesses in the top assets classes an increase of less than $1.30 in sales accounted for an increase of $1 in cost of sales. Thus, it would seem that even a comparatively modest improvement in the character and volume of its sales operations can have a major effect on net earnings of small business.

*Owner's Compensation in Small-business Profits.* No fruitful comparison of the profits of small enterprises can be made unless the compensation drawn by the owners of the business is taken into account. The small business is typically the source of employment for its owner. This is almost as true of the small corporation as it is of the unincorporated enterprise. In corporations with assets under $50,000, the officers comprise about one-fifth of the labor force and, of course, its highest paid segment. For companies with assets up to $50,000, the compensation of officers totaled roughly fifteen times the reported net profit in 1941, the best of the prewar years. All three of the classes with assets of up to $250,000 reported a larger amount for aggregate salaries to officers than the reported net profit.[1]

After deducting officers' compensation, the corporations in the lowest asset class showed a net deficit for every year in the 1930's.

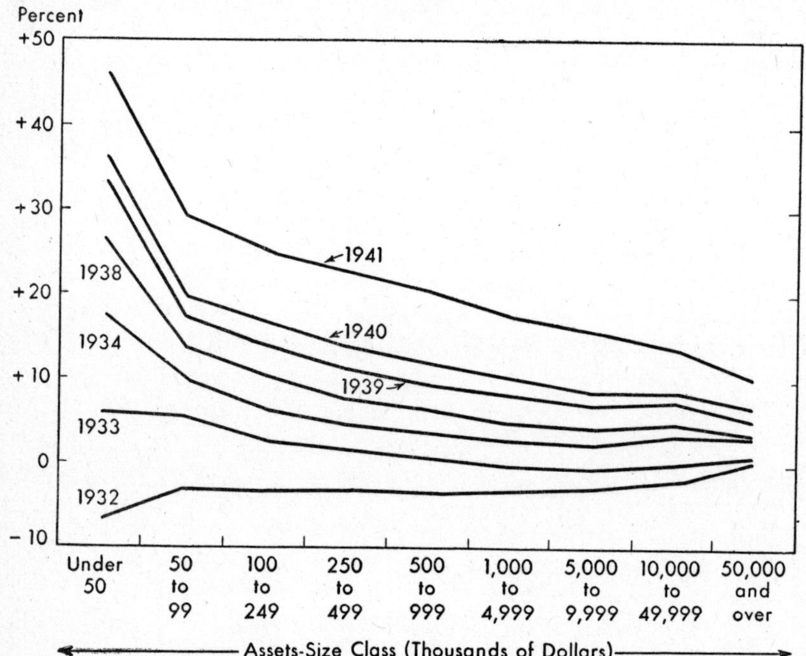


CHART 5. Ratio of net profits before taxes and officers' compensation to equity, all corporations, by assets-size classes. (*U.S. Department of Commerce, based upon data of the U.S. Bureau of Internal Revenue.*)

But the total return, *before* deducting officers' compensation, presents a different pattern. Instead of the average net profit ratio rising with successive increases in size of business as seen in Chart 4, the curve of profits before deducting officers' compensation (Chart 5) shows the smallest firms at the highest level, the profits ratio tapering off with increase in the size of business.

A typical corporation in the assets class under $50,000 had no net funds available from current earnings for officers' compensation

[1] J. L. McConnell, "Corporate Earnings by Size of Firm," *Survey of Current Business*, May, 1945, p. 7.

in 1932, but the return to owners rose to around $4,600 per firm by 1941.[1] By contrast, the deduction of officers' compensation has a hardly appreciable effect on the earnings ratio of firms with total assets over $5 million.

The drastic effect on reported net earnings that can be produced by fluctuations in the compensation of officers tends to blur the profit picture. We can therefore get a truer idea of the net profits of small businesses by arbitrarily assigning an average rate of compensation for officers to firms in a given size class. Consideration must also be given to differences in the going salary rates of owner-managers as between manufactures and distribution or between distribution and services and among different lines of industry. Such an adjustment has been worked out by the Business Structure Unit in the Department of Commerce. Some of the results obtained from the analysis on that basis are pointed up in the accompanying charts (No. 6, by industry groups; No. 7, for specific industries).[2] Taking the year 1939, the firms with assets below $50,000 show up less favorably than those in any of the higher classes. In the more prosperous year of 1941, the rate earned by the smallest businesses on their equity, before taxes, begins to match the rate for big business. The upper levels of small business and the firms in the intermediate size classes (up to $10 million) show a higher ratio of net profit to equity than do those in the big-business class.

*Industry Variations.* The pattern of profits by size varies from one major branch of industry to another. In *manufactures* the firms within asset classes from $50,000 to $500,000 compared favorably with the largest in rate of return on equity. But in *wholesale trade* the highest rate was earned by the smallest class in 1941 and by the group between $50,000 and $100,000 in 1939. From there on the intermediate classes, though below the rate of the smallest firms, nevertheless had a higher rate than was earned by the firms with $50 million or more in assets. In *retail* trade the contrast between the 1939 and the 1941 curves is very marked. In 1939 there was a substantial rise in the rate of profit from the assets class

[1] *Ibid.* (Finance companies not included in this estimate.)

[2] See also Appendix Table 3, Adjusted Corporate Net Profit before Taxes, by Asset Size.

under $50,000 to the big-business classifications. In 1941, however, intermediate firms did better than the large ones. In *service* industries the year 1941 was outstandingly a year of high profits

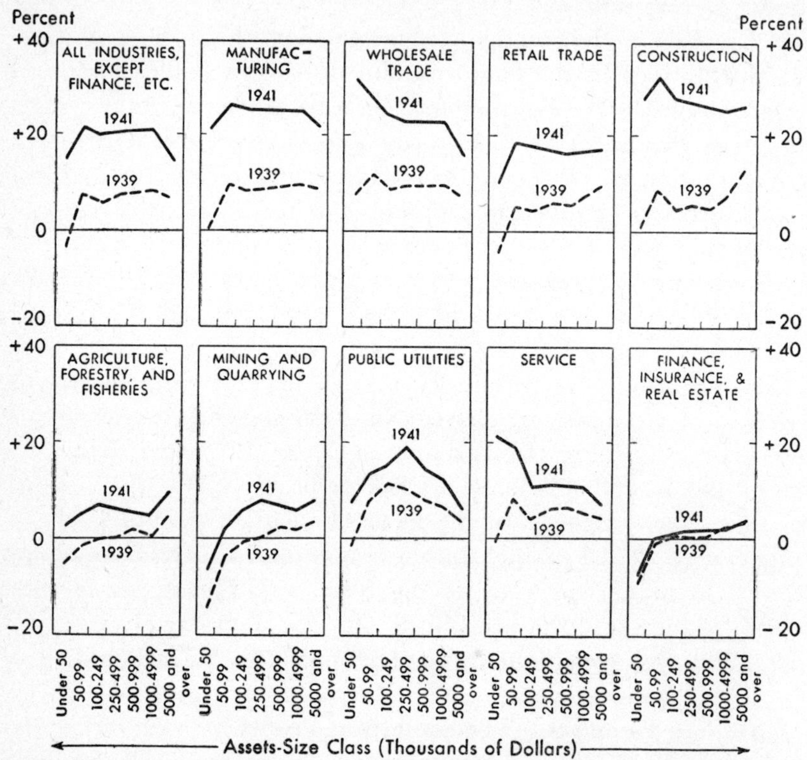


CHART 6. Ratio of adjusted net corporate profits before taxes to equity, all nonfinancial corporations and industry groups by assets-size classes. Adjustment consists in applying average going rates for owner's compensation. In the case of mining and quarrying, capital assets were substituted for equity in all assets-size classes under a million dollars, to correct, in part, the distorting effect of prior-year losses. (*U.S. Department of Commerce, based upon data of the U.S. Bureau of Internal Revenue.*)

for small firms, with a marked drop in the rate of profit after the hundred-thousand-dollar level of assets was passed.

*Manufacturing Profits.* Opportunities for a statistical analysis of variations from one industry to another exist mainly in manufactures, for which the most detailed breakdowns of the Statistics of Income are available. The data on corporate income point up the connection between profits and size that stems from the

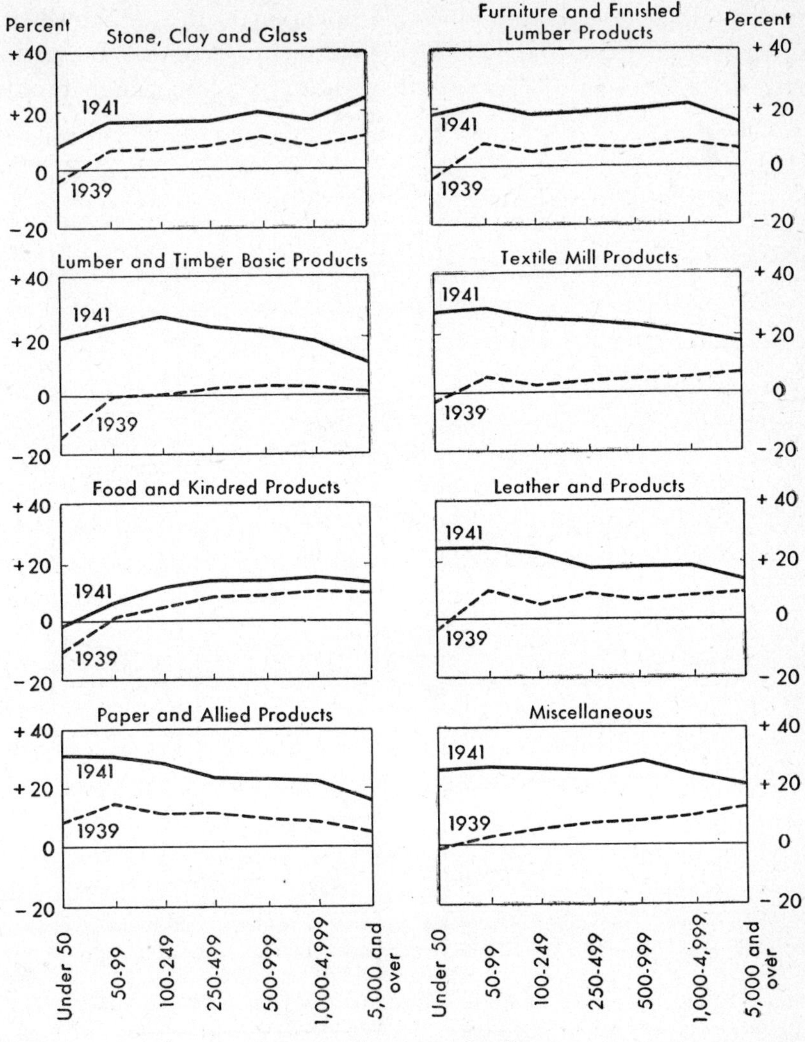


CHART 7*a*. Ratio of adjusted corporate net profits to equity. (*Bureau of Internal Revenue, Statistics of Income, and U.S. Department of Commerce, Business Structure Unit.*)

tendency of small business to concentrate in lines requiring a high ratio of man power to mechanical equipment and in which small machines are efficient operating units. Among the small manufacturers are the apparel lines, which have tended to reach their

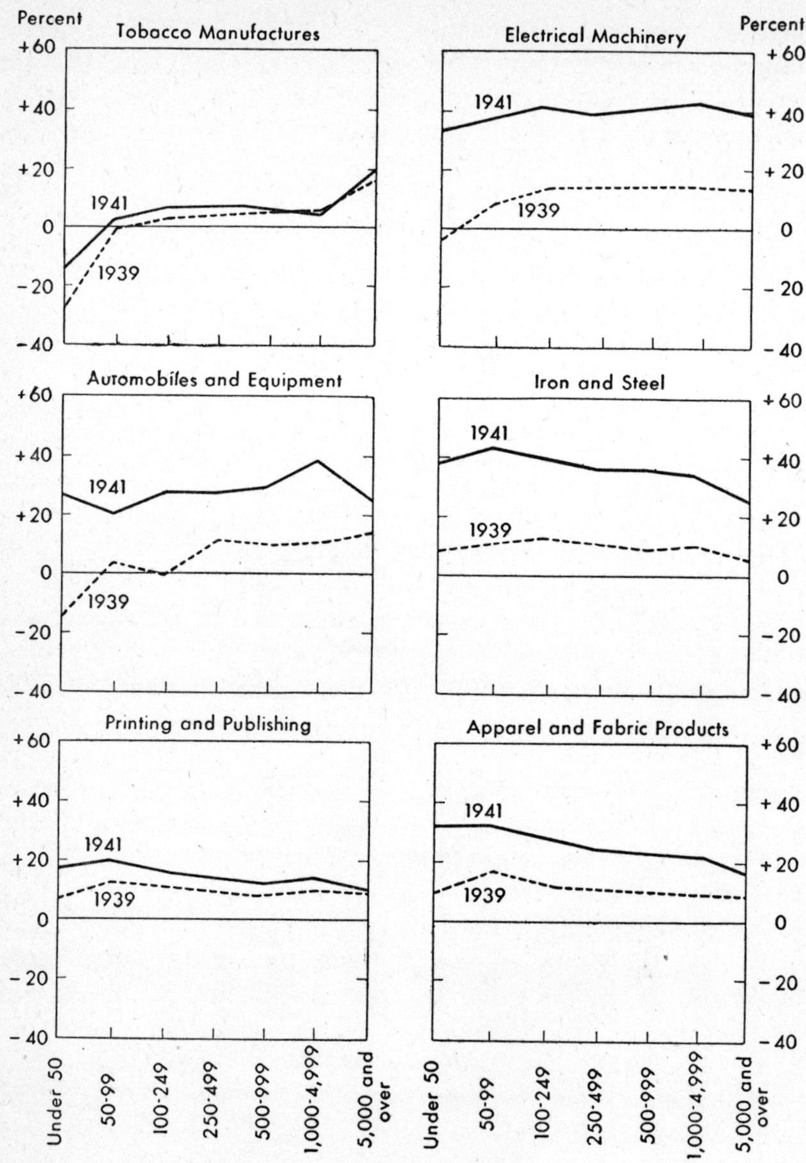


CHART 7*b*. Ratio of adjusted corporate net profits to equity. (*Bureau of Internal Revenue, Statistics of Income, and U.S. Department of Commerce, Business Structure Unit.*)

peak of profits at the assets class of $50,000 to $100,000; the ratio tapers off from there on. Printing and publishing profits likewise reach a peak ratio near the $100,000 assets level and taper off as greater size is attained. Leather, paper, and rubber products show a similar tendency. But at the other extreme are examples in petroleum, mining and quarrying, electrical machinery, and tobacco, where small enterprises either were unable to keep up with costly technological advances or national advertising of manufacturers' brands left the smaller firms behind.

Of the 21 branches of manufactures for which data are available in the Statistics of Income, all but 8 attain their highest ratio of profits to investment below the million-dollar level of assets for 1941; and for more than one-third profits tend to be greater among small businesses than among the largest in 1939. Undoubtedly, therefore, a considerable number of the small firms do substantially better than the average for their assets class.

*Retail and Service Profits.* Although the retail and service trades are strongholds of small business, there are nevertheless some significant differences in the profit position of small business when specific trades are compared. The following details are for 1942, during which the improvement in earnings of small business in the retail and service fields continued.[1] In food stores the ratio of profits to equity rises steadily from the lowest size level to the assets class of $250,000 to $499,000, after which it tapers off. For filling stations there is a sharp rise from the smallest size class to a peak in the next higher size classification. Eating and drinking places showed their highest profits ratio in the assets class of $50,000 to $99,000, while those under $50,000 of assets had a substantially higher profit rate than the group above $5 million. In the general area of department, dry goods, and general merchandise stores, the best showing was made by firms above $250,000 of assets.

The small firms invariably made their best showing in average profit ratios in the service industries. In the case of hotels and other lodging places the highest profit ratio was earned by the companies in asset classes under a quarter million dollars, and the least favorable average was reported by hotels in the size brackets above a million dollars of assets. For motion-picture theaters the

[1] See Appendix Table 4.

highest profit ratio was recorded in the smallest size group, with a declining ratio as size increased.

Taking the profit picture of business as a whole, the middle size—from $250,000 to $1 million—appears to represent the high plateau of the profit curve.

## HIDDEN "EFFICIENCY" FACTORS

Emphasis in this discussion of small-business efficiency has necessarily been on cost comparisons and rate of profit because they are most amenable to quantitative measurement. Even these leave much to be desired because of the varying interpretations that can be given to figures bearing on small business or profits. It is not safe, for example, to assume that firms with the lowest cost are necessarily those with the best profit showing. On the contrary, some of the most successful small businesses depend not on the gains of large sales but on the deliberate featuring of a highly personalized service—high in quality, convenience, and accommodation—for which the buying public is willing to pay a price premium that leaves the small enterprise a wide margin over the additional cost involved. This is especially true in retailing and the service businesses, although it may well apply to craftsmanship in lines of manufacture like furniture, jewelry, and fashion items.

This implies that some firms may be efficient in the sense that they have worked out the right combination of goods and services to command the highest premiums in the market.

Again, one may look at the year-to-year returns reporting the great majority of the small-business corporations in the deficit column and still have strong mental reservations about the validity of the returns as indicating no profits. It may be said of the high-salaried owners of some of these small companies, as it was said of the Iowa farmers in Los Angeles, that by staying in the red throughout their working lives they were able to accumulate enough to retire in Southern California. On the other hand—such is the degree of variation in small business—the use of net investment or net equity often provides a low base on which to figure profits, especially when the main capital of the enterprise is in the hand and the head of the owner himself. A small profit may thus give a high profit ratio, since the investment in education, training, and experience that may precede successful operation of a small business cannot be included in the Statistics of Income.

In addition to these variables in cost or profits measurement, another aspect of efficiency in small business defies any balance-sheet analysis. It is known that there are a great many small businessmen—how many can only be guessed indirectly from the nearly two millions of multiple job holders revealed by the Census—to whom the relatively small returns of the business side line represent a highly efficient use of part time. A professional man may be the owner of a parking lot, retail shop, or similar venture. In the case of the part-time one-man firm a small return from the business, coupled with the personal satisfaction derived from contact with customers, may represent an alternative to unsatisfactory employment opportunities. A weighing of alternatives would justify the operation of the business as representing not only the most efficient use of the individual's time and effort but the best social contribution from the community's standpoint.

Such considerations affect the small-business population. They also help to explain why some small businesses continue as acceptable enterprises over a long period despite the fact that their paper profit is far from impressive.

## SMALL BUSINESS EFFICIENCY AND THE INVESTOR

Compared with big business, small business is notable for a lack of uniformity in the results achieved. From the standpoint of the investor, this makes discrimination a necessity. Knowing that a superior small business can often outdo its larger competitors in economical operation and satisfactory rates of profit, the investor nevertheless needs to know the marks of superiority. Investment in a small business to be managed by one or two men requires a degree of intimacy with the enterprise that is not called for in the case of the big business. For this reason investment in small business is likely to be local, so that the investor has access to a knowledge of the setup to which he is committing his funds. The investment in a small enterprise is more nearly an investment in a man and in his ability or product than it is an investment in a line of business.

*The Middle-size Firm as Investment Outlet.* The scale of operations at the intermediate size approaches the point at which less personalized measurements apply and the abilities of others, besides the firm's leading spirit, begin to play a more important part in its efficiency. The product and the processes likewise become more important as determining factors. The intermediate-size business is not too large for well-integrated management, economy, and profitability. Because it is not wholly the reflection of one or two individuals, it is capable of surviving the original owners, hence a better investment for the nonparticipating investor. The available data on costs and profits point to the middle-size business—especially in manufactures—as offering the best promise for the development of new employment in thriving, independent, competitive enterprises. Unquestionably, investment in this field, too, must be highly selective. But one can more readily conceive of investment ratings being established for such businesses by competent investment management concerns to which the individual investor could turn for the placement of savings.

*Summary.* It is evident that small business can be conspicuously in the red or conspicuously in the black. A slight shift in the character and volume of business done can mean a sharp change in the rate of profit of the small business. The average small business seems to have ample leeway for utilizing its personnel and facilities to better advantage at the expense of only a slight increase in costs. The fact that so many small firms were able to pull out of the red in one or two years with the upturn after 1939, even though their share in total prosperity was relatively small, may point a moral. It suggests that a little further push in the direction of a more informed type of small-business operation could pay worthwhile dividends in improved financial condition to many small firms. The ways in which small business can be aided toward that goal is the subject of the ensuing chapters.

# VI. MANAGEMENT AND RESEARCH

In looking at the small business scene we have repeatedly found sharp contrasts in the degree of success achieved by competitors of the same size and type of business and under similar external conditions. These divergencies show up in the records of survival and failure, in which boom years furnish as varied a pattern as do depression years. They come out in comparisons of unit costs, where the best as well as the poorest records are made in small business. The highest profit rates and the highest loss rates appear in small enterprises. Some firms with apparently respectable financial ratios have been rejected as credit risks, while others with lower ratios but greater promise are able to fill their credit requirements. From the composite the inevitable conclusion emerges that the caliber of the management[1] has, on the whole, been the most decisive factor influencing the success or failure of the small enterprise.

## WHY SMALL BUSINESS NEEDS GUIDANCE

Small business has demonstrated notable hardihood in the face of revolutionary changes in business organization and techniques. The number of small firms has remained steady despite the development of mass production and large-scale distribution. Small business has quickly responded to new opportunities opened up to it by big business. It has come through serious depressions, and in the aftermath of the Second World War we find small business generally in the most confident mood that it has known for more than a generation. Small-business enterprisers may draw from the historical picture a justifiable inference that as a class they have been alert, intelligent, and resourceful.

[1] The term "management" will be employed loosely to include the three aspects of the executive function: (1) *administration*, which involves the creation of plans and the determination of policy; (2) *organization*, to facilitate smooth and coordinated functioning of the various parts of the enterprise; and (3) *management*, in the stricter sense of carrying out the administrative plans through the supervision and control of operations.

*Management Factor in Survival*

These evidences of survival power in small business do not mean, however, that small business can afford to be complacent about its ability to hold its place in the competition that lies ahead. Just as the cases of business failure cannot be taken as proof of a general lack of business acumen on the part of small enterprisers, so the fact that small business has managed to carry on should not be taken as proof that small enterprises in general are competently managed to exploit their full possibilities. The occasional genius who achieves outstanding success by instinct or even while apparently breaking orthodox rules of management is interesting as a special case, but he does not provide the specifications upon which to shape general policy in the field of small-business management. As against the success stories of neophytes who made good with a shoestring and a stout heart, we should keep in mind the sobering evidence of Federal income tax returns from small corporations as summarized by the Bureau of Internal Revenue.

It will be recalled that in most years of the prewar decade the majority of the 300,000 corporations with assets under $100,000 reported a net deficit instead of a net income. We have no reason to believe that if we had access to a parallel record on the more than two million nonincorporated firms, with typically smaller capital and a smaller fraction surviving the first three years of operation, we should find any smaller percentage of deficit cases than is revealed by the small corporations.

Even among small enterprisers who have managed to succeed by their wits while their businesses were within the compass of one-man control, weaknesses in management have come to light and proved crucial when the business grew to a stature that required some recognition of departmental organization and discipline. As one credit manager of long experience put it, he has watched "successful little fellows in the process of growing toward bankruptcy."

The war period provided small businesses with favorable conditions that stimulated an increase in sales and disposal of previously slow inventory items. The fact that so marked an improvement in the financial position of small businesses could be effected in so short a time and with such comparatively small changes in the volume and character of the merchandise offered is instructive. It demonstrates what significant changes in the profit position can be achieved with minor changes in operation. During the postwar period external circumstances will not provide the corrective that a scarcity market in wartime afforded. More positive efforts will be required of small business to create prosperity for itself. However, the war experience that pulled half a million small businesses out of the rut of red ink furnished some criteria for their successful operation and profitable growth.

*Rising Caliber of Competition*

To point out that small business needs to raise the level of its management is not to be patronizing toward small business. Big business, for all its tremendous advantages in financial resources, physical equipment, and top-flight know-how, recognizes and acts on the need of having its organization, policy, and operations continually tested from within and by outside counsel. The postwar small enterpriser cannot afford to be less realistic about his position. While his operations do not have the complexity of the highly departmentalized organization, the small owner-manager is required on a smaller scale to meet the same general problems as his large competitor. His personnel may consist entirely of himself. Even so, he must plan to coordinate the functions of buying, selling, financing, record keeping; he, too, needs continuous appraisal of his activities to see if they add up to a successful total operation.

In keeping informed on current changes—whether in the character of the community and habits of consumers or in processes of production and sources of supply—the direct experience of a single small enterpriser has obvious limitations. His success is related to the economic environment of which he is a part; yet he is usually too harried by the work at his elbow to get a clear view of his position in that environment. He needs qualified counsel outside his shop to help him take an unprejudiced look at his business, discovering flaws to be corrected and opportunities of which he should take advantage.

In the postwar economy only a part of the small enterpriser's competitive problem is to hold a place for his small business against big business. He must also reckon with the competition of other small and intermediate businesses that are geared to new standards for small-business management. Even the small country store dare not remain in the cracker-barrel stage. The hamlet has been brought too close to the urban center for the local establishment to hold its customers by virtue of its location alone. To succeed in small business during the next generation will take ability to cope with a better informed competition and with more resourceful consumers.

### *Public Pressure on Small Business*

Small business has not been immune to the increased role of government in our economic life. As with the rest of the community, a larger percentage of its earnings must go into taxes. More of the small businessman's time and thought is demanded to keep adequate records concerning pay rolls, terms of employment, pricing methods, income deductions, etc. (This is not entirely a loss to him; failure to keep records revealing costs has been a notable weakness in small-business management.)

Every small enterpriser who sets up a business establishment thereby commandeers the capital, goods, and services of creditors, suppliers, employees, and government, all contributing to his exercise of the privilege of business operation. He thereby creates a corresponding public interest in the way he utilizes the resources thus made available to him. Sickly small enterprises represent a social cost to all those connected with the small business, whether in the role of landlord, creditor, servicer, or consumer. Whatever progress can be made toward raising the level of management in small enterprises is that much gained toward a better performance for our economic life generally and serves to safeguard the continuance of small business as a stimulating factor in the economic scheme.

## FACTORS RETARDING MANAGEMENT GUIDANCE

The small enterprise that is short on management guidance may be so because of the psychological bent of the small-business owner. He has chosen to be his own boss partly because he wants things his own way and is often impatient of formal controls. He has confidence in his own ability.[1] By temperament he would rather find his own way to success by trial and error than accept standardized guideposts to a surer path. Disciplining of his operations appears as red tape, hemming him in and reducing the flexibility that he deems vital. That may be only another way of saying that he has not been effectively exposed to the kind of counsel that he could appreciate as helping to remove obstacles from his path, make his efforts more fruitful, and free him for more rewarding exercise of his initiative.

The small enterpriser's prejudice against formal controls may have been reinforced by the relative fruitlessness of his occasional search for management miracles. The highly departmentalized organization charts that he has seen in trade or technical journals, for the smooth routing of formal operations, materials, or even correspondence, would mean little to the small foundry or dress manufacturer. Neatly packaged success stories showing how engineering problems have been solved by a big company with but 3 per cent of its revenue from sales set aside for technological research prove little to the firm with gross output under $100,000. Refined analysis of distribution costs, to determine what lines should be weeded out, often meets with the reaction from a small retailer that to discover his costs by a distribution analysis would cost him more than he could save by cutting out the line or that what he could save on paper by weeding out accommodation items he would lose in good will of his customers.

The tailoring of management guidance to the requirements of the small independent business has proved difficult of practical achievement. The small shop or store cannot be expected to provide its own objective means of scrutinizing its management except in an elementary way. The really small store will have to be serviced from the resources of agencies in a position to mass-produce guidance for that particular store and for many like it. The somewhat larger firm of moderate to intermediate size—particularly in manufacturing—has need of a less expensive over-all

[1] In the interviews conducted by the National Opinion Research Center on behalf of this study, 60 per cent of those interviewed placed ahead of all other reasons for entering business the desire for independent accomplishment. When asked what factors may have tended to handicap them in their growth, 1 in 12 who noted difficulties mentioned the possibility of their own shortcomings.

management counsel than is now available to it through use of separate limited services of a lawyer, an auditor, an engineering consultant, and an advertising agent, whose combined services still leave large gaps in the guidance of the management as a whole.[1] The problem is to bring essential management guidance to the small business on terms that the small enterprise can afford and through media to which small business will respond.

This chapter is not intended to resemble a manual or even the summary of a manual on the management of a small business. The purpose here is to point up the problem areas of management to which small business should give special attention at this time if it is to hold its own during what promises to be a highly competitive, quick-moving postwar generation. With these problems in mind, one may then look into the resources that can be tapped to supply small business with necessary tools of management.

## PROBLEM AREAS IN SMALL-BUSINESS MANAGEMENT

Of immediate and prime importance in the effort to reduce the social waste of short-lived business ventures and to increase the net contribution of small business to the economy is the guidance of new and prospective enterprisers. In the common interest they should be helped to see if they are ready for the venture and to learn how to make a promising start. With more than a million new business entrants in the two years following the end of hostilities, and many more in the mood to undertake their own businesses,

[1] Of the 600 small firms in the National Opinion Research Center study, approximately two-thirds employed an accountant or attorney to help them with tax reports. One firm in 9 indicated that it had looked for additional professional advice on management problems, but in 3 out of 5 cases this reference to outside professional advice meant that they got some service from trade associations or trade journals, while another fourth consulted a CPA beyond the routine matters of tax reports and checking accounts. Among the nearly 90 per cent that used no outside professional advice on management problems, only 1 out of 16 felt any need of such aid.

As to the expense of individualized professional management counsel, a partner in one of the nationally recognized industrial-counseling and market-research agencies, who has been actively interested in the problem of aiding small and intermediate industrial concerns, expressed pessimism over the development of that type of clientele by his firm. He indicated that the small company, lacking its own staff services, had a variety of problems needing attention and that the amount the consultant felt such a client could be charged for an adequate checkup fell far short of the cost of handling the account. This view was confirmed by executives of other leading industrial counseling firms as far as their own agencies were concerned.

the training and counseling of the new or potential enterpriser is a matter for national policy—a postwar challenge to the absorptive power of our business structure.

*Rebuilding Lines for Postwar Markets*

Many established small businesses have the problem of determining their objectives for the postwar markets in much the same way as the new business. Small manufacturers carried war contracts, which gave them new know-how and a new outlook. They may have acquired additional equipment, additional floor space, and perhaps an expanded organization. There is a natural urge to build up postwar lines to utilize these new resources.

Distributors who found themselves unable to obtain merchandise in their prewar lines took on new ones, some of which proved highly successful under wartime demand. They, too, have been loath to go back to the prewar line and must give relatively more attention to the expansion of the newly acquired lines.

A large fraction of the business population is located in places that have undergone radical changes in the size, character, and mode of living of the community. Some of the migrants have remained in their wartime communities and are a new factor in the local peacetime market.

Against the background of such changes, alternatives have to be weighed in determining what product lines to build. On the production front, for example, can the firm safely concentrate on precision work, or should it return to the less exacting popular line? Shall it produce for the general trade or as supplier to one or two large manufacturers? Shall it continue the close ties with the wartime prime contractor or reach out with a diversified line of its own? In seeking outlets, shall the firm sell chiefly through wholesalers or shall it deal directly with the retailer? Shall it contract its output with the large chain or other private brand retailer, or shall it produce its own brand? Shall it concentrate on the local market or attempt to spread its market area? If the business is a retailing or a service enterprise, shall it do a strictly cash business or offer a liberal credit policy?

To an alert firm, the selection of the line of goods that it is best able to produce and market, considering its financial resources, location, access to markets, and the character of its competition, is a continuing subject for reexamination. In the transitional postwar years the decisions on line building can be the chief factor in success. Right decisions may depend on the initiation of the small businessman in the fundamentals of scientific management: defining the problem; gathering the facts on materials, methods, and potential markets; translating them into a plan, organization, and procedures; controlling the execution; and testing the results.

Some of the postwar changes in markets and materials are readily recognized, so that the problem is largely one of getting a more detailed analysis of the apparent condition and arriving at a working program. But not all the changes affecting his future can be seen by the naked eye of the small enterpriser. In his complete absorption with current business he may, for example, be unaware of technological developments of which his competitors are taking advantage.

As a random case in point, we may take the small manufacturer of men's clothing. During the war he easily disposed of all the civilian clothing he could manufacture in addition to military orders. His initial postwar concern was to get sufficient merchandise. Yet a group of bankers who are close to the financing of the clothing industry have pointed out to the author, in conversations on the financial requirements of small business, that some of these same manufacturers whom they backed liberally during the war are regarded as poor risks in the postwar period. The bankers believe the small manufacturer cannot possibly market a line of low-priced men's clothing in competition with big firms that not only made wartime strides in mass production as manufacturers but have been going heavily into retailing. Such large manufacturers, distributing through their own retail outlets, have first-hand experience with the consumer to guide their decisions as to styles and price lines. The small manufacturer does not have an equally sensitive barometer in gauging his operations.

A pool for the analysis of market behavior seems called for, both for the small manufacturer and for the distributors of his product, at the same level of expertness as that available to big business. Otherwise, the small manufacturer may have to work solely to the order of the big department store, chain store, or mail-order house.

The small enterpriser must learn to seek and to use the standard market information. A harried small enterpriser, however, can hardly be expected to have the time and opportunity to analyze the pertinent data. The smaller he is the greater his need to have the data digested for him by private or public agencies competent to sift out the portions of information that suit his purpose. The accountant, lawyer, or banker, whom he has learned to use for counsel, are unlikely to be of help in an appraisal of markets. To aid the small businessman in this regard, basic information must be available on the population changes in his neighborhood, the age distribution of the families, their incomes, and their buying habits. Some small businessmen will themselves be able to translate these facts into an appropriate buying and selling program, but persons familiar with the use of such data will be needed in most instances wherever a real effort to aid small business is undertaken.

Many small businessmen do reasonably well through observation alone, without the benefit of accurate measurement and objective guidance. But for most the uninformed process of cut and try is a precarious one. If it does not result in early failure, it puts the small enterpriser in the large class that makes no headway. In any event it is not likely to increase the contribution that the small enterprisers as a whole can make to the nation's aggregate production and sales.

*Organizing for Control of Performance*

Under the impetus of wartime demand, small business generally registered a large increase in total profits and financial resources. The comparative ease with which this was done in many cases has its potential dangers.

With heavy and often undiscriminating demand running in their favor, small enterprisers enjoyed a rapid turnover of their stocks with a minimum of need for exercising careful judgment in their selection. The problem was not to clear slow-moving inventories but to keep inventories from running below requirements. The small firm bought and sold under any conditions that the traffic would bear. To get some uniformity in price control, the Office of Price Administration had to fix definite dollars-and-cents prices on staple cost-of-living items rather than depend on the retailer's own calculation of margins and markups. In dry goods, where the large number of items made fixed prices impractical and markups were fixed instead, the OPA found itself practically helpless to cope with the jumbled or nonexistent records of the retailers. The agency had to depend on manufacturer's ceilings as a basis for determining whether retail prices were in line.[1] When relief from ceiling prices was asked for, the inability to present an accurate picture of costs and net profits often prevented relief from being granted.[2]

With the wartime seller's market still prevailing, small businesses have suffered very little from the neglect of controls commensurate with their expanded production and sales. But that is only a respite. A similar indifference marked the operations of those favored by wartime windfalls after the First World War. A few of the war babies of that period succumbed to their carelessness in the fall of 1920 and during 1921. Others did not feel the full impact of inadequate organization and controls until a decade thereafter, when the depression either wiped them out or left them with little to show for the carefree prosperity of the previous decade.

Since then, bookkeeping among small firms has been extended to meet the requirements of the income tax, sales taxes, and social-security deductions, not to mention the wartime impact of rationing, priorities, and price control. The next needed step is a more informed use of such records as guides in the control of inventories,

[1] This contrasted to the situation among the department stores and chain stores, which generally assigned a special man or section to the handling of price ceilings, liaison with OPA officials, the preparation of correct tags, etc.

[2] Though the problem of inadequate records bulked largest in small-scale retailing of food and apparel, even the better disciplined industries presented difficulties in determining costs for price ceilings. For example, the Washington representative of the American Institute of Laundering reported as follows:

. . . "to mention some of the things which our industry representatives have learned about the problem confronting OPA officials: First, some of the accounting systems used by some laundries are alarmingly inadequate. Some of these requests for price adjustment are so poorly prepared that skilled laundry owners, who have spent a lifetime in the business, simply cannot make head nor tail of them. It is only fair that I make that statement . . . because it is actually true . . . and because if OPA officials made it there would be some who would misunderstand. In one case, after submitting three sets of figures, the laundryowner stated, 'These last figures were actually taken from the books' [Question: Where did the others come from?]" *The AIL Member*, May 19, 1944 (American Institute of Laundering, Chicago).

in the effective use of personnel, in making decisions on financial policy.

While the pace of wartime and reconversion business has made it difficult for firms in all lines to take hold adequately of the organization problems attending expanded volume, the need is most acute in the case of manufacturing firms that grew large on war work. With Uncle Sam as the willing buyer, the provider of specifications, and often the provider of appropriate tools as well, production could be expanded with little or no attention to questions of market organization and selling policy. There was little time to correct the overcrowding of responsibility on certain individuals or the wastes of overlapping authority and imperfect coordination.

*Standards and Tests.* The small business seldom takes the trouble to match its costs or the performance of materials, man power, and equipment against appropriate standards of efficiency for the type and size of business concerned. In recent years progress has been made in simplifying the techniques for cost control on the production lines, so that they may become applicable to the smaller establishment. Likewise, norms have been computed of the percentages that specific items of expense may reasonably bear to total operating expenses and costs of distribution for items of different turnover rates for a number of lines of distribution. Quality tests, too, have become generally available. It seems fair to say, however, that the great majority of small enterprisers are unaware of the significance of such standards, are indifferent to them or—more to the point—are at a loss as to how to apply them. Many firms, as the record convincingly shows, have failed without realizing that the chief source of their trouble was not lack of capital or external economic forces but rather the cumulative effect of substandard performance and cost leaks that they were unable to detect.[1]

To strengthen his chances of survival in the stiff competition of the postwar years, the small businessman should be made more widely aware of the availability and uses of standard costs, the

[1] The findings of the Department of Commerce in the 1931 study of failures in New Jersey (cited in Chap. IV) revealed that one-fourth of the firms kept no books or formal records.

simpler financial ratios, and other operating standards whereby the small firm can test and improve its performance.[1] Here local banks and the credit departments of the suppliers to small business would seem to be the logical sponsors and "persuaders" in making tests of performance a matter of habit with the small business.

### *Technological Progress*

To prosecute the war successfully, industry had to find substitutes for scarce materials, to break down complex operations and scarce skills into simpler components, to find quicker means of performing old jobs, to create more effective machines with relatively less input of time and effort per unit. To encourage these advances, the government supported an unprecedented program of research by the managements furnishing war material. It was inevitable that the direct benefits of this huge investment in research on the part of Uncle Sam should go largely to big business, which handled the major responsibility of wartime production. Big business can be trusted to capitalize on the momentum given by wartime research in further refinements of product and procedures in the physical sciences, engineering, and personnel administration. The application of war-found methods to civilian production will become increasingly evident with the years.

Some of the results of wartime research are the property of the government, which financed the development of the new processes. Many of these are available to small businesses in a position to take advantage of the opportunities such publicly owned technological resources provide.[2] The bulk of the small manufacturers do not, however, have the facilities for utilizing this new knowledge in experimental improvement of their products. Small business needs pooled laboratory resources for product development at reasonable cost. Pending private development, some service in this area could be provided for by the Bureau of Standards.

The general level of wages promises to continue substantially higher than the prewar level. To match these higher wages with

[1] See *Distribution Cost Analysis, 1946,* and other cost studies in the U.S. Department of Commerce Economic Series. The Department of Commerce also furnishes information on privately issued manuals for specific industries.

[2] See the Alien Property Custodian, *Annual Reports,* 1945 and 1946.

an increase in the volume of goods and services, the productivity of labor must be raised. More effective use of labor, without unreasonable exploitation or industrial strife, will require a high degree of skill in "human engineering" by all industry. The small proprietor will have to give increased attention to the organizing of his own time and the efforts of his employees, who must ordinarily be more versatile than those in the large establishment.

Labor relations should get the benefit of factual analysis for the small as well as the large businessman. Irritations must yield to specifications of job requirements, so that union rules can be adapted to the characteristics and limitations of the small enterprise. Only through advances in this direction can the small enterpriser be expected to meet increased wage rates without adding disastrously to labor cost and forcing his prices out of line with his big competitors.

### *Safeguarding Continuity*

Small enterprises as a class have notoriously neglected to ensure the continuity of their establishments as going concerns when the original owner is no longer able to carry on. We are not concerned here with legal factors determining the life of a corporation as against that of a partnership or individual proprietorship. We are concerned with the problem of training understudies to take over when the innovator of the small business retires or dies.

The small enterpriser has often been an individual who made up in ambition and resourcefulness what he lacked in formal education. He may have been an immigrant who got his start as a hod carrier and became a contractor, a peddler of junk who established a foundry, a clerk in a country store who built up a successful dry-goods house, a pharmacist's assistant who evolved as owner of a diversified line of drugs and sundries. The man sees himself as the business, and so, typically, the self-made small enterpriser has run his business as though he were expecting to live forever. He has been loath to share his authority, to build up assistants to the status of co-managers. Aware of his own lacks, he has encouraged his children to seek higher learning and to go into the professions rather than into apprenticeship in his own business.

Two results have all too frequently ensued. One is that as the original owner has lost his youthful zest, the business settled into a static condition without anyone in a position to challenge unprogressive policies and give new life to the management. The other is that when the successful proprietor is ready to retire, none of the employees has been placed in the position where he can become part owner or even where he can readily assume executive direction. With the death of the owner, other members of the family seldom have the know-how to put in the right kind of manager or to take charge of the business themselves.

A successful small business has usually progressed to a point where its purchase is beyond the means of the outside individual with the needed managerial experience. In such situations the chain store or the large company seeking a promising subsidiary is likely to come forth with the best offer to buy. The merger of the successful retail store or small manufacturing plant with a larger organization is at least as likely as the transfer of such firms to other small independent enterprises when the retirement or death of the original owner occurs.

Following the First World War, mergers increased fourfold during the decade of the 1920's. By 1929 the net loss by merger, in the number of manufacturing and mining firms reported, rose to 1,245 for the year.[1] The Department of Commerce has likewise noted an increase in mergers during and since the Second World War. Between 1940 and 1946, the number of corporate mergers recorded by Moody's and by Standard & Poor's involved the elimination of 1,658 companies in manufacturing and mining. Within this group the annual figure rose consistently from 111 mergers in 1941 to 419 in 1946.[2] Among the reasons given are (1) the large amount of liquid assets in the hands of large companies which see the opportunitity to diversify their lines through absorption of smaller firms, (2) uncertainty on the part of small enterprisers as to the peacetime future and the desire to cash in on their wartime increases, (3) the strain and weariness of small enterprisers who

[1] Willard Thorp, "The Structure of Industry," TNEC Monograph No. 27, Washington, D.C., 1941, p. 233.

[2] See *Report of the Federal Trade Commission on the Present Trend of Corporate Mergers and Acquisitions*, Washington, D.C., 1947.

have no immediate successors to take over the management and wish to be relieved of further responsibility.[1]

Another potent factor in the retirement-mindedness of small business owners, expressed in unsolicited comments by more than a third of the small firms interviewed in the National Opinion Research Center field study (November, 1944), is the fear that their competitive position will be weakened through their inability to get labor terms that fit their businesses; these are not based on big-business conditions except as the labor agreements by the larger firms set the pattern. Finally, fear of inability to cope with rising material costs and the current price structure is reported. The desire to pull out and "let the big fellow do the worrying" reflects the lack of adequate managerial subordinates or successors upon whom the owner could put some of the new burdens he is loath to take on.

[1] Indicative of the character of the trend is the following report taken from *Business Week*, Oct. 7, 1944:

"A new method for meeting the postwar hazards to small business is being demonstrated by Continental Industries, Inc., New York. Continental is a management and finance concern which buys up well-established small or medium-sized manufacturers and provides them with top executive talent. Thus, a number of companies can combine to acquire skills in finance, renegotiation, reconversion, product redesign, market planning, and salesmanship comparable to their big competitors.

"Last month Continental Industries announced the purchase of its eighth company, the Quality Hardware & Machine Corp., Chicago, makers of machine-tool products and metal stampings. Other members of the family are Franklin Machine & Foundry Co., Providence; A. W. Harris Oil Co., Providence; Kensington Shipyard & Dry Dock Corp., Philadelphia; Walsh Holyoke Steam Boiler Works, Holyoke, Mass.; Liberty Motors and Engineering Corp., Baltimore; Braeburn Alloy Steel Corp., Braeburn, Pa.; J. Sullivan & Sons, Philadelphia (makers of tapes and bindings). Other firms will be added. The eight already acquired have a total annual output of some $150 million and average about 600 employees each.

"Quality Hardware will continue to make tools, dies, jigs, gauges, special machinery. But plans are already set for postwar expansion of output through a line of home appliances. . . . There are suggestions in the Continental Industries idea that may have a bearing on the broader small business picture. To such manufacturers it applies the good old maxim, 'In unity there is strength.' The merging of plant activities under Continental Industries is another manifestation of a trend by smaller companies, fearful of the shock that will come when war orders dry up, to merge or sell out while the going still is good.

"Wall Streeters are watching with interest the acquisition by large companies of smaller concerns which promise to extend the purchaser's peacetime markets."

The selection and training of successors should be basic in management plans of small enterprise to ensure its continuance as an independent business. The offer of successorship would in many cases serve to hold the competent employees who might otherwise leave the small firm.[1]

*Approach to a Guidance Program*

Enough has been said to indicate that postwar small business is confronted with problems of management that cannot be solved adequately without supplementing the isolated and limited individual experience of the small enterprise. How can small business be provided with the tools of management needed to keep abreast of business progress?

Bearing in mind what a conglomerate of enterprises comes under the general title of small business, what existing management resources can be tapped and what needs to be developed?

Obviously, when we are thinking of mass education in management, we are not regarding it as a substitute for the work of the experienced industrial counselor, who helps a company in the formulation of an organization plan and does an unbiased testing of the soundness of the market, production, or financial program. It is to be regretted that more firms do not give themselves the benefit of such a checkup from the business doctor or have to regard a periodic review of the company's operation as a luxury that cannot be afforded. It is hoped that business-research and industrial-management associations will stay with the problem of devising a type of expert management checkup for the individual firm that the latter can afford as a profitable expense. We need not wait, however, until that day comes to pass before taking advantage of

[1] Among suggested financial plans for ensuring successorship is for the business to carry insurance on the life of its owner, with the successor as beneficiary. The principal of the policy is adjusted to the expected value of the claim of the owner's heirs in the firm, so that they can be bought out by the designated successor with the proceeds of the policy. The premium on the policy may be taken into consideration in fixing the salary of the beneficiary. This is a variant of the method of offering shares of stock as part payment to the employee who is being groomed for the post of executive. Of course, some firms may find that the premiums required to insure the estimated value of the partner's interest would make too heavy a fixed charge against earnings for the firm to bear.

opportunities for raising the level of business management among small enterprises generally.

In considering feasible proposals, it must be remembered that a minority of small firms belong to national and interstate trade associations, subscribe to a trade journal, and are otherwise in the know of conditions in the industry. For the majority, especially the million and a half firms that employ no help, most of the catechism of generalized management principles must be discarded in favor of a simpler demonstration of the basic bread-and-butter routine. Why these routines make sound policy must be explained in dollars-and-cents terms applied to the enterpriser's own situation. For the smallest firms, education in management comes most logically and effectively from suppliers and the others with whom the enterpriser does business.

## SOURCES OF MANAGEMENT GUIDANCE

Few small businessmen are totally devoid of personal contacts from whom they can learn some elements of management. The salesman who visits the factory or store has been trained to sell his product in terms of the kind of market it will reach; in his sales talk he may offer a comparison of costs with similar products and occasionally give some advice on how to display the product to the best advantage. The banker or lending agency can offer counsel on the customer's financial program. The accountant and auditor and occasionally the lawyer have an opportunity to appraise and to point up elements in the business that may need strengthening.

For the small businessman who is prepared to take the necessary time, a wealth of literature is available from which he may do his own planning for effective management. Some of the written materials have been especially designed to meet the postwar situation. The Association of Consulting Management Engineers prepared a series of handbooks for the CED especially to assist the small and medium-size business. Under the general title "Planning the Future of Your Business" are separate handbooks for industrial employers, retailers, and wholesalers. Government agencies for management guidance (to which a following section will refer) have issued special booklets on the requirements of particular lines of business.

Suggestions contained in such manuals can be followed up by consultation with available agencies. The alert enterpriser will be at no loss to find them. Local market data are obtainable through the local chamber of commerce or the district office of the Department of Commerce. State universities maintain research bureaus and experimental laboratories to aid in market research and product development. Trade associations and trade journals are usually prepared to supply standard accounting systems suited to small enterprise. A few large companies make their laboratory facilities available for technical analysis to small firms in non-competing lines. The problem is not a lack of availability of sources but rather how to make small enterprisers aware of the opportunities in the use of such facilities.

Occasional advice received through regular business activities becomes more meaningful when it can be fitted into an organized pattern of thought. Such a pattern can be developed by the small enterpriser through his own reading and reflection. But the stimulus to a habit of analysis will, as a practical matter, have to come from sources directly concerned with the gains to be had from bringing management guidance to small business. The sources to be considered here include large dealers, trade associations, and public and private educational agencies.

### *Counsel through Suppliers*

Suppliers are more likely to concern themselves with their customers' management problems when an exclusive relationship exists. Thus, for example, an automobile agency makes regular reports to the manufacturer on the size and character of sales as to cars, accessories, or services. In return the dealer is given the benefit of training and guidance in many aspects of the business, such as repair methods, record keeping and record analysis, sales-promotion methods, and quotas or standards against which the individual dealer's own performance can be tested. In these circumstances the distributor is made aware of the factors in successful management; he is helped to work out his particular problems and keep up the level of accomplishment.

The manufacturer-agency relationship has several counterparts between wholesalers and retailers. With the development of centrally supervised chain stores and manufacturer-owned distribution outlets, independent enterprises have sought ways of gaining comparable management service. This need became particularly apparent to the wholesalers whose prosperity depends on the ability of their independent customers to cope with department-store, chain-store, and mail-order competition. Beyond providing independent retailers with special brands and giving them the benefit of local advertising and promotion, some wholesalers have undertaken directly to guide the managements of the retailers within their orbit.

Independent wholesalers often have encouraged and financially supported the organization of a voluntary retail chain. The wholesale house has supplied the members with exclusive private brands and assistance in their promotion. The wholesaler's sales force in such an arrangement constitutes a group of merchandising counselors who cooperate in the efforts of the voluntary chain.

The grocery field offers the most numerous examples of the big-brother relationship between wholesaler and independent retailers. One of the most instructive cases, however, is to be found in the dry goods and variety-store field.[1] The retailers selected by the wholesale house are located so that the units are not competitive with each other. The service furnished the retailer includes (1) appraisal of the location and, where necessary, relocation to a promising site; (2) provision of a standard store front and supervision of store layout; (3) planning of a financial program and an operating budget (with appropriate forms, such as the accompanying sales quota chart); (4) selection of merchandise suited to the character of the community served; (5) programming of merchandise promotion, in which a calendar of merchandise to be featured is prepared in advance for the ensuing months; (6) window- and store-display services supplementing the layout guidance; (7) a training and rating program for the accounting and sales personnel, as well as the owner-managers; (8) a periodic field appraisal of the operations in the stores and a financial

[1] The procedures described follow the general plan of Butler Bros. of Chicago in their administrative direction of the Ben Franklin group of variety stores and their system of Federated Stores, which operate in the moderate-price apparel and dry-goods field.

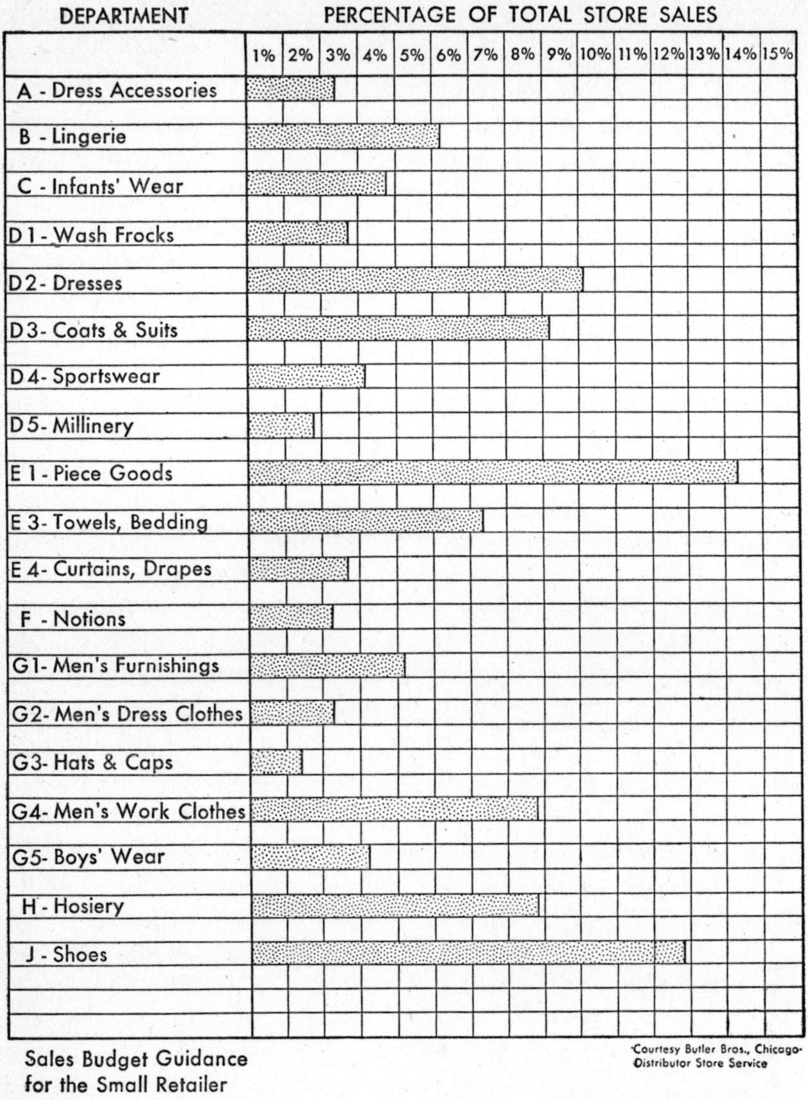

DEPARTMENT

PERCENTAGE OF TOTAL STORE SALES

1% 2% 3% 4% 5% 6% 7% 8% 9% 10% 11% 12% 13% 14% 15%

A - Dress Accessories
B - Lingerie
C - Infants' Wear
D 1 - Wash Frocks
D 2 - Dresses
D 3 - Coats & Suits
D 4 - Sportswear
D 5 - Millinery
E 1 - Piece Goods
E 3 - Towels, Bedding
E 4 - Curtains, Drapes
F - Notions
G 1 - Men's Furnishings
G 2 - Men's Dress Clothes
G 3 - Hats & Caps
G 4 - Men's Work Clothes
G 5 - Boys' Wear
H - Hosiery
J - Shoes

Sales Budget Guidance
for the Small Retailer

Courtesy Butler Bros., Chicago-Distributor Store Service

CHART 8. March departmental sales chart. Take into consideration merchandise deficiencies (together with any special local buying habits) and plan your promotional program accordingly.

appraisal by the home office, with recommendations for strengthening operations that show weakness.

In the example given, the charge for the management services thus rendered, under the contract with the dealer, will vary according to the maturity, efficiency, and stability reached by the outlet. But it appears to amount on the average to about 1.5 per cent of gross sales. Expansion cases, distress cases, or other special problem cases may require additional time and involve appropriate supplementary charges.

Similar services are provided by the voluntary mutual chains and cooperatives. They involve varying degrees of adherence to agreed rules by the dealer and the management agency, manufacturer, or supplier.

Such arrangements are irksome to many of the small independent proprietors who prize highly a complete freedom to buy their commodities wherever they please. Many refuse to relinquish their individuality for the use of a group name, whether it be a label of District Independent Grocery Association or designation as a Ben Franklin Store. Among more than two million small enterprises a large number are certain to prefer to build their business success on the basis of an individuality clearly distinguished from their competition. These firms will want the opportunity to pick and choose more freely the kind and extent of guidance they will buy, whether from the accountant, lawyer, advertising agency, or engineering counsel or from a public source of information.

Differences in the degree of acceptance of management guidance have been and will remain a factor determining the character of the services available. In this connection the trade association has a potential to be more completely realized.

### *The Trade Association in Management Guidance*

A trade association is generally an association of competitors within the same line of business; hence its natural areas of service are those in which the competitors have a common interest. Self-protection has traditionally motivated the formation and conduct of the majority of trade associations. Scrutiny of their activities indicates that in addition to holding conventions for mutual inspiration, they have been occupied largely with legislation and politics to limit the area of competition or to promote activities that would mean additional business to the group.[1] A number of the local retailers' associations formed in prewar years had as their original purpose a campaign for punitive legislation against chain stores.

An evident process of education has been going on, however, with the result that technical and advisory services, standardization of accounting methods, studies of industry costs, and labor relations, are increasingly becoming major fields of trade-association activity. That emphasis is most apparent among the larger and better financed associations, which maintain technical staff.[2]

One of the most fruitful activities of the well-established trade association has been in the development of standard accounting for the trade. Without uniformity in accounting practice, information gathered for the benefit of the industry—whether by government, research foundation, or trade association—was found to have little value for comparison purposes. Uniform cost-accounting systems have likewise tended to make competition more intelligent. Association secretaries point out, for example, that indiscriminate price cutting, as well as overpricing, becomes less common in a line of business where the individual firms are informed as to the relationship between unit costs and prevailing price levels.

The trade association has proved a useful medium for securing over-all statistics of an industry. This can be accomplished by routine statistical reports supplied by the members where an association is well staffed, or the association may confine itself to

[1] See C. J. Judkins, *Trade and Professional Associations of the United States*, U.S. Department of Commerce Industrial Series No. 3, Sec. 2, 1941.

[2] Judkins points out that among the 1,900 national trade associations listed in 1941 the average annual income was $15,000, that the majority of the national and interstate trade associations had a membership of less than 200, a staff of less than 4, and annual receipts of less than $20,000. The local associations tend to have smaller incomes and to narrow their activities to legislative and governmental problems.

The files of the Small Business Division in the Department of Commerce reveal that some 40 attempts have been made to organize "small-business" associations, but they usually have been short-lived. About 15 are currently in operation (June, 1946); their membership is small in number and of limited influence. As yet their emphasis is almost solely on legislative action. The small business generally looks to the association within its own trade as its natural medium. (Departmental Memorandum, U.S. Department of Commerce, Small Business Division to the Secretary, May, 1946.)

digesting and interpreting for the industry national and regional data made available by government bureaus. Information is disseminated through its own or affiliated trade publications.

As a control on standards prevailing in the industry, the association may carry on experimental laboratories. The American Institute of Laundering, for example, operates a full-fledged commercial laundry for demonstration purposes. It enables the institute to set up standard costs and to test laundering practices. Its research work includes reports on the behavior of different fabrics, information on cleansers that may be injurious, and setting standards of approved practice.

In general, trade associations are not expected to perform services for the individual member unless the results of such services are equally available to all the other members. The trade association is not precluded, however, from performing the useful function of a clearinghouse and intermediary for any member requiring aid in his product development or market research. The trade association is in a good position to maintain an active directory of available research facilities, to refer its members to appropriately specialized research laboratories or market-analysis agencies, and to make these facilities available under a standard contractual arrangement worked out on behalf of association members.

### *Labor-Management Cooperation*

Development of the large industrial union, adapted to bargaining with big business, has called attention to the shortcomings as well as the opportunities of small business in its labor relations. A sizable portion of small business—especially the very small enterprises—is still not unionized, but organized labor is a far more important factor in small business today than it was a generation ago.

The small enterpriser has the advantage of a more intimate contact with his employees and can make direct personal adjustments, whereas the large business has the problem of communication through formal channels. Some outstanding examples of good labor relations, in both union and nonunion establishments, are to be found among businesses of moderate and intermediate size. These have pioneered in providing the conditions that combine high security of tenure and high labor efficiency. On the whole, however, small business has not kept pace with big business in meeting the standards of good labor management.

The typical small business of yesterday was notorious for irregularity of hours and disregard of the rudiments of good physical working conditions. The differences here between small and big business are gradually but certainly being reduced. Standardization of wage rates and of working rules, through union activity, has likewise served as a salutary discipline upon small-business management, leading to the more effective utilization of man power.

In the hiring of labor, small business frequently complains that it gets the fringe workers, especially when hiring is done through a union in an industry where big business is dominant. Part of this difficulty is the result of slowness by small business in adopting social-security measures provided by larger concerns. Among these are health insurance and medical care, pensions, paid vacations, death benefits, and recreational facilities. Insurance companies have yet to develop group insurance for small firms at rates comparing favorably with those feasible for large business units. In this area the trade association may be able to perform a useful function by pooling its membership for insurance purposes.

Occupational standardization under union rules carries a threat for the small enterpriser, especially in general service lines. A primary advantage of small business lies in its flexibility; on the labor side that requires versatility on the part of all who work in the small enterprise, whether as owner, mechanic, or chore boy. In the survey conducted for this study by the NORC a common complaint by the proprietors interviewed was that the usefulness of their employees has been reduced by union regulations, that the men are unwilling to do needed work if it conflicts with union rules, with the result that more men must be hired than can be fully utilized. This is a moot question, as well as an important one, and requires objective analysis. It would be in the interest of both management and labor in each industry to make a careful study of the special problems that confront the unionized small enterprise—strict adherence to craft lines, classification of workers, number and distribution of working hours, overtime provisions, etc. Such a study should reveal the nature of the adjustments required to preserve jobs of maximum usefulness and earning value in the smaller enterprise.

In an industry where small-business units predominate and industrial discipline among enterprisers is relatively lax, the caliber of management prevalent in the industry may become a prime concern of the labor organization affiliated with it. Although organized labor's primary activity has been to obtain for the laborer a fair share of the value added by labor, the efforts to improve his status have in some industries led to deeper interest in the problems confronting management.

In some sections of the apparel industry, which is mainly one of smaller enterprises, the management counseling facilities of the labor organizations seem to be greater than those which the owners command. The International Ladies Garment Workers' Union maintains a staff of engineers to check on weaknesses in management that retard the prosperity of the industry or prevent a given firm from meeting the conditions of the union contract. The union will appraise the operations of the firm and uncover practices that may account for excessive production costs. The appraisal, made with the consent or on the invitation of the owner, seeks to provide the means for meeting all or a feasible portion of the union's terms. In the apparel field, where the fear of migration of style leadership to other parts of the country is a mutual concern of management and labor in a given territory, counseling between management and labor is clearly a common protection.[1]

[1] The value of union-management cooperation is a highly volatile and debatable question at this time. Before the Senate War Investigating Committee on Manpower Problems and Their Effect on War Production, Mar. 9, 1945, George Romney testified on behalf of the Automotive Council: "A dangerous illusion in this country is the idea that union representatives can help management apply good managerial practices, particularly those involving discipline. There have been a few exceptional cases, but almost invariably they result in partisan efforts to replace union representatives who supported management action."

But see *contra*, Knickerbocker and McGregor, "Union-Management Cooperation: A Psychological Analysis," *Personnel* (American Management Association), November, 1942, p. 525. "If the union has gotten as big a piece as possible [by collective bargaining] there remains another way—to strive to increase the size of the pie so that there will be more for everyone who partakes of it. The concept of union-management

*Credit Associations*

Local credit associations are formed primarily for exchange of information concerning the credit habits of customers. Through state and interstate federations, the local service has been extended. The National Association of Credit Men, as a professional agency, helps to keep its members informed on trends in such matters as business failures and their causes, amounts of outstanding credit, and changes in credit practices. Only in rare cases, however, have credit associations taken advantage of their strategic position to aid systematically in educating their small-business customers in the rudiments of sound credit practice. No group could be found whose clinics on credit management would be taken more closely to heart by the average small dealer than those conducted by the credit men upon whom he depends for goods, services, and funds.[1]

The problem of the banker making loans to small businessmen would be considerably lightened if his borrowers were in a position to answer the questions that the banker must have answered before an intelligent decision on credit granting can be made. The banker, like the creditor, has the advantage of strategic relationship, and management guides issuing from that source may be expected to carry correspondingly great weight with the average small manufacturer, retailer, or service enterpriser. A definitive pamphlet on "What the banker wants to know about the prospective borrower" would not lack in readers.

---

cooperation springs from the latter point of view."

The motives underlying union activity for improved management of industry were expressed in a report of the executive board of the Amalgamated Clothing Workers of America, as follows: "The conditions which the best organized workers obtain in any industry are the compound result of general economic circumstances, of the technology and the general prosperity of the respective industry [as well as] the bargaining strength of the union and the general level of legislative protection that labor enjoys. . . . The possible progressive advance of the industry is the limitation which union workers must reckon with and which intelligent unions must impose upon themselves for fear that some day they may find themselves in no man's land. " (Thirteenth Biennial Convention, 1940).

[1] If the credit men of large manufacturing and wholesale houses were to undertake a systematic program for the guidance of their customers in credit management, they could find useful discussion materials, supplementing their own experience, in current Dun & Bradstreet publications, which deal with the use and interpretation of financial records: the occasional reports, *Dun's Statistical Review* (monthly), and *Dun's Review* (monthly).

### *Management Guidance by Educational Institutions*

Preoccupied with the development of professional skills and catering mainly to students at ages when the prospects of becoming business owners are still remote, the professional school has not featured the management problems of the small enterprise in its curriculum. There are signs, however, of a growing concern on the part of collegiate schools of business with the management problems of the small enterpriser. Bureaus of business research affiliated with educational institutions commonly supply research materials on costs, markets, and other industry trends. Less frequent but significant experiments have been undertaken by business schools in conducting courses, institutes, and clinics on management problems in cooperation with local chambers of commerce, professional groups, trade associations, and labor unions. They open a promising area for pioneering in adult education—one in which the teaching skill of the professional educator has to be combined with the wisdom and experience of successful business managers so that small business may increase its contribution to the general prosperity. (A fuller treatment of present practices and the possibilities along this line is given in Chap. IX, Education and Public Policy.)

### *Government Agencies*

Over-all guidance of national economic policy as a function of government has become established in the thinking of the American people. We have looked to the federal government to supply our basic data on the number and character of our population, number and size of businesses, and on trends in production, prices, money and banking, pay rolls, employment, etc. These are valuable tools in the formation of administrative policy for those who know how to use them. Big business has had the know-how for making direct use of them. In specific lines of business, a few trade associations and leading trade journals reinterpret these data indicating their application as guides to management.

The government went considerably beyond the mere dissemination of business information during the war. The SWPC, for example, aided in breaking down large prime contracts into segments that smaller establishments could handle. It reached out among small manufacturers and acquainted them with production opportunities; it helped them to get their contracts and to get them financed, and it put them in touch with technical advisors to facilitate performance.

A carry-over of some of the guidance functions of the SWPC was contemplated in the organization of the Office of Small Business as a peacetime agency within the Department of Commerce. In practice, the program of this new agency has been focused upon a study of the needs of small business, the supplying of information, and the stimulation of its use through business-educational institutions. The scope of the aid offered to small business has been somewhat reduced from the original plan.[1] The agency has been instrumental in the development of management courses, conferences, and research projects among educational institutions and trade associations.

Whether or not the counseling services of the Office of Small Business can constitute more than a paper program will depend largely on three factors: (1) the Department of Commerce must be able to recruit personnel of the quality and experience to command the respect of those who are to have the guidance, (2) the Congress must recognize the value of the program by making adequate financial provision to attract high-grade personnel and to localize the service, and (3) business groups must encourage the fullest use of the facilities offered.

As part of the general effort to help veterans to gainful civilian employment, the government assumed the obligation of counseling those wishing to venture into small business. The Department of Commerce and the Veterans Administration have cooperated in supplying manuals on how to operate various types of small business. These are of value not only to the prospective entrants but also to those who are already in the lines of business described. A

[1] The Department Order No. 12, issued early in 1946 (U.S. Department of Commerce) divided the Office of Small Business into seven divisions including a Business Counseling Division, an Area Development Division, and a Special Services Division. The *Manual of Orders* issued by the Undersecretary in June, 1947, retained four of the original units: (1) Management Division, (2) Industrial Production Division, (3) Finance and Tax Division, and (4) Business Practices Division. [As this goes to press, continuance of the Office is threatened by lack of Congressional appropriation.]

similar service has been performed by state industrial and business-promotion departments.[1]

The Bureau of Standards, both on its own account and in cooperation with trade associations and industry foundations, has contributed to the standardization and simplification of styles, processes, sizes, etc., as well as to the establishment of quality standards, in the effort to eliminate wasteful practices and reduce costs. The importance of that work justifies more effective dissemination than it has enjoyed.

*Province of Public Guidance.* The growing activities of government in the field of management guidance has raised the issue of the division of this responsibility between public and private agencies. Government's wartime activity to expedite production needs no explaining here. A stimulant to the expansion of government aids for business management was the recognized need to maintain peacetime production and employment at a level substantially over the prewar level. The services of the government in this regard are intended to supplement and not displace the efforts of individual firms and the private associations. But debate will continue on how far a government agency like a Federal or state Department of Commerce should be expected to go in the way of rendering direct management services through local clinics and through attention to individual requests for aid. Some pressure is found both in and out of government to have the Department of Commerce do for small business as complete a job in management guidance as the Department of Agriculture does for the American farmer. The reception of this suggestion by small businessmen, as it affects competition among themselves, is a mixed one.

An important difference between the competitive situation in agriculture and that in nonfarm business has a bearing on the acceptability of management services rendered by the government. Generally speaking, the farmer raising a given crop is not an individual competitor of his fellow farmers. His product is marketed in bulk with that of others raising the same crop. They share in a total market at a common price. Conditions are good

[1] A list of small-business manuals issued by the U.S. Department of Commerce will be found at the end of this chapter, also a list of the series on small-business management problems issued by the New York State Department of Commerce.

or bad for cotton or tobacco rather than for cotton farmer A as a competitor of cotton farmer B. Although general business conditions affect all business, a business proprietor is more immediately concerned with how he can hold his own in direct competition with competitors, whom the customer has the alternative of choosing in preference to himself. He may not, therefore, be enthusiastic about government management guidance that would tend to strengthen his competition, although he himself might also profit thereby.

As a practical matter the general information supplied by government agencies as a guide to management is used most effectively by big business. Small business might get equal benefit from the information if it pooled its resources and had a local business association or trade association do the work necessary to make the data applicable to the areas served by the small business. Small businessmen are usually far from appreciating the uses to which information supplied by government agencies can be put. Government, therefore, is placed in the position of having to serve as a public school, to provide the citizenry with elements of business education that will enable small businessmen to contribute more effectively to the total economy. The more widely the rudiments of management become known to the small businessman, in his preliminary training and through current practice, the less need there will eventually be for the government to concentrate on such things as business-management clinics.

The boundary line between the services to be rendered by government to small business and those which private agencies provide should not be regarded as fixed. It is one that must shift according to the level of management literacy that has been attained.

### *Raising the Social Performance of Small Business*

In discussions as to how to aid small-business management, iconoclasts occasionally ask the question, "What for?" Is the effort to establish formal management-guidance programs for small enterprisers worth while when many of them do not feel they have need of such help? Is it going to help the small businessman to ply him with information about management aids, controls, and precautions that may even stifle his venturesomeness and undermine confidence in his own judgment? Isn't it better to let the small businessman live and let live as he may—as he has been doing all these years—rather than prod him toward higher goals? Will cleverer management by one small business tend to crowd out other small-business competitors rather than to make a dent in the big-business competitor? Aren't we making it tougher for new entrants if we raise generally the standards of business management for small business?

There is a distinction to be made between improving management in small business and staging a race to see what small businessmen will be eliminated. We are assuming that the postwar period provides large opportunity to raise the total of production and employment. Managerial competence is required to make the opportunity a reality. It is logical to assume that if more small businessmen are taught and apply the rudiments of sound management, small business in general will provide a greater total product, sustaining more jobs and greater aggregate real income.

We expect no millenium to result from better education of the small businessman in the field of management. Nonetheless, the operations of 3 million small enterprises involve a substantial portion of the nation's resources. In encouraging small business to observe more widely the rules of intelligent management, we are in a sense demanding that important resources of the nation shall not be wasted through blundering use of them. Insofar as stagnation and failure among small businesses can be avoided through informed management, both the capital of the nation and the values in a virile small-business population are conserved.

## SMALL-BUSINESS MANUALS ISSUED BY THE U.S. DEPARTMENT OF COMMERCE

*Economic Small-business Series:*

- Credit Sources for Small Business, No. 46
- Distribution Cost Analysis, No. 50
- Small Business and Government Regulation, No. 58
- Record-keeping for Small Stores (Prepared for Senate Small Business Committee). Senate Committee Print No. 2, 79th Cong. 1st. Session (Rev. 1945), 94 pp.

Store Modernization Check List, 1942, 9 pp. A guide for a systematic inspection of store facilities.

Veterans and Small Business, 1945, 45 pp.

What It Takes to Be a Retailer, 1945, 7 pp.

*Industrial Small-business Series:*

Establishing and Operating Your Own Business, No. 19

Establishing and Operating a Metal Working Shop, No. 16

Establishing and Operating a Shoe Repair Business, No. 17

Establishing and Operating a Small Sawmill, No. 20

Establishing and Operating a Grocery Store, No. 21

Establishing and Operating a Service Station, No. 22

Establishing and Operating an Automobile Repair Business, No. 24

Establishing and Operating a Beauty Shop, No. 25

Establishing and Operating a Real Estate and Insurance Brokerage Business, No. 26

Establishing and Operating a Painting and Decorating Contracting Business, No. 27.

Establishing and Operating an Electrical Appliance and Radio Shop, No. 28

Establishing and Operating a Retail Bakery, No. 29

Establishing and Operating a Hardware Store, No. 31

Establishing and Operating an Apparel Store, No. 32

Establishing and Operating a Dry Cleaning Business, No. 33

Establishing and Operating a Laundry, No. 37

STATE OF NEW YORK DEPARTMENT OF COMMERCE SMALL-BUSINESS SERIES

No. 1 Starting Your Own Small Business in New York State

No. 2 Financial Services for a Small Business

No. 3 Picking a Location for a Small Business

No. 4 Insurance for a Small Business

No. 5 Purchasing and Inventory Control for a Small Business

No. 6 Record Keeping for a Small Business

No. 7 Advertising for the Small Business

No. 8 Use and Control of Credit in a Small Business

No. 9 Regulations Affecting Small Business

No. 10 Publications for a Small Business

# VII. MEETING FINANCIAL REQUIREMENTS

In current discussion of small business, the center of the stage has been held by financial problems. Of the nearly 400 Congressional bills introduced in recent years on behalf of small business, the majority were measures involving financial aid or protection. Lack of capital or credit, we have noted, has been a ready-to-hand explanation for a host of difficulties. Feeding funds more liberally to small business is the obvious panacea that the small businessman's well-wishers have to suggest for strengthening the position of small-business enterprise in the economy. Our concern in this chapter is to appraise the financial requirements of small business and existing facilities for encouraging new enterprise as well as enabling established small business to operate effectively.

The end of the war found small business riding a crest, and in the early postwar years the level of operations continued above the prewar plane. Unquestionably the recent success of many small enterprises may be attributed at least in part to the abnormal demand of wartime and transitional markets. Their present comparatively strong position is of itself no assurance that we may not be back again, after a readjustment period, to the conditions of financial stress that have been the experience of small firms in prewar years. What weaknesses are discernible in the structure of financial resources available to the small business? What additional facilities, if any, appear to be needed for the greater assurance that the legitimate requirements of small business will be met in the years ahead?

As a point of departure for the appraisal, the abundant testimony bearing on the financial plight of small business in the past may be reduced to the following summary statement of the situation, as viewed by debtors vs. creditors:

*From the Enterpriser's Standpoint*

Small firms, including many with good commercial credit ratings, have been unable to obtain needed term credit through their banks. Even on short-term borrowing, apparently sound firms have been cramped by inadequate bank credit except in generally prosperous years.

Restriction of credit allowed by banks for working capital and current operations has compelled small business to depend unduly on mercantile credit and on rescue loans by finance companies. Fixed assets have been sold to replenish current funds. Small enterprisers have been unable to take advantage of commercial discounts and have often been restricted to the suppliers who will carry slow accounts and charge accordingly.

The cost of borrowing is much higher for small firms than for larger ones, the differential being greater than the difference in risk warrants. Even so, the percentage of credit refusals is much higher for smaller than for larger enterprises.

Sources of investment funds for small, private ventures have been drying up. Especially after the depression years of the 1930's, savings for investment have gravitated to tax-exempt bonds and securities of big-name corporations.

Flotation of the securities of small business through regular investment channels is practically impossible or prohibitively high in cost. Banks shy away from capital loans to small business.

The traditional means of growth through plowing back of profits has been curtailed by tax rates that draw off earnings needed for consolidation and expansion of the business.

*From the Standpoint of the Credit Institutions*

The counter case, that of the credit sources, runs about as follows:

The financial position and prospects of the majority of small firms are in doubt; even those apparently profitable have relatively small equities and heavy short-term debt; their current assets are mainly in inventories and accounts receivable, the value of which may be indeterminate. Small enterprisers commonly have inadequate accounting and comparatively little insight into their own financial position.

Long-term loans demand continuity of business; small enterprise is as uncertain as the life and continuing capacity of the owners.

The small businessman is overly sensitive to interference with his control and often refuses reasonable guidance in connection with financial aid. The cost of keeping track of small loans and investments in small business is high, and even going interest rates do not cover the expense.

Banks have a primary obligation to depositors to maintain liquidity. Credit institutions have an obligation to the economy to keep inefficient firms from extending themselves, to prevent undue losses to creditors and the violent business reaction that must result from liberal support of uneconomic enterprise.

In spite of all these difficulties, banks are anxious to lend to deserving small enterprises, but there are comparatively few credit-worthy takers of the credit that is available.

Thus we find a range of viewpoints from those who believe that small business suffers a serious lack of financing, which undermines the economy, to those who hold that credit institutions protect the economy as well as depositors by not making funds too freely available to borrowers whose abilities are unproved.

It is difficult to make a decisive summation when everything everybody says is true up to a certain point and in its application to particular cases or areas of business. We know that currently the banks have ample funds which they are more than willing to lend. But we also recall that in the early 1930's banks and creditors, in taking measures designed for their own safety, contributed to the wiping out of small enterprises whose loans were called and that public measures had to be invoked to relieve the credit stringency.

The establishment of the Reconstruction Finance Corporation and the amendment of the Federal Reserve Act by the insertion of Sec. 13B reflected pressing needs for financial resources that were not available through the ordinary channels of credit. In order that smaller manufacturers might play a larger part in war production it was necessary to establish the SWPC, with its special facilities for procurement and management guidance paving the way for additional financial support from the banks and the RFC. These special agencies were also enlisted in smoothing the conversion of smaller war plants to a peacetime basis.

While these agencies have provided useful experience in dealing with credit needs not met by customary sources, the additional facilities furnished by them touched directly only a small percentage of the great mass of small firms. They touched practically none of the very small firms, those with three or less employees, which make up the bulk of the business population. In a great part of the work of the SWPC, in particular, the financing was related to the filling of orders. It did not relate to the conditions of normal production, where financing is dependent upon the ability of the small enterpriser to make and hold his place in the market. On that broader front the problem of financing small business remains.

Because of the great variety of situations involved, both as to types of firms and the different types of credit that they may need, it would be well at this point to indicate the separate categories that require consideration, from short-term to equity financing.

## TYPES OF FINANCING REQUIREMENTS

At the risk of rehashing what will be familiar knowledge to the reader, the types of financing required by small business are reviewed briefly here to provide a framework for analysis.

### *Short-term Credit*

The ordinary requirements for short-term credit are periodically to build up inventories of materials for processing or of merchandise for sale, to take care of pay rolls or current operating bills until payment has been received from sales, occasionally to take advantage of the opportunity for a "good buy." Short-term bank loans may enable the small business to discount its bills and thus avoid the premium on extended commercial credit, which often puts the small businessman at a fatal disadvantage. For such short-term borrowing, the business seeks (1) ordinary mercantile credit from the supplier, usually 30 to 90 days; (2) bank loans, normally from 2 to 6 months; (3) loans from banks and finance companies against accounts and notes receivable, inventories, or other collateral, with repayments spread over a year.

The short maturity fits into the usual situation of the small owner-manager whose capital is largely in his own person, his earnings record and know-how.[1]

[1] Compared with large companies, the small corporation typically has a very low base of permanent capital, including that represented by long-term debt, for the

*Term Loans*

The credit demanded by the enterprise seeking to manufacture or take on a new line; improve plant, machinery, and equipment; or increase its working capital for expanding operations requires a longer maturity than is ordinarily contemplated in mercantile or current banking credit. To carry out such an operation the borrower requires a repayment schedule commensurate with the rate at which he may be expected to realize on his program of readjustment and expansion.

Where the large firm can issue its own debt paper and offer it to the highest bidder, the small businessman usually depends on a relationship of confidence with a single bank willing to go along with him in his requirements and ambitions. Local banks have often made term loans to a borrower acquiring new assets or for refunding of obligations in the guise of short-term lending. The 90-day note is given with the expectation on both sides that it will be met with a part payment and that the balance will be renewed for successive 60- or 90-day periods. This arrangement enables the small business to get long-term credit but places the enterprise in a very vulnerable position when business is unfavorable.

The recent participation of the Federal Reserve banks and the RFC in term lending to small business has served to call the attention of the commercial bank to the possibility of extending the programmed loan—with maturities of one to five years or even longer—to the area of small business. It is as yet, however, a very minor fraction of commercial banking for the small enterprise.[1]

amount of business it does. (This is due largely to the nature of small business, which concentrates in lines requiring a minimum of physical equipment but even within the same industry the small firm has a relatively lower capitalization than its big-business counterpart.) The balance-sheet analyses of the Bureau of Internal Revenue for 1939 and 1941 show that the profit-earning firms in the assets classes under $100,000 averaged about $6 of annual sales for every dollar of capital assets (less reserves) whereas among firms in the big-business class (those with total assets of $50 millions or more) the aggregate of net capital assets exceeded their gross annual sales. (*Statistics of Income for 1939*, Part 2, Table 6, p. 146; and *Statistics of Income for 1941*, Part 2, p. 142.) See, also, Charles L. Merwin, *Financing Small Corporations in Five Manufacturing Industries, 1926–1936*, Studies in Business Financing, National Bureau of Economic Research, Inc., New York, 1942.

[1] Neil H. Jacoby and Raymond Saulnier, *Term Lending to Business*, National Bureau of Economic Research, Inc., New York, 1942, p. 35.

*Equity Capital*

Equity capital includes original investment in the firm and permanent additions to that investment for expansion of the business. Typically, the capital for new small enterprise is furnished by the owner-enterprisers themselves, occasionally supplemented by interested relatives or friends. Additions to the capital investment in the small business have traditionally been made by plowing back earnings.

The risks of starting a small enterprise are such that the privilege of entry must naturally depend on the willingness of individuals to risk their own savings in the venture. This is not the province of bank credit. But when an enterprise has proved its earning capacity and requires additional permanent capital for expansion, banks have occasionally been called upon to extend credit to provide such capital, enabling the firm to develop more rapidly than it could through the normal reinvestment of its surplus. Banks have done this through mortgage loans against existing assets or in rarer cases by combination of character and collateral loans programmed on an extended repayment plan.

The boundary line between the term loan and the capital-investment loan is unfixed. The immediate purpose of the loan may be to give the business more elbowroom in the way of working capital and funds for plant improvement; but earnings from the expanded operations are counted upon to translate the increased liabilities into additional equity by the time the loan has fully matured.

Business credit from suppliers is more widely available to the small enterprise than is any form of bank credit or equity capital. That is evident from common observation of small-business operations and is supported by such studies as have been made of credit sources, including sample interviews made for this study. Currently, we have availability of short-term bank credit and an increasing disposition on the part of commercial banks to make longer term loans.

## AVAILABILITY OF BANK CREDIT

In past studies of credit rejections the greater part of the unsatisfied demands of small business applicants was for longer term credit

—a year or more. Whether or not the banks have fully carried out their responsibility to make adequate credit provisions for small business has long been a moot question. One reason for the conflict of opinion is the fragmentary nature of the factual evidence. When businessmen appear before a Congressional committee to report their inability to obtain credit, the bankers are not ordinarily on hand to check the businessman's statement of his case and its validity as applied to small business in general. Studies made of the availability of bank credit date back to the difficult years of the 1930's, when banks, sensitive to the large number of bank closings, were keeping their depositors' funds liquid—presumably spurred to this practice by the watchful eyes of the bank examiners. The evidence obtained from four representative studies during that period is worth reviewing for the light it sheds on the nature of the difficulties encountered.

*Census Study of 1935.* The broadest of the prewar surveys of credit difficulties was made in 1935 by the Bureau of the Census at the request of the Business Advisory Council of the Department of Commerce.[1] The findings were based on reports from manufacturers with 20 to 125 employees—in the upper size stratum of small business. Of the 6,158 cases tabulated, it was found that 71 per cent were regular borrowers from commercial banks and that 29 per cent were nonborrowers or had no credit experience. Nearly 90 per cent of the borrowing firms depended entirely upon bank credit for additional working capital. Of the 4,387 borrowing concerns, 45 per cent reported difficulties in obtaining credit. This percentage was fairly representative of the situation in specific areas; the percentage of credit-difficulty cases was as low as 32 in only one of the Federal Reserve districts, all of which were sampled. Credit rejections were reported by manufacturers of foods and textiles, as well as by producers of heavy goods.

For long-term loans about one-fifth of all the concerns depended upon their banks (a slightly lower fraction for those with credit difficulty); another fourth got long-term funds through mortgage loans and sale of stocks or bonds. But it was stated by 40 per cent

[1] Bureau of the Census, Business Advisory Council of the Department of Commerce, *Survey of Reports of Credit and Capital Difficulties by Small Manufacturers*, Washington, D.C., 1935.

of the firms without credit difficulty for working capital, as well as 48 per cent of those which reported credit trouble, that they had no available sources for long-term credit.

In an attempt to test the common claim of the banks that they were always ready and willing to meet the legitimate credit requirements of all creditworthy borrowers, the Census study analyzed the financial position of firms whose applications had not been fully met. Among the 1,954 cases of reported credit difficulty, financial condition was as follows:

| | *Per Cent* |
|---|---|
| *a.* Current ratio* of 3 or better | 23 |
| Current ratio of 2 or better | 42 |
| *b.* Net worth † to debt ratio of 3 or better | 33 |
| Net worth to debt ratio of 2 or better | 50 |
| *c.* Both of above ratios 3 or better | 18 |
| Both of above ratios 2 or better | 33 |

* Ratio of current assets to current liabilities.

† Ratio of owner's equity in the business to the firm's total obligations.

Those with ratios for (*a*) and (*b*) above of 2 or better were examined for Dun & Bradstreet rating: 38 per cent of them were rated *high;* 26 per cent, *good.*

Thus, apparently 20 per cent of those who complained of credit difficulties in the survey for the Business Advisory Council would have been considered eligible borrowers in terms of the position revealed by their financial statements and their commercial credit standing with respect to promptness in paying bills.

Unfortunately, no analysis was available of other factors considered by the banks upon which the rejections may have been based.

*Rejections in Chicago Area Sample.* Additional reports on credit availability, likewise made in the 1930's, bear out the findings of the Department of Commerce study. One of these, made by C. O. Hardy and Jacob Viner, analyzed nearly 2,000 credit refusals in the Chicago Federal Reserve district for the interval between the general closing of the banks by Presidential order on Mar. 6, 1933, and Sept. 1, 1934. Approximately nine-tenths of the applications studied were for loans under $10,000. In the judgment of the two authors, the rejected firms rated as follows:[1]

[1] C. O. Hardy and J. Viner, *Report on Availability of Bank Credit in the Seventh Federal Reserve District,* Washington, D.C., 1935, p. 10.

TABLE 37

| *Merit Rating* | *Per Cent* |
|---|---|
| Good | 32.0 |
| Good if reduced | 7.1 |
| Questionable | 24.6 |
| Information insufficient | 11.4 |
| Not good | 24.9 |
| Total | 100.0 |

*Refusals and Restrictions in Manufacturing.* Two studies by the National Industrial Conference Board, based on experience from 1929 to 1938, indicated that the smaller firms (capitalized under $500,000) had proportionately more rejections of their credit applications than those in the higher brackets.

The following tabulation is taken from the first of these studies, which included the credit histories of 3,438 firms primarily in manufacturing lines, over the period 1929–1932.[1] It will be

TABLE 38

| *Capitalization* | *Total number of concerns reporting* | *Concerns with no bank-credit experience* | *Number of concerns dependent on banks* | | *Ratio of refusals, etc., to total dependent on bank credit, per cent* |
|---|---|---|---|---|---|
| | | | *No credit difficulty* | *Credit refusals or restrictions* | |
| Total | 3,438 | 1,322 | 1,650 | 466 | 22.0 |
| $50,000 and under, very small | 176 | 50 | 74 | 52 | 41.3 |
| $50,001–$500,000, small | 1,350 | 442 | 706 | 202 | 22.2 |
| $500,001–1,000,000, medium | 438 | 175 | 230 | 33 | 12.5 |
| Over $1,000,000, large | 1,124 | 556 | 513 | 55 | 9.7 |
| Unclassifiable | 350 | 99 | 127 | 124 | 49.4 |

noted that in this sample the percentage of refusals or restrictions of credit incurred by the very small firms—those with assets under $50,000—was more than four times as high as for the firms with capitalization above a half million dollars.

That study was followed up by the NICB with one for the period 1933–1938,[2] in which a sample of 1,755 firms likewise

[1] Ralph A. Young, *The Availability of Bank Credit*, National Industrial Conference Board, New York, 1932, p. 71.

[2] L. H. Kimmel, *Availability of Bank Credit, 1933–1938*, National Industrial Conference Board, New York, 1939, p. 66.

revealed a concentration of credit restrictions among the smaller firms. The breakdown of refusals by asset size was as follows:

TABLE 39

| *Capital employed* | *Per cent of total firms reporting* | *Per cent of firms reporting refusals of bank credit* |
|---|---|---|
| Total | 100.0 | 100.0 |
| $50,000 and under | 12.9 | 31.8 |
| $50,001–$500,000 | 39.0 | 49.4 |
| $500,001–1,000,000 | 7.9 | 7.1 |
| Over $1,000,000 | 36.0 | 9.1 |
| Unclassifiable | 4.3 | 2.6 |

In this sample, 20 per cent of the concerns reporting credit refusal or restrictions were rated *high* or *good* by Dun & Bradstreet. Reasons given for rejection were mainly that (1) funds were desired for a longer period than the banks could consider, (2) borrowers were already receiving up to the legal limit that the bank was permitted to give any one borrower, (3) loans were of a type disapproved by the bank examiners, (4) borrowers had unsatisfactory financial statements.[1]

*Loans by Finance Companies.* Small firms with limited access to regular bank credit have resort to the finance company, pledging their accounts receivable. Out of an aggregate of $2.6 billions of loans made against accounts receivable in 1941, about three-fifths were estimated to be with finance companies other than commercial banks. Apart from financing through factors, used by large as well as small firms, roughly half a billion dollars in accounts-receivable loans went through industrial banks and commercial finance companies, whose usual service and interest charges to smaller firms averaged around 20 per cent per annum.[2] Miscellaneous business loans made through small loan agencies frequently exceed 30 per cent per annum.[3]

[1] *Ibid.*, Chap. 3.

[2] Saulnier and Jacoby, *Accounts Receivable Financing*, National Bureau of Economic Research, New York, 1943, pp. 32–38, 131–133.

[3] See Small Business Loans and Risk Capital, Senate Small Business Committee Print 8, Feb. 24, 1942, pp. 58–59.

*Small Banks and Small Business.* Studies reviewing the unavailability of bank credit in apparently legitimate cases should not blind us to the more common situations in which the legitimate commercial loan requirements of small business are regularly being met. Far from shying away from small business, the average bank is, in itself, small business and is largely occupied with small-business loans. The number of commercial banks having deposits of $5 million or more was less than 15 per cent of the total of insured commercial banks in the country. On the other hand, 43.5 per cent of the banks had less than $1 million of deposits in 1940. A survey of bank lending made by the American Bankers Association (1940) revealed that the reporting banks had handled approximately 24.5 million credit transactions during the year for a total of $39 billion. On the basis of that survey the average new loan was $1,787 and the average renewal was about $1,400.[1]

The inference can be drawn from the studies of credit refusals that the small proprietor may have difficulty in stating his case for credit, even when his record apparently warrants credit accommodation. The ordinary contact between banker and borrower, especially in large urban centers, falls short of giving a clear insight into the needs and possibilities of the small business seeking financial support.

### *Expansion of Term Loans*

The extent to which the length of term caused difficulty on loan requests analyzed in the surveys of bank credit points to the view prevalent among commercial banks in the 1930's that employment of bank deposits for long-term loans was of questionable propriety. That view was undoubtedly more common in the 1930's than it is today. With the greater confidence given to banks by the insurance of their deposits, by Federal Reserve support, and by the present general high liquidity of bank assets, there has been an unmistakable trend toward looking with greater favor upon longer term loans. Bank examiners have been instructed to eliminate the automatic rating of "slow" for all unsecured loans running beyond 6 months. The requirement that the credit line must be

[1] Hearings, House Special Committee on Postwar Economic Policy and Planning, 79th Congress, 1st Session, Part 5, p. 2457.

cleared once a year has also become less rigid. The Federal Reserve and the Federal Deposit Insurance Corporation have given their blessings to longer term loans by small banks when suitably programmed as to payment.[1]

Both the Federal Reserve and the RFC have had a small part in the making of loans to small enterprises. Under the Sec. 13B Amendment of the Federal Reserve Act, passed in 1934, the Federal Reserve banks received a total of 9,291 loan applications for a total of $395 million during the first five years of operation. About 2,700 of the applications, with authorizations totaling $179 million, were approved and $123 million was actually advanced either directly or in collaboration with member banks.

A breakdown of the first 150,000 successful applications showed that 3.1 per cent of the aggregate amount advanced was in loans of $10,000 or less.[2]

On Dec. 31, 1941, the aggregate of direct industrial advances by all Federal Reserve banks was $9,504,000; in addition, the Federal Reserve had guaranteed commitments to member banks on industrial advances in the amount of $14,597,000. It is estimated that the maximum of Federal Reserve advances outstanding at any one time before the war was not more than $32 million and that about $27 million was the maximum outstanding in commitments shared with member banks.[3]

The RFC authorized loan disbursements of about $460 million over the period Feb. 2, 1932, to June 30, 1941. This total covered 9,713 loans or participation in loans to 8,021 enterprises—not far from 1,000 loans per annum. Approximately 54 per cent of the authorized funds were actually advanced. The distribution of the RFC loans by size of loan is indicated in Table 40.[4]

Of the $460 million, loans of not more than $100,000 total $158,450,000 for the nine-year period. Obviously, these are not impressive amounts; the ABA report for the single year 1940 dealt

[1] Jacoby and Saulnier, *Term Lending to Business*, p. 26.

[2] U.S. Senate Banking and Currency Committee, 76th Congress, 1st Session Hearings on S. 1482 and S. 2343, June, 1939, pp. 113, 115.

[3] From *Annual Reports* of the Board of Governors of the Federal Reserve System. See I. G. Gromfine, *Report of the U.S. Bureau of Labor Statistics on the Financial Problems of Small Business*, September, 1944, pp. 49–50.

[4] *Report of the Reconstruction Finance Corporation*, Second Quarter, 1941, p. 65.

TABLE 40

| *Size of loan* | *Total amounts authorized (000)* | *Per cent of total* | *Total number of loans authorized* | *Per cent of total* |
|---|---|---|---|---|
| Total | $460,375 | 100.0 | 9,713 | 100.0 |
| $5,000 and under | $8,477 | 1.8 | 3,656 | 37.7 |
| $5,001–$10,000 | 12,356 | 2.7 | 1,537 | 15.8 |
| $10,001–25,000 | 33,268 | 7.2 | 1,853 | 19.1 |
| $25,001–50,000 | 42,633 | 9.3 | 1,087 | 11.2 |
| $50,001–100,000 | 61,716 | 13.4 | 789 | 8.1 |
| $100,001–200,000 | 62,286 | 13.5 | 415 | 4.3 |
| $200,001–500,000 | 87,701 | 19.1 | 274 | 2.8 |
| $500,001–1,000,000 | 45,755 | 9.9 | 62 | 0.6 |
| Over $1,000,000 | 106,183 | 23.1 | 40 | 0.4 |

with loans totaling $39 billion. Nevertheless, the small-business loans by the Federal Reserve and the RFC served a useful purpose, improving, by their example, the standing of term and capital loans to small business among the rank and file of commercial banks in the larger communities.

### *Wartime Financing to Small Business*

The war undoubtedly enlarged the horizons of the banking fraternity with respect to credit for small business. This was due partly to public pressure and partly to a recognition by private banking of its wartime obligations.

To give smaller business a larger share in war contracts than it obtained in the first months of the war, ordinary banking credit had to be supplemented and the lending process speeded up to a wartime tempo. The SWPC, established under the SWPC Act of June, 1942, was designed to serve this purpose. The SWPC facilitated loans by agreeing to repurchase them from the banks. It also participated directly in bank loans and, where banks would not lend, made direct loans which were processed through the RFC. Rate of interest under direct SWPC loans was uniformly 4 per cent, while the banks charged up to 6 per cent for the loans made by them. Where the SWPC offered to repurchase, it protected its commitments with ½ to 1 per cent charges to the banks on the guaranteed portions of the loans.

*Meeting Postwar Credit Needs*

The question was naturally raised, at the war's end, as to whether or not the special aids rendered to small business by the SWPC and cooperating agencies should be carried over in suitable form to help in meeting peacetime credit requirements. When President Truman terminated the SWPC, he turned over its financing functions to the RFC and its educational functions to the Department of Commerce.

*Support of Federal Agencies.* The strong public sentiment to support an expanding volume of credit demand in the postwar period was met with an announcement by the RFC in March, 1945, of "blanket participation in loans made by bankers to business enterprises." The RFC Circular 25 described the plan as follows:

> Reconstruction Finance Corporation has adopted a program which in effect provides for a practically automatic guaranty of 75 per cent (or such lesser percentage as may be requested by the bank) of loans made by approved banks to business enterprises which meet the requirements of the Blanket Participation Agreement. . . . Under this program such loans would be made by banks upon terms and conditions satisfactory to them without the necessity of filing loan applications with the RFC as heretofore.
>
> This action has been taken in order to adequately and promptly care for the large volume of applications for loans which it is anticipated may develop during and subsequent to the period of conversion from a wartime to a peacetime economy.

After operating under this program through 1946, the RFC announced its discontinuance in January, 1947—partly to coincide with the original expiration date of the RFC and in view of the uncertainty of its extension beyond 1947, partly because the need for such blanket guarantees of bank loans did not appear urgent at the time.

Meanwhile, however, legislation was introduced in Congress to enlarge the powers of the Federal Reserve Bank in the guaranteeing of small loans. The bill S.408 was introduced in the 80th Congress, 1st Session, on Jan. 27, 1947. Under its provisions the Federal

Reserve banks could guarantee term loans of individual banks up to 90 per cent of their value. The powers would be extended to include new as well as established enterprises, and the term limit set at ten years. The guarantee privilege would thus be available as a regular feature of the established banking system.[1]

## THE BANK CREDIT PROSPECT

Optimism on the part of small business concerning its current credit position is reflected in extended interviews with the heads of 584 small enterprises in a random sample of firms coming within the conventional small-business classifications, conducted for the CED in November, 1944, by the NORC. Only nine firms among the nearly 600 reported any credit problem, and in all nine cases the need of credit was for long-term working capital.

*Analysis by ABA.* On the capacity of the commercial banks to meet postwar credit needs, the chairman of the Postwar Small Business Credit Commission of the ABA presented, as the war's end approached, an analysis along these lines:

Of some 2.2 million active businesses listed with Dun & Bradstreet, 1.5 million have a net worth under $5,000. For those in this group seeking credit, the average requirements may run from $500 to $2,500. Assuming that half of this group would want to borrow as much as $5,000, the total amount of loans involved would be $3,750,000,000, or less than 10 per cent of the total loaned by the banks in 1940.

The next group, comprising 520,000 enterprises with net worth between $5,000 and $100,000, may average between $20,000 and $30,000 in credit needs per firm. If 50 per cent of this group were to borrow $30,000 each, the total of $7.8 billion would be less than one-fifth of the amount loaned by the banks in 1940.

Assuming, likewise, that among the 46,000 firms with net worth between $100,000 and $1 million, one-half were to borrow as much as $250,000 each, the total of roughly $5.8 billion in credit would run about 12 per cent of the bank loans in 1940.[2]

On this basis, somewhat less than half of the volume of loans

[1] This bill did not become law in 1947; its provisions were again endorsed in the Board's Annual Report for 1947 (p. 11).

[2] Statement of Robert M. Hanes, before House Committee on Post War Economic Policy and Planning, May 4, 1945.

made by the banks in 1940 would be a maximum requirement for businesses with net worth under a million dollars. Meanwhile, since 1940 bank deposits have more than doubled.

*Commercial Credit Expansion.* It was expected that with the resumption of peacetime business, the demand for bank loans would increase sharply. That expectation has been fulfilled. The volume of outstanding loans of commercial banks increased by more than $5 billion during the 12 months of 1946; this was the largest increase in any year since 1919–1920.[1] Among the factors reflected were the cumulative demands upon banks to assist in the GI program for veterans entering business, other business entries and resumptions, and programs of reconversion, reorganization, expansion, and a general face-lifting of enterprises to meet peacetime competition.

An extensive study of loans by member banks was made by the Federal Reserve System toward the end of 1946. The aggregate, exceeding $13 billion, was a new high for commercial loans. The study revealed that among small enterprises—total assets under $50,000—the ratio of term loans to total borrowings had risen from the prewar period, amounting to 30 per cent of the small-business indebtedness to the banks. The pattern was not appreciably changed, however, insofar as the character of the lending was concerned. Lending to small business was still mainly secured with real estate as the usual collateral. Four out of five loans to small business were for a year or less. The small banks, especially those in the smaller communities, devoted relatively more of their loan funds to the smaller enterprises.[2]

## UNSATISFIED CAPITAL REQUIREMENTS

As far as ordinary bank credit is concerned, and this may now include intermediate term credit of the 1- to 5-year variety, one sees no need for new public credit agencies. The chance for

[1] *Federal Reserve Bulletin*, March, 1947, p. 235.

[2] See the following issues of the *Federal Reserve Bulletin:* Albert R. Koch, "Business Loans of Member Banks," March, 1947, p. 258; Donald McC. Holthausen, "Term Lending to Business by Commercial Banks in 1946," May, 1947, pp. 502–503; Tynan Smith, "Security Pledged on Member Bank Loans to Business," June, 1947, pp. 666–667; "Member Bank Loans to Small Business," August, 1947, pp. 963–965. See also *Monthly Review* (Federal Reserve Bank of St. Louis), May, 1947, pp. 52–53.

improvement would be in the increasing ability of the banks to adapt their resources more effectively to small-business needs.

The sector of small-business financing that remains least adequately cared for and in the long run has the most crucial implications for the American economy is the supply of the more permanent or venture capital for small, independent enterprises.

Banks and public credit agencies can, within limits, help in supplying working capital that may ultimately create additional equity. They may stretch loans to five years where there is collateral in real estate, equipment, or inventory covered by warehouse receipts. But they cannot be expected, with the funds of depositors, to assume the risks that go with ownership of enterprise. Bank credit is no adequate substitute for direct investment of individual savings in specific business ventures, which in the last analysis gives meaning to the concept of an economy of free enterprise. On the other hand, the migration, urbanization, and industrialization of our society during the last half century have tended to break down the personal ties of family and neighborhood that gave rise to the informal pools of risk funds with which many a nineteenth-century enterprise was launched. The present-day equivalent of Uncle Bill and Aunt Susie must be found in a more impersonal source of capital funds—the more so since the tax levels on business and individual incomes have slowed the rates at which earnings can be plowed back for business growth.

*Market for Small Issues.* From the standpoint of what small business can contribute to future employment, the problem of attracting outside risk-capital centers on enterprises employing from 8 to 100 workers in a range of net worth from $20,000 to $500,000. These now represent somewhat under 10 per cent of the total business population, a total of perhaps 250,000 enterprises, employing about six million workers.[1] They include a large majority of the manufacturing firms. Securities offered by such firms would be for the most part in issues of less than $250,000. The difficulty experienced in marketing such issues through present channels and the prohibitive expense of flotation have been statistically summarized in two studies by the SEC. The report

[1] See paper by Roy A. Foulke, submitted to Senate Special Committee on Small Business, 78th Congress, 1st Session, Committee Print No. 15, p. 17.

issued by the commission in June, 1939, covering small issues between July, 1933, and June, 1937, revealed that (1) within a year after the effective registration date the issuers were able to sell only 23 per cent of the securities registered; (2) of the 584 companies in the sample one-third failed to sell any part of their securities. Of those which reported sales, new ventures sold only 27 per cent of their issues, while established concerns sold 44 per cent of the amount registered; (3) of the reported sales, about 71 per cent were made within three months after registration. Once the campaign period was over, the sales were reduced to a trickle.

In the commission's study of May, 1940, the high cost of these generally unsuccessful efforts to float the issues of small concerns was made evident. Corporations attempting to sell bond issues of $250,000 or under paid an average of $8.40 for each $100 bond sold, $16.40 for each $100 of preferred stock, $22.80 for each $100 of common stock. These costs were nearly double those incurred for issues between $1 million and $5 million, on which the averages were $4.50 per $100 of bond sales, $8.20 for each $100 of preferred stock, $15.40 for each $100 of common stock.[1] The findings confirm the general opinion that the established investment channels, on the record to date, hardly serve to float any substantial number of securities or to find individual investors for new independent enterprises or going concerns of moderate size that need outside capital for expansion.

In the flotation of securities there are inescapable fixed items of underwriting expense—registration, legal, accounting, engineering, printing, listing, etc.—that apply to small and large issues alike. And it is obvious that it takes more selling effort to market the security of an unknown than of a big-name business enterprise with whose standing the prospect is familiar. As a result, the investment banking house ordinarily regards a flotation under $1 million as unprofitable. The larger investment bankers are prone to consider an undertaking even between $1 million and $5 million as one of doubtful advantage. For stock flotations in amounts of $100,000 or less, regular channels of underwriting are practically unavailable.

[1] Cited in *ibid.*, p. 19.

## *Meeting Financial Requirements*

Our discussion of small-business requirements has not disposed of the question as to the adequacy of the existing facilities for financing small business. One could still take the position that small business bids for capital and the favor of the investor just as do other sources of investment; hence, that small business is getting as much as the market believes it deserves. A genuine need may stem, however, from social lag in the meeting of legitimate economic requirements. It is quite conceivable that the concentration of investment effort upon large-scale enterprise and governmental activities has created a gap in facilities designed to maintain the balance between small and large business—a balance especially needed in a society that regards freedom of competitive opportunity as a socially desirable aim.

The degree to which small business has felt pinched for financing has been related, of course, to the general business situation. Evidence has been noted that in the 1930's many small firms with apparently legitimate claims were unable to obtain the credit needed to carry on. The lack was chiefly in sources of long-term loans for working capital or more permanent capital requirements. There is some evidence that term lending by the banks has been extended, but to obtain such a loan the small business still must have ample physical collateral to insure the loan, whereas the larger firm in similar circumstances may obtain unsecured credit. Difficulties in obtaining loans up to the requirements of the small business have often reflected the fact that the small firm had an inadequate equity base to begin with.

We do know that in the current pattern of the investment market the efforts of small concerns to float securities have seldom been successful and have nearly always proved prohibitively expensive. Despite the special GI provisions for financing veterans and the special legislation to facilitate reconversion, the total of the business population had by the beginning of 1947 not yet caught up with the long-term trend.[1] When postwar material shortages are

[1] The Office of Business Economics in the U.S. Department of Commerce has projected the trend in the business population for the years 1929–1940 and finds that "As of December, 1946, the actual number of firms in operation was within 65,000, or 2 per cent, of the number expected on the basis of the prewar relationship with the general level of business activity." See "Business Population and Turn-over," *Survey of Current Business*, July, 1947, p. 15.

no longer a deterring factor, the requirements of capital facilities to permit new and expanded enterprises should be expected to increase.

The frequent claims of the lack of capital facilities before the Congressional Small Business Committees have not added up to a statistical measurement of the extent of the lack. Nor does the use that was made by small business of the special facilities offered by the RFC, the Federal Reserve, or the SWPC produce incontestable proof that the lack of financial resources is deterring new enterprise and stunting small-business growth. The same must be said for the observed decline in the importance of personal support by relatives and neighbors. The total picture has, however, led competent observers to a conviction that there is urgent need for a new approach to the problem of supplying equity capital to small business.

On this score, a memorandum prepared by the Filene Foundation in 1940, preliminary to the launching of the New England Industrial Development Corporation, contained the following typical observation:

> First, as to the question of the need for fixed capital for small business: There is no disagreement among economists, businessmen, and bankers whose statements are here reviewed that small business lacks adequate capital. There is little or no disagreement that our financial mechanisms are not set up so as to provide equity capital for the smaller business units. At the same time, there is no disagreement that there are many sound small businesses which could profitably use additional equity or risk capital (*i.e.*, common stocks) were they able to secure it on terms comparable to those on which the larger business units secure their capital. Second, as to the question of semifixed capital, that is to say, long-term loans for small business—loans for working capital, for the purchase of equipment, and so forth, for terms of 5, 10, or even 15 years: *The weight of the evidence and opinion presented is that the need is real and definite.*[1]

A similar conclusion was reached by Roy Foulke of Dun & Bradstreet, who, on the basis of long study of the capital and credit position of small businessmen, stated that "under the existing setup of our economic structure we find no organized source or sources to

[1] Cited in R. L. Weissman, *Small Business and Venture Capital*, Harper & Brothers, New York, 1945, p. 45.

provide long-term money or permanent capital to intermediate-sized concerns."[1]

*Foreign Experience.* Consideration of small-business financing as a growing problem has not been confined to the United States. Before the First World War it had been the common practice over Continental Europe to operate "mixed banks," which combined capital loans and equity participations with ordinary short-term lending. However, the experience of the 1920's and 1930's created a growing sentiment for the separation of capital financing from commercial banking. In practically every European country there was a trend toward the formation of special banks—not constrained by the considerations of liquidity deemed necessary to protect demand deposits—to care for the capital requirements of small business. France had its Credit Artisanat (1923) supplementing the Banques Populaires and Credit Mobilier, which had been established earlier. Belgium established special guaranty banks both for artisans and independent professional people—the Fonds de Garantie and the Caisse Centrale. In Germany, several of the provinces established Industrieschaften, as well as the more general Bank für Deutsche Industrie Obligationen. Denmark and Sweden had their Industrial Credits companies.[2]

In Great Britain the growing acuteness of the problem of financing new and independent enterprises, especially in the smaller brackets, led to the formation of the Royal British Commission on Finance and Industry, generally known as the Macmillan Committee. The report of that committee, presented in 1931, stressed the existence of an area of unsatisfied demand for business capital—the widely discussed "Macmillan gap"—and recommended finance agencies expressly designed to facilitate the growth of new and small enterprise in Great Britain.[3]

The validity of the demand for additional means of supplying equity capital is not discounted by the specific cases where small businessmen have succeeded in mobilizing new capital. The total

[1] *Small Buiness: Access to Capital*, U.S. Senate Small Business Committee, Senate Print No. 15, 78th Congress, 1st Session, p. 19.

[2] Kurt Grünwald, "Industrial Credit Survey 1919–1939," *L'Egypte Contemporaine*, Cairo, Nos. 203 and 204, February, March, 1942.

[3] A note on the new British financing facilities that have been established as a result of the recommendations in the *Macmillan Report* will be found on p. 177.

problem of capital financing, in an area covering three million small enterprises, is too large and varied to be disposed of by pointing to individual cases in which small enterprises have found a solution. Nor has the aggregate problem been met by the efforts of small-town banks, which have typically been the most generous in stretching their facilities to meet the capital requirements of small enterprises.

That the need exists on a broad front has been recognized in a number of proposals for the creation of new facilities, which merit consideration at this point.

## PROPOSALS FOR NEW FACILITIES

Proposals that have been made to create additional machinery for supplying ownership capital or long-term debt capital to small business may be differentiated according to the degree in which they are organized as private business ventures for profit. They may also be appraised in terms of the likelihood of their satisfying the mass market for small-business capital. We shall consider, in turn, the community agency for industrial development, the adaptation of private investment banking to provide small business capital, new governmental agencies that would engage directly in the financing of small business, and, finally, extension of the present private banking system to cover investment in small business.

### *Community Industrial Development*

The privately sponsored civic corporation for the financing and development of new and expanding local enterprises has emerged in a number of communities. The general purpose is to bring the enterprise that needs capital into contact with the sources of funds seeking investment outlets, to make investments from the community fund, or to aid a business in obtaining additional financing. In a sense, it is an effort to reproduce, through a formal organization, the equivalent of the practical neighborly interest in a local venture that used to develop spontaneously in the more simple social structure of an earlier period. At the same time, it recognizes the fact that technical expertness and respected judgment are, under present conditions, more necessary than good will to attract funds to new ventures. Industrial-development corporations may also be concerned with steering local problem cases out of their difficulties, although they are designed primarily to bring new enterprise to the community.

*Examples.* An early experiment in this field was the industrial-development company created by the Boston Chamber of Commerce in 1911. From 92 subscribers an underwriting of $500,000 was obtained "to be loaned to small enterprises to expand or enlarge their businesses, if sound and legitimate and possessed of good prospects of success." Apparently the first publicity campaign of the chamber was very effective, since it claimed to have received more than a thousand inquiries during its first year. Of these, 58 were considered worth looking into. They resulted in an authorization of 11 loans, aggregating $51,000; only two of them appear to have turned out satisfactorily. As reported by the New England Council, the experiment was discouraging in respect to the character of the applicants and the great risks involved. At any rate, "the company ceased operations in 1914 after discovering that there was no real field in its activities."[1] The experience of the Boston Chamber of Commerce gives point to the attitude expressed by a number of other chambers, that the business of attracting capital to local enterprise is a full-time job for a separate trained organization devoted solely to that purpose rather than for a chamber of commerce.

Among the older development corporations that are still active are the Industrial Corporation of Baltimore, the Easton (Pennsylvania) Guarantee Fund, and the Louisville Industrial Foundation, each of which has operated for about 30 years. Of the more recent entrants into the field, typical examples would be the New England Industrial Development Corporation, the Economic Development Council of Kansas City, and the Wyoming Valley Industrial Development Fund. In all there are about fifty community agencies that might properly be listed as industrial development corporations, although more than twice that number are known to have been started.

The most frequently cited example of the successful community organization to encourage independent enterprise is the

[1] See *Financing of New Industries*, Report of the Subcommittee of the Industrial Development Committee of the New England Council, Oct. 31, 1940, pp. 4–5.

Baltimore Corporation. The fund originally invested in the corporation by a group of leading citizens is utilized primarily to facilitate the making of investigations and appraisals of applicant enterprises and the maintenance of engineering and related facilities for counseling. When a new proposition is found promising, the directors of the corporation may invest personally in the venture or find other members of the community who are interested. The organization has a standing list of such prospective investors. The Baltimore Corporation has, according to its director, been able to support itself by means of the fees charged for engineering and counseling services to companies seeking its advice.

The Louisville Industrial Foundation represents a second type of community development corporation. In that case there is a pooled investment fund contributed by civic leaders. From the fund, investments are made directly in small enterprises entering the community or in a local enterprise requiring reorganization or expansion. This type of organization may foster all forms of enterprise whether big or small, public or private, that hold promise of expanding employment in the community.

The Economic Development Council of Kansas City is essentially a privately sponsored research foundation which carries out product-development research for individual firms on a fee basis at the same time that it attempts to discover new opportunities for investment capital in the area. The Wyoming Industrial Research Foundation,[1] supported by appropriations from the state government, seeks to discover new uses for the state's resources with the object of encouraging private capital to invest in Wyoming.

The New England Industrial Development Corporation, founded by Lincoln Filene and associates, presents an excellent case on the field that needs to be cultivated. According to its prospectus,[2] the corporation has the research, financial, and counseling services of more than 50 private and public organizations which "flow out as specialized services to the individual small manufacturer, to the community seeking new industrial development, and the persons or organizations interested in undertaking

[1] Not the Wyoming Valley (Wilkes-Barre, Pa.) Industrial Development Fund.

[2] *A Report of Progress, 1940–1944*, by the New England Industrial Development Corporation, p. 1.

new industrial ventures or the establishment of branch industries in New England." The services to individual enterprises, investors, or communities are offered on a fee basis kept to a minimum in accordance with the limited dividend character of the organization.

The SWPC, through its district offices, attempted during the war to encourage the formation of industrial development corporations in a large number of communities in order that small enterprise might have better access to investment funds. The early liquidation of the SWPC negated these efforts, but it was indicated that the Department of Commerce, through its small-business staff and field offices, would make the encouragement of community industrial development corporations one phase of its activities.

*Limitations.* On the record to date, the industrial-development corporation has barely scratched the surface of the problem of supplying capital for small business. The Baltimore Corporation, with its long and respected career, has given help to an average of eight cases per year over the 30 years of its existence.[1] Its field has been primarily the intermediate-size business; practically none of the loans or investments it has recommended have been for less than $100,000. The aggregate of its financial operations over the 30-year period is about $25 million.

The Louisville Industrial Foundation invested an aggregate of $3.3 million in 60 firms over a period of 27 years (1917–1944). These funds were distributed as follows:[2]

TABLE 41

| *Type of investment* | *Number* | *Amount* |
|---|---|---|
| Completely new enterprises | 13 | $899,120 |
| Brought-in enterprises | 12 | 708,477 |
| Recently founded enterprises | 8 | 296,550 |
| Old established enterprises | 11 | 699,800 |
| Public enterprises | 2 | 200,000 |
| Refinancing operations | 14 | 496,331 |
| Total | 60 | $3,300,278 |

[1] A great deal of the respect it has acquired is attributed to its director, G. Harvey Porter, who has served in this capacity since its inception, and who would probably have performed equal service as industrial counselor under other auspices.

[2] "Louisville Industrial Foundation, A Study in Community Capitalizations of Local Industries," Research Department, Federal Reserve Bank of Atlanta, February, 1945, pp. 36–38.

The New England IDC, established in 1940, apparently made only slight headway in financing local small business, although it has been helpful in furnishing financial and managerial guidance to clients. In 1943 the corporation's representative recommended to the Senate Small Business Committee the establishment of a holding company for investments in small firms backed by government guarantees.[1]

From the histories of the leading industrial-development corporations one gains the impression that they have been highly selective in their search for ventures of unusual promise, with emphasis on the development of new manufacturing processes. This tendency is natural and desirable in an organization that is characteristically a civic enterprise.

Although the type of community endeavor exemplified by the industrial development corporations has been helpful as far as its activities have reached, these activities have touched only a negligible fraction of small business and its capital requirements. The effort to supply capital requirements of small business must obviously be made on a much broader front if an improvement is to be made in the total situation.

*Investment Company for Small Business*

An interesting approach to the problem of filling the need for small-business risk capital without resort to government operation is found in the plan proposed in 1945 by the Committee on Small Business of the Investment Bankers Association. It is to encourage establishment of local investment houses specializing in small-business financing. The chartered investment company would acquire, retain, and sell securities or debt paper. Operations would be limited to the communities of the Federal Reserve bank district in which the investment house is located, and no loan or issue would be for more than an established maximum ($100,000 was originally proposed). The chartered investment company could be started with a minimum of $25,000 of paid-in capital.[2]

[1] See Hearings before the Special Committee to Study and Survey Problems of Small Business Enterprises, U.S. Senate, 78th Congress, 1st Session, Part 15, Feb. 23, 1943, p. 2157; also *Business Developments* (Chase National Bank), Feb. 15, 1945.

[2] See "Capital for Small Business," a statement on national policy by the Small

The company would have the privilege of supplementing the investment of the stockholders through the sale of debentures to the Federal Reserve bank up to three times the amount of the paid-in capital. The debentures, placed at low interest rates and with an extended term for amortization, would provide supplementary capital with which the investment company may expand its operations. Funds obtained through debentures would also supply the leverage for making possible a reasonable net return to the stockholder.[1]

In the IBA proposal provision is made for the sharing of the composite risk by those financially aided. In addition to the Class A shares for its subscribers, the investment company would issue Class B junior shares to the borrowing firms.

> Whenever a loan was made or securities purchased, the investment company could require the borrowing or issuing company to employ up to 10 per cent of the cash proceeds of the transaction in the purchase of Class B shares. . . . The actual amount of shares so purchased . . . would depend upon the investment company's evaluation of the risk and, also, upon bargaining between the two parties.[2]

The IBA proposal accepts the premise of the industrial-development corporation that investment support of small business must come mainly from the area neighboring the small enterprise; hence the company must be a local institution. It draws frankly upon the willingness of the government to do something for small

---

Business Committee of the Investment Bankers Association of America, Chicago, 1946, 14 pp. (mimeo.).

[1] Thus, in principle, the proposed investment corporation for small business would resemble the traditional British investment trust of the nineteenth century. The BIT issued common stock for its own operating group and issued preferred stock and debentures or other senior stock to provide it with additional funds. The British-type investment trust was instrumental in developing new shipping lines, mines, "plantations," and manufacturing establishments. It held the new securities during the period of development and went into new ventures with the profits from the disposal of old securities. In practice, the proposed small-business investment corporations would differ from the British investment trust in two respects: Instead of roaming the world, as did the BIT's, it would operate within the local area where it is established; and instead of placing its debentures with private investors at 4½ to 6 per cent, it would obtain its senior Funds from a Federal agency at interest close to the Federal Reserve rate.

[2] IBA, *op. cit.*, p. 3.

business, by tapping the Federal Reserve System for additional working capital obtained in exchange for low-interest debentures.

The plan recognizes the riskiness in general of investment in small business and avoids promising simultaneously to service the small enterprises with management guidance and protect investors—at least for the present—at interest rates as low as those granted to larger business with facilities for continuing self-appraisal.

That the IBA proposal did not command vigorous support is not surprising. As the framers of the plan have pointed out with notable candor, "Investment bankers as such are not investors but are merchants of securities. Thus, they do not purchase new security issues to hold but to resell as promptly as possible to others."[1] Apart from the limited market of a localized operation, there is serious question as to whether or not personnel drawn from the investment banking field is likely to reach to small firms that, though deserving, may be in need of continuing management guidance and of being carried along for a considerable period.

Before questioning whether the possibilities of the private banking system for supplying capital have been fully explored, let us review the proposals for new government lending agencies.

### *Direct Government Financing*

Ever since the depression of the 1930's there has been support in Congress for supplementation by the Federal government of the existing facilities in long-term and equity capital for small business. The authorizations to the RFC and the Federal Reserve banks previously referred to were aimed primarily at distress cases. The wartime lending powers given the SWPC reflected the fear of shutting out small business from substantial participation in the war effort unless the government got behind small business with credit guarantees and direct loans. With postwar requirements in mind, members of the Senate and the House introduced a score of bills for a new government agency to meet the capital requirements of small business.[2] Legislation was also introduced to establish a system of Federal insurance of small loans.

[1] *Ibid.*, p. 7.

[2] See I.G. Gromfine, *Financial Problems of Small Business*, Bureau of Labor Statistics, September, 1944, p. 78, for a tabular comparison of 16 Congressional proposals.

With the fast tempo of business in the immediate postwar period, the pressure to enact new legislation to supplement existing facilities temporarily subsided. But one must expect that a recession would revive the interest in the creation of new governmental facilities.

Some of the legislative proposals for a new government financing agency call for a Federal lending agency, empowered to provide long-term debt, with or without collateral, with varying limits or maturity up to 20 years. Others go beyond term banking to set up Federal investment corporations which may acquire equity securities, as well as bonds, mortgages, and other evidences of debt. Usually the proposals for a Federal investment corporation authorize the purchase of preferred stocks but omit common stocks to avoid the criticism of government ownership in small business. Securities taken by the Federal corporations are exempted from the rules of the SEC.

The majority of the bills call for the capital stock of the government lending or investment agency to be subscribed by the Treasury, although a few name the RFC or the Federal Reserve banks as subscribers. In at least one case provision is made for subscriptions by the public, with the unsubscribed portion to be taken up by the RFC. Where the Federal Reserve System is authorized to establish the financial corporation, the Treasury is directed to purchase the FDIC stock from the Federal Reserve banks as the basis for the initial capital. For additional capital, debentures of the corporation would be bought by the Treasury or guaranteed by the United States government.

A good composite of the usual provisions in proposed measures for a small-business finance corporation is contained in a bill introduced by Congressman Randolph of West Virginia, which provided as follows:

Sec. (3) For the purpose of providing funds or credit, with or without guaranty as to principal and interest, to a commercial, industrial, or mining business, the Corporation is authorized and directed, subject to such regulations and requirements as its board of directors may prescribe,

(*a*) to make loans to and discount or purchase the obligations of such a business;

(*b*) to purchase preferred stock in a corporation or joint stock association engaged in such a business;

(*c*) to discount for or purchase from a financing institution obligations of, or preferred stock in a corporation engaged in, such a business;

(*d*) to make loans to a financing institution on the security of such obligations or preferred stock; and

(*e*) to guarantee any financing institution against loss of principal or interest on loans made to such a business and on purchases of preferred stock in such a business; to make commitments to purchase and thereafter to purchase any such loans, discounts, or purchases.

The Corporation shall have the power to make or acquire any such loan or obligation with a maturity of not less than one year and up to ten years, and the Dorporation shall have the power to purchase any such preferred stock provided the issuer of the preferred stock is obligated to retire the same within ten years, except that the board of directors shall have power to extend such period for not to exceed ten years; and all such loans, obligations, or preferred stock shall provide in a manner satisfactory to the Corporation for installment payments on the loan or obligation, or periodic retirements of the preferred stock. . . .[1]

Whatever the variations among the proposals in the specific powers granted, they are based upon the common premise that it is necessary for the government to step in with a more versatile financial backing for small business than has been available through private investment channels, the banking system, or the RFC.

That brings us to the significance of the double-barreled feature of the powers contemplated for Federal financing agencies in proposed legislation. For example, in the quotation from the Randolph Bill, above, it will be noticed that the Federal agency is in one aspect of its operations a banker's bank—a facility for discounting the term obligations of financial institutions or purchasing their securities and guaranteeing loans made by the financing institution. In that respect the Federal agency is designed as a rear line of defense against strain on our private system of finance, while the latter continues the direct dealings with business. But at the same time the Federal agency is authorized to deal directly with business firms—to make loans to them, with or without collateral, and to purchase their securities.

[1] H.R. 2994, 79th Congress, 1st Session.

There is much to be said for the general purpose of broader directives to back up the banking system and the financial institutions. If the powers of direct lending were granted as emergency powers, to be used only in a crisis that the existing financing institutions could not meet, then the Federal agency could be a valuable contingent resource. That purpose could be served by the RFC or Federal Reserve Board. But the legislation would authorize direct lending to or investment in small and intermediate business. If this means that the Federal lending or investment agency is intended to enter upon financing of small business from the start as its routine activity, then we should face the implications of public machinery so employed.

The stated objective of any new Federal finance agency for more adequately supplying small-business capital is to foster decentralization of business enterprise through more independent owners. To speed that end, the new government agency presumably must be more liberal in its lending practices than the private investment sources and the banking system, including the RFC and the Federal Reserve System, have been. In other words, the chances henceforth to be taken by government, if it directly finances small business, should be greater than private bankers or investors have on the whole been willing to take. At the same time the government is expected to make its funds available at figures below the rates heretofore regarded as prohibitive for small capital issues and long-term commitments. Some bills specify 4 per cent. The combination of these requirements adds up to a prospect—considering the scale on which the government agency would operate—that the total of defaults will be on a larger scale than heretofore unless a new level of small-business efficiency somehow emerges. It must also mean that small businesses which might otherwise have dropped out or have kept their operations within the capacities of their management will linger until their windfall of government support has run out. Ultimately, we must expect to find in the lap of the government agency an accumulating residue of defaulted debt and ownership paper of the enterprises assisted; on foreclosure, the government becomes the big owner of small business.

If the number of failures is to be held down, we must contemplate, along with the financing, a considerable amount of continuous investigation and guidance of the firms to which funds are granted. New techniques of flexible repayments, varying with the prosperity of a given season, must be invoked. In the case of the Federal Reserve loans under 13B, the complaint was frequently made that the expense of supplying the Federal Reserve Bank with the information it wanted, in order to service its 13B loans, was inordinately high, and that this was in part an explanation of the small number of firms that proceeded to qualify for loans. The same complaint has been made before Congressional committees with respect to RFC loans. Even so, the Federal Reserve banks avoided showing a deficit only by omitting to allocate full administrative overhead to the 13B program. RFC losses on small loans were offset by profits on loans well above the small-business level.

It is hard to escape the conclusion that direct Federal financing of term capital to small business is destined to become a subsidy program if it yields to public pressure or else fail in its liberal objectives if it hews to the line of conserving its capital. Either the subsidy would be needed to cover the costs of adequate financial and management guidance, or it would be incurred in covering the losses on unproductive loans. The disposal of its defaulted claims on the unsuccessful small businesses would involve, in any event, a more direct participation of the government in the disposition of small-business enterprises.

These considerations are not dissociated from the issues of practical politics that are involved. An unpublicized reason for securing a new agency is that the Federal banking system is not too sensitive to outside persuasion. Federal agencies like the War Production Board, the OPA, and the SWPC had painful experience with the political pressures brought to bear upon them to stretch a point in behalf of a constituent. Congressmen, among others, had to act as go-betweens—often reluctantly—in the attempt to get special favors for home-town enterprises. One cannot appraise the projected scheme of a system of governmental investment corporations for small business without recognizing the fact that such pressures must enter appreciably into the situation, although the bulk of the personnel in the setup be sincere and competent.

The experiences of the 1930's and of the war period give strong support to those who ask for preparedness through adequate governmental facilities to meet any crisis that may develop as a result of the unavailability of financial resources to small business. Establishing a line of defense to be used when and if existing means fail to meet an emergency seems wise. It is taking an unnecessarily long chance, however, to launch for this purpose a brand-new Federal finance corporation limited to a hazardous business in which the prospects of breaking even are doubtful. Legislation looking toward more liberal financing might well concentrate on enlargement of the lending powers of the Federal Reserve banks and the RFC, with an unmistakable mandate from Congress to reduce the inhibitions and make full use of such powers. By an equally clear mandate, the direct lending should be invoked only as the existing facilities fail to support deserving small business.

*A Note on Proposed Insurance of Small Loans.* Proposals for insurance of small loans were made by the SWPC and embodied in Congressional bills on small-business financing. Obviously, they reflect the hope that the protection thus afforded may encourage a more liberal credit treatment to small-business applications without jeopardizing the liquidity of bank deposits. The sponsors of loan insurance usually draw an analogy between it and forms of governmentally sponsored insurance already established. The precedents generally cited are the insurance of housing loans by the Federal Housing Administration and the insurance of deposits by the FDIC. The analogy seems spurious in several respects, which may be briefly noted at this point.

In the case of housing, the basis of the insurance is, of course, the real estate itself. The life or condition of the security is hardly disturbed if the property is transferred from the defaulting owner to a new owner who assumes the obligations involved. Moreover, the size of the loan is geared to tangible values that provide an actuarial basis for insurance risk. If anything, the effect of FHA insurance has been to protect the tangible value of the amounts secured, by the application of stricter standards of construction than had formerly applied within the given price ranges.

Back of the insurance of deposits, we have total assets of the banks, our currency reserve, the U.S. Treasury as guarantor for a large fraction thereof, and a comprehensive system of controls over the treatment of deposits. Together these safeguards have made a small fraction of 1 per cent of the total deposits sufficient to build up a surplus in the FDIC.

Indeed, a criticism coming from small banks has been that their opportunities to make loans are, in effect, reduced by the restrictions of the examiners of the FDIC—inasmuch as the FDIC is concerned with holding down the risk and increasing its own protection against banks that loan too freely.

The insurance of small-business loans involves a very different situation from that just described. The explicit objective is to make banks freer to liberalize their lending policy. The banks are to be encouraged to lay their burdens on the insurance system in order to overcome the fear of riskier small-business loans. If the system of insurance is not to discourage this objective, it must either (1) place a very high premium on the insurance or (2) accept losses beyond the actuarial basis of its premiums.

Unlike deposits, which have a uniform dollar value regardless of the name to which they are credited, the small loans represent a broad range in the degree of soundness or unsoundness. As a practical matter, the banks would probably have to insure the whole portfolio of their small loans, just as deposits are lumped for FDIC insurance. A uniform premium covering all small loans must increase the expense to the sounder borrowers in order to cover the weaker.

The conglomerate of small loans, under a liberal policy, offers little promise of the type of standardization that has made the FHA and FDIC financially successful. On the other hand, if such standardization of practice be developed, the very objective of liberalizing loans to small business would be defeated.

It would seem sounder to give fuller trial to the guarantee of and participation in the small loans of the individual banks by the Federal Reserve System and the RFC, since in that way the responsibility for the small-business loan would be retained where the responsibility for a character loan should lie—on the lender and the borrower.

## CAPITAL FINANCING THROUGH THE BANKING SYSTEM

The discussion up to this point has called attention to the lacks in measures developed thus far for small-business financing. The adequacy of the private efforts has been questioned, and the wisdom of direct government financing has been challenged. Is there any other promising alternative? Let us reexamine the potentialities of the banking system on this score. Whatever the complaints about the bankers, the fact remains that the small business looks chiefly to the local banker to aid in its operation and development.

The banking system, out of the trials and errors of the last two decades, has extended its credit frontiers. Gradually, commercial banks have been increasing term loans, both secured and unsecured, for working-capital purposes. Were it not for the element of liquidity in the interest of demand depositors, the banks would appear as the logical agency through which to accomplish the growth of small enterprise. Under prevailing conditions, however, the bank may fail the small enterprise at the stage when credit requirements of the business go beyond working-capital needs into the area of permanent capital.

Wc must face the fact that the traditional type of individual investment in a new enterprise, on the basis of neighborliness and personal confidence in friend or relative, has been passing out of the picture. The growth of large cities and the increasing complexity of our economy have diminished that kind of investment. We also have to reckon with the long-term trend in taxation, which leaves a smaller percentage of earnings to plow back into the business. With the drying up of former sources of individual equity capital, expansion of the smaller firm's permanent assets will increasingly have to depend upon an advance of funds to the business to be repaid from future earnings over an extended period. In other words, the creation of additional equity for an established small firm becomes increasingly a lending operation rather than a permanent investment of ownership funds by the financing agency. This condition is accentuated by the fact that the small enterpriser characteristically is jealous of his managerial control and hesitates to take in outsiders as the price of obtaining new capital.

With this background it seems essential to find some way of utilizing the banks as an instrument for effecting the growth of small-business capital. The operation of investment affiliates by commercial banks during the booming 1920's fell into disrepute because of abuses that developed from their unregulated practices. But that experience does not preclude the consideration of capital banking protected by adequate sanctions and controls. With the precedent set in the capitalization of the Federal Reserve banks, it should be feasible for the commercial banks in each Federal Reserve district to be authorized to subscribe a percentage—let us say up to 3 per cent—of their capital and surplus in a district capital bank, with branches as need develops. The capital bank would operate under authority of the district Federal Reserve bank and under policies broadly laid down by Congress and carried out by the board of governors of the Federal Reserve System. The capital banks would provide a logical place to which the commercial bank, itself a stockholder, would as a matter of course refer its creditworthy client for a capital-loan program. Capital-bank financing could be supported by collateral, securities, receivables, or certificates of indebtedness, both secured and unsecured.

There is some room for debate as to whether or not an investment bank that is an integral part of the banking system should be expected to engage in buying and selling of venture shares—specifically common-stock issues. At least in the early stage of the experiment, it would seem prudent for the financing done by the capital banks to be essentially on a credit-granting basis. Preferred stocks would be callable on a prearranged program with the bank. Common stocks could be issued with the bank, as stockholder, sharing in earnings and in the increase of equity values but with redemption features to be exercised by the issuing firm within agreed time limits and adjustments of transfer value, so that the small firm could regain its full control of the venture. A further possibility, with time and experience, is that the capital bank, as an operation under the Federal Reserve System, may be put in a position to place its debentures or rediscount paper with the Federal Reserve banks at rates low enough to permit a fair return on the expanded employment of its funds.

While the capital bank here suggested is conceived in the first place as an accommodation available to the bank depositor and his bank, it need not limit its operations to clients referred by its bank stockholders. It may well be permitted to accept long-term obligations of finance companies, business associations, and other enterprises coming within the area of small and intermediate business. Nor is it a necessary part of the plan that private investors be excluded from subscribing to the capital of the bank even though the plan is conceived in the first place as a project to be inaugurated by the commercial banks of the district.

The financing of capital operations involves different psychology and different methods from those involved in the conduct of a commercial bank for depositors. It requires personnel not inhibited by orthodox banking traditions. A bank specializing in permanent capital should be in a position to develop new techniques for the financing of small enterprise, for which the times call. It could, for example, modify the traditional procedure of regular payments of the same amount at each due date by adjusting the size of payment, the interest rate, and service charges to the position of the enterprise, to general business conditions, and in line with central banking or monetary policy at a given time. It could receive more liberal payment in stock as an offset to granting interest rates lower than the risk of the enterprise would ordinarily command. A capital bank must be prepared to furnish the advisory services needed in the successful financing of small business. But here the capital bank would have a valuable ally in the commercial bank, whose information and regular banking facilities would be joined with those of the capital bank in helping the small enterprise through its vicissitudes.

Where the small-town or neighborhood bank may be limited mainly to retailers or a limited line of industry for its banking market, the capital bank could encompass an area large enough to permit diversification of investments, with correspondingly better chance of offsetting losses with gains. Given the necessary freedom of action within a framework of reasonable banking supervision, the capital bank should be able to come out with profits justifying the venture. Yet the size of the dividends that such an enterprise will earn for its member banks, even after the initial experience-building stage, is secondary to the larger issue. That issue is whether private financing enterprise will adequately serve small business or, by default, the financing of small business will be brought under a Federal program whereby government itself becomes the investor in small business.

A system of capital banks along the lines here described would appear on its face to have potentialities for small-business financing on a far broader front than is possible with the volunteer corporations that have been discussed, and it would not invade to any major degree the area of venture capital to which their activities contribute.

## TAX POLICY FOR SMALL BUSINESS

The discussion of the financial problems of small business has served to highlight the importance of ability to convert profits into permanent capital. The small business is generally started with the savings of its owners, and its growth must likewise depend largely on what the owners can save out of profits, in view of the difficulties of the small enterprise in acquiring outside capital. There is, moreover, the question of retaining control, which again places the emphasis on creating new capital out of the firm's earnings rather than from outside sources. Thus, in the mind of the small enterpriser tax payments are apt to be reckoned as an additional barrier to survival.

Since we are assuming that the expansion of small business is important to a balanced, productive, competitive economy, the effects on new and small business must be considered in framing the postwar tax structure.

The lawmakers have not been unmindful of the claims of small business in the intricate politics of taxmaking. The difficulties of trying to give fair treatment to small business in the tax structure are increased by the fact that the interests of small business are too varied to permit a united front on many of the questions that arise. There are conflicts of interest between the small corporation and the small partnership, between the new business and the established small business, between owners of small enterprise who are in the high-income brackets and those near the bottom of the personal-income scale. What is sought is the area of tax policy in which the self-interest of small business most nearly coincides with the general economic welfare.

For a more systematic treatment of tax policy and the part of small business therein than is appropriate here, the reader is referred to the tax policy statements of the CED and the tax studies of Professor Groves of its research staff.[1] The objective here will be the more limited one of indicating briefly how the interest of small business is tied to the general goals of the tax

[1] See *A Postwar Federal Tax Plan for High Employment*, August, 1944, and *Taxes and the Budget*, November, 1947, policy statements by the Research and Policy Committee of the CED; also, Harold M. Groves, *Production, Jobs, and Taxes*, McGraw-Hill Book Company, Inc., New York, 1944, especially Chap. III; Groves, *Postwar Taxation and*

system as a whole and what aspects of tax policy should receive special emphasis by small business.

*Relation to General Tax Reform.* The earlier analysis of business profits has made it clear that small business tends to experience a sharper drop in income when business is generally low and a sharper rise in profits when business activity is high than is the case with the more broadly based big enterprise. Hence, small business has more than proportionate dependence on any characteristics of the tax system that tend to sustain the total of employment and the aggregate demand for goods and services.

Small business, as we have seen, has concentrated in retailing and consumer services, residential construction, and apparel and food manufactures. A tax structure that would release additional funds for consumer spending is therefore especially significant for the well-being of small business.

Concretely, this means that when supplies have caught up with postwar shortages, foreign relief, and defense, small business should support a program that keeps the mass of consumers in the market through the scaling down of personal income tax rates. Likewise, excise taxes, which tend to reduce the net volume of consumer purchases, should be eliminated, except for special cases such as gasoline, liquor, and tobacco. Heavy reliance on sales taxes as a revenue source requires levying the tax on articles of mass consumption. Release of most of the more than $3 billion now collected as sales taxes will aid substantially in sustaining the volume of business in areas upon which small business depends.

Small business, of course, has a direct interest in the reduction of income tax rates, since risk capital is dependent upon the availability of individual savings and the plowing back of earnings into the business.

*Recent Tax Relief.* The Revenue Act of 1945 repealed the excess profits tax, the capital stock tax, and the declared-value excess profits tax. On corporate income, reductions were made in the surtax for smaller companies, so that the combined rates for normal and surtaxes were reduced from 25 to 21 per cent for

---

*Economic Progress*, McGraw-Hill Book Company, Inc., New York, 1946, especially Chap. IV.

corporations in the income brackets under $5,000 and from 27 to 23 per cent on incomes between $5,000 and $20,000.

*Business Income Tax.* Small business, like big business, is interested in the reduction of taxes on business income, in avoiding the repressive effects of having corporate income taxed both at the source and as dividends of stockholders. How far a business corporation is properly subject to taxation of its income as a corporate entity, apart from its stockholders, is still a moot question. As a practical matter the corporation tax looms so large in total revenues of the government that expectation of its early elimination seems unrealistic. Graduation of the corporate tax to favor the smaller corporations, in the low-income brackets, may be defended on the ground that their ability to survive and grow is more seriously affected by their ability to increase capital through earnings.

For the really small business, particularly with net income under $10,000, the distinction for revenue purposes between corporate and individual ownership is negligible. The aggregate government revenue from the corporate tax on firms with incomes up to $10,000 was estimated at between $90 million and $100 million (as of 1945).[1] The chief reason for a corporate tax on the small corporation would therefore seem to be mainly as a means of equalizing the advantages of the corporate form as against individual ownership.

Permitting the small corporation the option of being taxed as a partnership would mean that where the partnership plan was elected, the income of the business would be taxable to the stockholders under the individual income tax without regard to whether or not it was distributed as dividends. This would permit the small incorporated business to enjoy the advantage of the corporate form without having to assume the Federal corporate income tax.

*Depreciation Allowance.* The small business, particularly the new business, is subject to the disadvantage of being taxed on business income required for reinvestment and growth. The lack of legal and accounting facilities available to the big business limits small firms in utilizing depreciation allowances to full advantage. Small business, therefore, has a special interest in the proposal for accelerating the depreciation allowance in the first years, so that

[1] Unofficial estimate submitted by a staff member of the Fiscal Division of the Budget Bureau.

the bulk of the fixed assets would be depreciable within the first five years. The adoption of such a formula under the Federal revenue system would mean that small business could recover its capital for reinvestment within a shorter period. Such accelerated depreciation would also meet one of the larger elements of risk in small business—that of being left behind in competition with improved equipment. There are obvious administrative difficulties in the proposal, but the adoption of a formula that makes the rate of amortization highest in the early years would not seem impracticable.

*Fluctuating Income and Carry-over.* The small business, subject to wide fluctuations in income, is unduly penalized when its owners must pay out in taxes during a good year more than is offset by the drop in taxes in subsequent deficit years. The principle of averaging taxes over good and bad years, sound for all business, is often vital to the survival of small business. The present carry-back of 2 years' losses is of no use to new ventures, and a 2-year carry-forward is hardly enough to overcome the lean years. The privilege of carrying losses back for 1 year as well as forward over a five-year period, as recommended by the CED Research Committee, would be a constructive improvement over present provisions. A system of averaging of individual incomes over a given period would serve, likewise, to eliminate the present discrimination against persons whose incomes are irregular.

While these suggestions are made from the viewpoint of what is desirable for small business, their constructive implication is for the national economy as a whole. Small business—limiting the term here to firms of less than 100 employees—contributed nearly 45 per cent of all nonagricultural employment in 1939. If it is to do as well in the maintenance of high postwar employment, with the present handicaps in enlarging its capital, a tax system that has as little repressive effect as possible upon investment in small business must be regarded as essential for the survival and growth of small business.

## SUMMARY

In meeting its financial requirements small business has the least difficulty in obtaining ordinary business credit from suppliers. In bank credit the difficulties increase as the requirements move from short-term to long-term loans. The major financing problem of small business is the difficulty of obtaining adequate permanent capital.

The record is not sufficiently clear to say if the banks have been overcritical of loan applications by small businesses. The main studies made during the early 1930's reflected the bias of a depressed period; they need to be supplemented by continuing systematic analysis of small-business loans and the nature of the risks involved in servicing them.

It is apparent that part of the small-businessman's difficulty in obtaining bank credit is his lack of accurate information on his economic position and his inability to state his case for credit purposes. This suggests the need of better understanding by the borrower of the considerations on which the bank gauges the creditworthiness of applicants for specific types of credit. A definitive manual, sponsored by the banking fraternity, explaining the criteria that have to be met could be a valuable aid toward mutual understanding between banker and borrower.

The credit problems of small business are accentuated by the fact that the position of the ordinary commercial banker varies, like that of his borrowers, with the level of business conditions. In their efforts to preserve liquidity the banks may fail the small business in times of stress when credit assistance is most needed. A shoestring equity position, which characterizes many small firms, tends to make short-term borrowing both more urgent and more difficult.

New facilities for capital financing are needed to offset the decline in traditional sources of personal financial backing for the small enterpriser. Neither the investment-banking nor community-development corporations are designed to meet the need on the scale required for healthy expansion of small business, nor are the commercial banks in a position to do so. The entry of the government into capital financing for small enterprise, with its grave potentialities for the future of independent competitive enterprise, appears likely unless adequate private facilities become available.

For financial aid the small enterpriser first looks to his banker; for the development of a new capital facility we should look to the banking system itself. There is a logical place for a network of capital banks under Federal Reserve supervision to which the commercial banks can refer the small enterpriser for his permanent capital requirements.

The capital banks should be free to develop new financing techniques, with management adapted to the special conditions and requirements of small enterprise.

In the field of taxation, the problems that bear most significantly on the small business are the maximum release of consumer funds, the opportunity for savings to be invested or reinvested in business venture, and the carrying forward of losses for business income tax purposes and the averaging of personal incomes over a period of years in order to cope with the fluctuations that are characteristic of small-business profits.

The sensitivity of the small business to the ups and downs of business generally means that its interests in the tax field are best served by measures that increase the prosperity of business as a whole.

The financial problem of the small business cannot be considered merely in terms of the total amount of credit or capital that can be made available. It is more pointedly a problem of understanding the nature of small-business risk and adapting the financial assistance—in character, timing, and quantity—to a considered program of development or rehabilitation in which the creditor and borrower are mutually aware of the factors involved.

Financial aid to small business cannot be considered apart from the problems of raising the level of small-business management and creating a climate of competitive opportunity for small enterprise. The position of small enterprise as competitor forms the subject matter to which the next chapter is devoted.

### NOTE ON BRITAIN'S CAPITAL BANK FOR SMALLER ENTERPRISES

The *Report of the British Committee on Finance and Industry* (Macmillan Committee), published in 1931, took note of the great difficulty experienced by small and medium-size enterprises in raising capital. It recommended (Sec. 404) that a private investment company be formed, devoted primarily to the capital requirements of the smaller industrial and commercial companies.

The Industrial and Commercial Finance Corporation, Ltd., established in July, 1945, followed the general lines of the recommendations in the *Macmillan Report.* It is a private enterprise, financed by a group of banks, including the Bank of England, British clearing banks, and the Scottish banks. It obtains no government assistance or subsidy. Its organization is independent, controlled only by its own board of directors. It is conducted on a strictly commercial basis. Its resources include £15 million of share capital; additional capital of £30 million is available under its borrowing powers (through debenture issues). Its stated purpose is to finance small and medium-size industrial and commercial businesses, particularly where they do not have access to the Stock Exchange and investment bankers. New as well as established enterprises may be served. The range of its financing is given as "any amount between £5,000 and £200,000, to any industrial or commercial concern operating in Great Britain which puts forward a sound proposal."

The following review of the activities of the corporation during its first year and a half is based on the first *Annual Report* and on statements by its general manager, J. H. Lawrie.[1]

*Character of Applications.* Applications received by the corporation fall broadly into two categories: those in which funds are required to cover the cost of reequipment or reconversion and those intended to finance a permanent expansion.

To meet the needs of the first group, the financing most often takes the form of a long-term loan, either secured or unsecured, to be repaid out of profits. Where the accommodation is not backed by equivalent security, the corporation may receive redeemable preference shares or a combination of preferred stock and a mortgage on fixed assets.

The second group covers a variety of situations, including new companies as well as those entering upon a major expansion. In some of these cases the corporation's financing is designed for an interim period until the company is in a position to resort to a public offering of its shares, the proceeds of which are to redeem the obligation to the ICFC.

Where small private companies or family businesses are involved, with a desire to retain control, the financing is often sought against limited-term debentures to be paid off out of profits. However, "the Corporation usually attempts to show such people that this point [of avoiding the sharing of ownership with outsiders] is less important than having a balanced capital structure, and that it is very unwise for a small business,

[1] J. H. Lawrie, "Financing the Small Business: The ICFC at Work," *The Banker* (London), August, 1946. Also First Annual Report and Statement of Accounts of the Industrial and Financial Corporation, Ltd., London, December, 1946.

especially in its early stages, to be highly geared and weighed down with prior charges."

The clientele consists of those whose capital requirements fall between £5,000 and £200,000.

*Sources of Applications.* Referrals of an applicant may be from the member banks, from professional firms, or from direct application by prospective borrowers. No fee is paid for introducing business to the corporation.

*Management Counsel.* The corporation maintains a liaison department for the express purpose of keeping in close touch with its customer's operations. Representatives of the liaison department pay regular visits to their customers, offer financial and managerial guidance for the protection of the corporation, the customer, and the commercial bank where it is also involved. The corporation regards the work of the liaison department in helping clients to adjust themselves to postwar competitive conditions as one of the most valuable services that the corporation can render to the industry.

Arranging the financial terms so as to improve the prospects of the business, the corporation "encourages a policy of ploughing back a proportion of the profits remaining after meeting directors' remuneration, redemption sinking fund payments and reasonable dividends. *This policy is encouraged even where the Corporation holds participating dividend rights.*" Periodic information is required of a borrowing or issuing firm so that adjustments in the financial program may be made to conform to the general policy of conserving the strength of the firm.

*Financing Terms.* Cost of financing includes the following features: There is no fixed interest rate. In general, secured loans are at 4 to 4½ per cent. Unsecured notes and preferred shares are at slightly higher rates.

To avoid excessive interest rates the corporation may take additional shares in payment for managerial oversight to protect the transaction.

An additional fee may be charged, ranging from ½ to 1 per cent of the total financing, to cover the costs of preparing the financial program.

*Relations with the Banks.* The ICFC maintains close relationship with the banks, which are the corporation's shareholders. A dilemma to which the corporation must address itself when the firm requires long-term capital and does not have the financial position to command an unsecured loan is this:

If the corporation lends the funds to build a new factory or buy new machinery, the borrower will simultaneously need additional working capital in order to finance the increased scale of operations. For working capital the firm should naturally look to its commercial bank; yet the banker is not likely to make working-capital loans if the ICFC has tied up the assets of the firm to support the long-term financing. In meeting that situation the ICFC may limit its security to a fraction of the firm's assets and finance the balance through participating preference shares or it may use a combination of preferred and common stock.

The annual report states: "In general, the facilities extended by us make the customer a better customer for the [commercial] bank. In a sample of 89 cases of a straightforward kind, customers who had enjoyed previously overdraft limits aggregating £1,900,000 were granted new limits aggregating £2,890,000, based on their now increased resources." In other cases, ICFC financing reduced emergency loans—"overdrafts amounting roughly to £627,000, were brought down to new limits aggregating £495,000." The chairman of the board comments: "I do not stress these figures which are based upon an experience not yet very wide. They serve, however, to illustrate the complementary character of our facilities and those of the banks and the advantage of this to eligible customers."

*Extent of Operations.* During its first year the total facilities made available by the corporation have aggregated approximately £5 million. Inasmuch as the funds are required for plant, machinery, and construction, available funds are taken up only as customers are able to obtain materials and manpower with which to go ahead.

Of the 840 formal applications examined the first year, 133 were granted facilities; the distribution of the advances was as follows:

TABLE 42

| *Amount* | *Number of cases* | *Per cent of total* | *Aggregate amount (000)* | *Per cent of total* |
|---|---|---|---|---|
| £5,000–£10,000...... | 35 | 26.3 | £259.8 | 5.1 |
| 10,001–20,000........ | 32 | 24.1 | 505.2 | 10.0 |
| 20,001–50,000........ | 38 | 28.6 | 1,432.9 | 28.3 |
| 50,001–100,000....... | 19 | 14.3 | 1,449.8 | 28.6 |
| 100,001–200,000...... | 9 | 6.7 | 1,423.3 | 28.0 |
| Totals............ | 133 | 100.0 | £5,071 | 100.0 |

Of the facilities offered, 50 per cent was in the purchase of stock of the borrowing companies.

*Need for the Corporation.* With respect to the evidence of the need for the type of financing that the ICFC is performing, the management has this to say:

". . . some may think that the degree of success which the Corporation achieves will provide the answer to the long-debated question: 'Is there, or is there not, a Macmillan gap?' This view is probably misguided, because of the great changes that have occurred in the relations of finance and industry since the *Macmillan Report* appeared. Whether there was a gap in 1931 can never be proved; what is suggested by the experience of ICFC to date is that there is undoubtedly a 1946 version of the Macmillan gap. . . .

"Applications to the ICFC have been flowing in, not only in a steady stream but at an increasing rate, throughout this year [1946]. Even when allowance is made for the fact that many of them are due to reconversion, it still seems certain that there is likely to be a lasting demand for the facilities provided by the Corporation."

# VIII. COMPETITION—MEANS AND ENDS

IN THE COMPLEX market structure in which small business finds itself today, the enterpriser is often at a loss to lay out his course or see where he is tending. There is no question that at times he suffers from artificial constraints upon his competitive opportunity; at other times he is a conspirator in concerted efforts to limit competition. Extended hearings before the FTC and Congressional committees, together with the battle of counter-interests in connection with what is termed fair-trade legislation, have made public the dissatisfactions of small businessmen with their position in the market. But they do not provide a clear-cut answer to the question, "What does small business want?" Certainly there is no program that small business as a whole supports.

The effort in this chapter will be to point up the basic problem areas requiring consideration as matters of national policy, recognizing that a bird's-eye view will necessarily fail to show up certain aspects of the competitive market that may be of particular importance to some businesses.

## CONFLICTING TRENDS AND OBJECTIVES

In the 1880's and 1890's, public review of trade practices revealed what appeared to be deliberate and ruthless malpractice on the part of expanding business combinations aimed at eliminating smaller rivals. Big business gave consumers the doubtful benefits of cutthroat price wars, which paved the way for the buying up or bankruptcy of small competitors and subsequent control of markets by a monopoly. The Sherman Antitrust Act in 1890 was conceived as legislation to widen competition and to prevent destruction of the free market. Today's markets reflect some modification of that emphasis.

Of the swashbuckling type of cutthroat competition that precipitated the Sherman Antitrust Act, relatively few examples are now in evidence. In their cruder forms they have been largely rendered obsolete by Federal and state legislation and by the corrective activities of agencies like the FTC and the Antitrust Division of the Department of Justice.

The difficulties that confront small enterprises today have developed, in the main, out of basic changes in the industrial process. With the changes have come, moreover, new alliances of interest as between large and small concerns and somewhat different conceptions of what is competition and what is fair and unfair.

For most durable goods, for which maintenance service must be provided, the manufacturer-dealer agency relationship is now taken for granted. It is recognized, for example, that under traditional merchandising methods, through independent wholesalers and unaffiliated retailers, the widespread ownership of automobiles would not have come about so rapidly as it has with the direct participation of the manufacturer in the channeling of product and service to the consumer.

But mass production has brought changes in distribution of nondurable goods as well. And in this area especially, many cases can be cited wherein what is meat for some may be poison for others.

To take a well-known instance: A national manufacturer of soaps sees a discrepancy between the daily year-round use of his product by consumers and the periodic peaks and valleys in soap orders received from the wholesalers. The manufacturer thereupon moves into direct contact with the retailer and reforms distributor purchasing habits to obtain a flow of orders that will permit stabilizing production at the factory. As a result, wholesalers are eliminated from the distribution of a staple item.

Likewise, a central purchasing department seems a forward step toward efficiency from the standpoint of the large company that adopts it on behalf of all its branches. But the change is anathema to the local suppliers, who are crowded out by the policy of pooling orders through a central purchasing agency. A uniform brand price may be welcomed by the small dealer who fears competitive pricing on standard items, but it is a barrier to the retailer who wants to pursue an independent and aggressive merchandising policy. A geographic basing-point system may simplify the pricing problem for the manufacturer who sets the formula and may win approval from customers near the basing point but it may prove a hardship for customers unfavorably situated with reference to the basing point. Chain stores have provided a rich market for makers of store fixtures, and the gains go to small manufacturers of store fixtures as well as large, but that is no consolation to the independent storekeeper who finds it difficult to match chain competition in food, drugs, or accessories.

Does small business want resale-price maintenance? Is it seeking reform of the patent system? Do small manufacturers favor descriptive labeling? Does small business want restrictions against out-of-state commodities? In the ranks of small business one finds strongly held views on these questions, but the views are on both sides of the fence. And always there remains a group of small businessmen who merely drift with the tide.

The conflict within the small-business ranks was aptly lampooned in a verbal exchange reported from a convention of the National Small Businessmen's Association in Pittsburgh. The delegates had protested the taxi charge of 75 cents from downtown to the meeting hall. An official of the taxi company reminded a convention officer that five persons could ride in one cab, cutting the tariff to 15 cents each. "But Mr. Chairman," challenged a delegate from the floor, "it is not safe for five little businessmen to ride that close together. There's liable to be a fight."[1]

That small business is not a homogeneous group for which a common program of trade practices can readily be formulated is suggested by the lack of numerical strength of the so-called "small business" associations.[2] Small enterprisers tie to their own line of business rather than to other small business as such. With most small enterprises at the retail level, the interest in group activities appears to be largely localized. The demands of small-business groups concerning trade practices have been more directly reflected in state and local than in national legislation.

[1] Quoted from *Business Week*, Sept. 24, 1938, p. 18.

[2] The Trade Association Division of the Department of Commerce is unable to learn the numerical strength of the small-business associations, in number, listed in its *Directory of Trade Associations*, 1942. Among the staff of that division it was doubted, however, if the largest of the organizations labeled small business has as many as 5,000 members.

Such legislation reveals a significant shift in what small business considers fair competition. The small businessman is sincere when he speaks of his faith in a competitive system. His protests are against what he regards as unfair competition. The result, however, tends to be a concentrating on legislation that produces uniformities in the market, with the ultimate effect of narrowing rather than freeing competition.

With the foregoing in mind, what criteria have we for passing judgment on the good or evil of current trade practices in their effect on small business as a whole? Let us go back to the thesis that small business should be fostered to assure business competition and to preserve the economic freedoms provided by a system of private enterprise. Do current trade practices help small business maintain its competitive virility? We are concerned, furthermore, with the value of small business as a deterrent to the centralization of control over business activity, whether by private or public agencies. And, finally, current trade practices must meet the test of our common consumer interest: Do they work toward providing more and better goods—and freer choices—at progressively lower cost to the consumer?[1]

## CONTROL OF MARKET CHANNELS

Despite the cross currents and diffusion of objectives, it is fairly clear that hand in hand with the development of mass production has been the tendency to administer and standardize market practices.

### *Mass Producer in Distribution*

Over the past 40 years a growing area of small business has come to be occupied by satellites of the mass producers. Small manufacturers tend to make their livelihood supplying materials or parts entering into the output of automobiles, tractors, refrigerators, washing machines, electric-light bulbs, and other mass-produced items. Many small dealers are, in fact, agencies for the maintenance as well as the distribution of the products of the assembly-line system.

[1] See E. G. Nourse, *Price Making in a Democracy*, Brookings Institution, Washington, D.C., 1944, pp. 237–238.

Outside this satellite area the lessons learned of the advantages that go with large volume—standardized procedures, large-scale purchasing, cost analysis, and scientific management generally—have carried into the field of distribution. The consumer has welcomed the conveniences and price gains that have accompanied the growth of mail-order houses, large department stores, retail chains, and supermarkets. The example set by the merchandising methods of the large distributor companies has stimulated a process of imitation. In its course many small businesses have been modernized and have gained in strength. Many have dropped out through inability to keep up with the procession. Others have managed to continue only by accepting a standard pattern with radical limitations on their scope and their degree of independence.

In what ways specifically have the market relationships of small dealers and small manufacturers been modified by big-business leadership in manufactures and retailing?

### *Changed Position of Wholesaler*

Before the arrival of mass production and distribution, distribution methods were usually patterned by the wholesaler. The nineteenth-century wholesaler was a key factor in the economy. His working capital maintained well-stocked warehouses and provided credit for the retailer. The wholesaler frequently was the source of funds for the small manufacturer and relieved the manufacturer of the problem of doling out his product among the scattered retailers. The wholesaler's influence was felt in the determination of the manufacturer's selling price and profit margin as well as the retailer's cost.

With the development of big business in manufactures, the key position of the wholesaler was challenged. Where the wholesaler resisted the invasion of mass-produced items and tried to protect his traditional lines, he was progressively by-passed. The large retailer found it desirable to purchase in wholesale quantities directly from the manufacturer; the opportunity to do so was a major incentive to large-scale retailing.

At the same time the large manufacturer took the initiative in creating and directing consumer interest in his product. With national advertising, the product gained mass acceptance and the particular brand was impressed upon the consumer. When the consumer demanded the brand thus made familiar to the public, the retailer was impelled to obtain it, with or without the wholesaler. The pressure compelled the wholesaler to stock nationally branded items even if those items were also being sold directly by the manufacturer to retail outlets. Market leadership was slipping away from the wholesaler.

In some areas big business extended its distributive control even to the by-passing of the independent retailer. Tires, gasoline, cameras, and popular lines of men's apparel are now familiar items on which manufacturers not only direct the market channels and maintain standard prices for the retailer but also deal directly with the consumer through their own outlets. Such manufacturer retailing may be for demonstration purposes and continue side by side with the regular retailer, or it may be direct competition for the retailer, or—as in low-priced men's clothing—it may exclude the independent retailer from the manufacturer's line. The independent retailer has felt the pressure on his accustomed selling margins.

As a measure of defense the larger wholesalers have countered by establishing their own brand labels and cultivating a circle of independent retail customers. They have also encouraged or sponsored the organization of independent retailers into voluntary chains, with exclusive access to independent wholesaler brands. The small wholesaler who cannot establish his own brands takes the leavings. Either he fits into the conditions set by the large manufacturer, or he may have to seek crumbs in the way of odd lots in an informal and often precarious jobbing business.

### *Realignments of Manufacturers and Distributors*

In this situation one might expect the small wholesaler and the small manufacturer to get together, bringing the small manufacturer's lines to the shelves of the small retailer, particularly on commodities that are not mass assembly-line items. Why have the little fellows not joined forces? Immediate interests of both small and large distributors have played a part in preventing this alliance.

The small retailer, crowded by low-price policies of big retailers and cut-rate competitors, has tended to seek refuge in the well-publicized national brand, with its uniform pricing protected under so-called "fair-trade" legislation. The independent retailer thus lets the national manufacturer-distributor fight for him the battle against private brands that the chain stores and large department stores are in a position to promote.[1]

A uniform price for the nationally promoted branded article protects the small retailer against undercutting of price for this particular item, but it leaves him open to a new menace. Many manufacturers build volume not only by producing their own nationally advertised brand but by providing also the privately branded item featured by the large retailer. The prestige of the department store, chain, or mail-order house enables them to sell this private brand in successful competition with the "fair-traded" brand. If a large manufacturer of a nationally advertised brand will not produce a like item for a private brand, the big retailer can often turn to a small manufacturer for the product and may even set his own specifications and terms.

What has happened to the relationship between the small manufacturer and the small retailer? The independent retailer, limited in the stock he can carry, naturally gives precedence to standard brands on which the consumer has already been sold by national manufacturer advertising and for which the consumer ordinarily asks by brand name. For the small manufacturer and wholesaler to edge in with an item that must be merchandised by the retailer in competition with already accepted national brands is often next to impossible. The retail druggist, for example, does not see why he should try to sell an unknown brand of tooth paste, putting in effort to win the consumer to its acceptance, when he can sell the established brand on the easier basis of supplying what the

[1] The National Association of Retail Druggists, in its promotion bulletin "What about Fair Trade," (p. 5) puts the matter very frankly in question and answer form, as follows:

"Q. Has Fair Trade eliminated competition as a factor in selling?

"A. No, it has spread the benefits of competition. Before Fair Trade, price competition was between retailers, and only those consumers who had access to cut-price stores benefited. Under Fair Trade, the price competition is between manufacturers and *all* consumers get the benefits of price reductions."

consumer asks for. For the small manufacturer the cost of an effective advertising campaign may be prohibitive.

This inability to deal effectively with the small retailer plays the small manufacturer into the hands of the large retailer, whether chain or department store. In a seller's market, such as has prevailed during and since the war, the small manufacturer could have something to say about the terms under which he supplied his main big customer. The more common situation is one in which the large buyer can dictate terms in line with its own pricing policy. Where the whole output of the small manufacturer is contracted for, his position is that much more vulnerable.

The small retailer, having experienced the price-cutting tactics of the large distributor of the familiar national brands, has aligned himself under fair-trade legislation with the large manufacturer of the national brand—indeed, small retailers have frequently put the pressure on the manufacturer to "fair-trade" his product. To the large retailer is left the aggressive merchandising of the output of small manufacturers.

### *Sublimation of Price Competition*

Thus, the small retailer and the small manufacturer find themselves taking rather than making prices; they are on opposite sides of a struggle for markets, although logically they might be expected to work together, protecting a mutual interest as independent small businessmen. A more virile small business could be conceived if the little retailer, instead of primarily clerking orders on brands presold by national advertising, were more generally merchandising products of his own selection, showing the consumer that the small dealer can discriminate and give special value at a price. In the same vein the small manufacturer might better safeguard his independence and continuity by spreading his product among a number of customers rather than contracting the bulk of his output to one large distributor who calls the turn.

It may reasonably be argued that the situation as just described is an oversimplification of a mixed and complicated market pattern. The average small businessman may not recognize himself anywhere in the picture just presented. Except for dealers who hold specialized agencies, the small merchant usually stocks the less familiar brands along with those nationally branded items which he regards as "musts" in his stock. Likewise, only a part of small-scale manufactures is contracted to large distributors to the extreme of 100 per cent of the manufacturer's output. It is also proper to point out that price is not the only factor in competition. Even under fixed prices, one dealer may win customers from his rivals by exercising ingenuity in the display of his stock, in the character of his advertising, by promptness in filling orders, and in the many extra services whereby customer allegiance is gained. The dealer agencies operating under the same general rules of the manufacturer may, nevertheless, be competing aggressively with each other.

Conditions have not quite reached the point where the dominance of the largest distributors on the buyer side has completely deprived the small enterprise of initiative as a competitor. If that stage had already been reached, it would be too late to discuss the matter with any reasonable hope of stemming the tide. The trend in the direction of cribbing and confining small enterprise—even though often with the consent and help of shortsighted small business—should be reversed before such a stage is reached. To the extent that independent manufacturers and dealers restrict their elbowroom for alert imaginative merchandising, for aggressive promotion of promising lines, and for pricing to meet their own special requirements for growth, small business is in the process of forfeiting one of its main reasons for continuance.

We do not begrudge the prestige earned for a product or brand by the national advertiser. Nor do we begrudge the retail chain the benefit of its alertness in substituting for the national brand its duplicate at a lower price under its own private brand. There is no intent to minimize the part that prosperous big business plays in creating markets that small business shares. What we are concerned with is the need to keep small business free enough and flexible enough to steer an independent course. If the small manufacturer can make a product that could compete on the basis of price and quality, a dynamic economy would require that he not be restricted to a single outlet where the product loses its identity as far as its ownership is concerned.

When the lethargy of consumers or the timidity of small businessmen has reached a point where the introduction of new products becomes possible only at great odds, restoration of the balance is in order. Specific suggestions for strengthening the market position of the small enterprise are discussed later in this chapter, after we have examined related aspects of the problem faced by the small enterpriser in maintaining his competitive position.

## COMPETING WITH BUSINESS INTEGRATION

Laying down legislative regulations and penalties for practices that can be recognized as fraudulent or as clearly coercive both in purpose and in practice is a comparatively easy matter. But more subtle situations prevail; they may, in fact, have a much more decisive effect on the destiny of small business than the direct predatory action designed to injure competitors. In the experience of the courts with antitrust suits and in the investigations of the FTC, the moot questions that have often divided the bench and resulted in split decisions tend to hinge on this issue:

At what point do the competitive pressures exerted by the large organization add up to such interference with the competitive opportunity of other members of the industry as to constitute a restraint of trade inimical to the public welfare?

The implications for small business will be brought into sharper relief by seeing how they apply (1) in the competition between the big chains and the independent dealer, (2) in the control of patents, and (3) in the more general imposition of restrictive terms under which small customers and suppliers are permitted to operate.

*The Integrated Chain versus Small Business.* As has often been noted, the bulk of small enterprise is engaged in the distribution of goods and services—more than two million concerns operating at retail, about 150,000 at wholesale. The majority of the small distributors are engaged in the sale of foods, drugs, and apparel. Topping their list of complaints is the unfair competition to which they feel that they are exposed by the chain-store systems.[1]

To the extent that the problem created by the chains has been one of relative inefficiency being hard pressed by greater efficiency,

[1] See Biagio Di Venuti, "Small Business Problems—An Analysis of 3,390 Problem Discussions Presented to the Senate Committee to Study Problems of American Small Business," 77th Congress, 1st Session, March, 1941.

it has been essentially a challenge for small business to learn and apply the newer techniques—in merchandising, in buying, in selecting and supplying stock, in more aggressively advertising its wares to its particular public.

The economist can have little sympathy with the punitive tactics—especially conspicuous in state and local taxation—by which it was hoped to discourage the increase in the number of chain-store units. Warfare on that plane has done little to resolve the underlying economic issues. Indeed, the measures taken often boomeranged. In some states the voluntary chains of independent dealers found themselves placed under the same bans they had helped to legislate for others. Progressively increasing taxation in relation to the number of chain-store units did reduce the total number of chain stores, but with an increase in the number of supermarkets and in total sales by the chains. Many an independent dealer later wished that the chain store were back at his corner instead of diverting consumer traffic to the location where the new chain supermarket set up its more varied stock—plus ample parking space—under pressure of antichain legislation. The public's appraisal is that the chain justifies its existence when its larger buying power is employed to reduce distribution costs and pass the savings on to the consumer, when it adds convenience and attractiveness to the merchandise layout, when it keeps its turnover high and its stocks fresh. The independent can match these advantages effectively only with constructive countermeasures that will pay off in consumer acceptance—whether in additional accommodations, by stocking of special items, or through joining with other independents to offer the savings of mass buying, warehousing, and advertising. On this level competition may be tough but is not judged to be unfair.

But when the growth of the large chain takes a turn where it freezes out small business, not on the basis of greater efficiency but by abuse of far-flung power, we have a different problem in national policy. Here we come to the general ground on which any big business may run afoul of the Sherman Act, the Clayton Act, the FTC, etc.—the stifling of competitive opportunity.

Tomes have been written on the definition of restraint of trade and the ways in which the courts have reinterpreted the concept.

Instead of reviewing the historical development it will better serve our purpose to present the problem as it stands today by means of an illustrative case in the field of retailing, where the majority of small firms are to be found. Probably no single case in antitrust litigation points up the threats to small business that develop almost imperceptibly with the expanding operations of integrated business organizations as does the celebrated recent case involving the Atlantic and Pacific Tea Company. Here, in litigation that engaged the attention of government and business over a period of more than two years, virtually every aspect of the problems of unequal competition between the integrated chain[1] and the independent dealers operating at a single level has been brought into the open.

A remarkable feature of the opinion in the A & P case is that although the decision was unfavorable to the company, the Court took occasion to pay tribute to the accomplishments of the A & P chain in reducing costs to the consumer. There was no charge that the company was making excessive over-all profits. On the contrary, as the Court pointed out,

> To buy, sell, and distribute to a substantial portion of 130 million people, $1.75 billions worth of food annually at a profit of 1½ cents on each dollar is an achievement one may well be proud of.

The Court went on to say:

> Integration, whether longitudinal or vertical or both, is not, of itself, a violation of the law; but as I conceive the applicable legal formula, if the nature and actions of that integration are of such character as to reflect the inherent vice of unreasonable restraint of commerce or the inevitable evil of an attempted monopoly, then a violation of the law occurs. In other words, if, in spite of a declaration of innocence of purpose, conscious acts of a group are such as inevitably to work undue restraint of trade or a monopoly, in whole or in part, the actors thereby bring about transgression of the congressional rule of conduct.[2]

It would be hard to indicate at just what point the growth of

[1] The A & P operates at all the levels of the manufacturer: importer, processor, broker, wholesaler, and retailer; the independent dealers operate at only one level.

[2] *United States v. N.Y. Great Atlantic & Pacific Tea Co., Inc., et al.*, 67 Fed. Sup. 626 (D.C., E.D., Ill., 1946). Decision by Judge Lindley, Sept. 28, 1946.

the company and the integration of its departments had carried it beyond the limits of legal competition and made it a violator of the Sherman Antitrust Act. By the time the Department of Justice had got round to the prosecution of the A & P, the organization consisted of at least 12 corporations whose integrated operations embraced every stage, from shipping of the raw produce through canning, packing, processing, manufacturing, brokering, wholesaling, and retailing. The subsidiaries representing the different stages of production not only served A & P units but served outside competitors as well.[1]

The chain—which was doing 25 per cent of all the food retailing in some states—could operate the strictly retail business at a profit of less than 2 per cent and offset that with advertising allowances and other concessions granted especially to various subdivisions of the combine, amounting to a preferential advantage of 5 per cent or more on the total operation. In entering a new geographic area the company could plan for "introductory pricing," with programmed losses, for a period long enough to divert the business from established independent grocers. The losses of the introductory campaign were made up in part by the profits obtained in

[1] One component of the A & P, the Quaker Maid Company, Inc., described the following variety of operations in its food manufacturing plants at Rockport, L. I., Brooklyn, N.Y., and Terre Haute, Ind.:

"In these plants several hundred items of food and food products are manufactured, canned, packed, and processed, including baking powder, beans, peas, barley, bird foods, bird gravel, candy, cereal, cocoa, cod liver oil, condensed milk, currants, cream of tarter, flavoring extracts, fish, furniture polish, gelatin, gelatin desserts, puddings, ice-cream desserts, honey, jam, jelly, liquid ammonia, bluing, window cleaner, ketchup, chile sauce, macaroni, spaghetti, marmalade, mayonnaise, mustard, olives, peanut butter, pork sausage, seasonings, preserves, relish, rice, salad dressing, salad oil, sandwich spreads, salmon, spices, syrup, tapioca, tea, vinegar, and bulk bakery products, including fondant, lemon oil, cocoa butter, ground ginger, bulk preserves and jellies, and flavoring extracts. Such products are put up in packages, cans, and containers, and cases. Where same are put up for resale in A & P stores, they are put up and advertised under the A & P, Ann Page, Sultana, Iona, Sunnyfield, Flight, Worthmore, Crestmont, Round Trip, Carnival, Mellow Wheat, White House, Rajah, Victoria, Encore, Cold Stream, Nectar, Our Own, Mayfair, Matinee, and other private brands and labels owned and controlled by the A & P group. The products of the manufacturing plants operated by the defendant Quaker Maid Company, Inc., are distributed through the wholesale warehouses and retail stores of The Great Atlantic & Pacific Tea Companies of New Jersey, Arizona, and Nevada and are sold to others." [*United States v. New York Great Atlantic & Pacific Tea Co., Inc. et al.*, 67 Fed. Sup. 626 (D.C., E.D., Ill., 1946). Information filed by the U.S. Attorney, Feb. 26, 1944.]

supplying A & P processed goods to the competing retailers. In other cases A & P commanded discounts from suppliers that the latter could not give to other customers.

In the record of the multiplicity of operations carried on by the A & P, it was evident that competitors were being placed under handicap through a combination of activities by the A & P subsidiaries that emerged as unlawful only when seen in combination. This was exemplified by the transactions of the Atlantic Commission Company (ACCO), whose profits, obtained from sales and brokerage fees to independent wholesalers and retailers—while such charges were saved by A & P subsidiaries—served to strengthen the competitive position of the A & P retail outlets against the very independents who were ACCO customers.

Said the Court:

It is clear from this record that retail distributors of food products in the United States are engaged in a close contest. Profit margins are slight. The differences between profitable operation and loss is fractional in character, between success and failure astonishingly small. There is constant incessant struggle for advantages. In such a situation, where margins between profit and loss are so small, any dealer engaged in the contest, having secured an unfair advantage over his competitors however small it may be, will be likely to upset or reverse a small percentage of profit in his competitor and convert it into a loss. When the net profit is in the neighborhood of 2 per cent, an advantage of 5 per cent in buying by one dealer immediately places him in an overpowering position as far as his competitors are concerned. So if any element of A & P's profits in competition with others arises from an illegal factor or an illegal function, even though the percentage resulting from the use of that factor or that function is small, it may be sufficient to change a competitor's profit into losses. Such a result, of course, is interference with open competition, under restraint of trade.

Again,

It is probably true that many actions of defendants of which the government complains, standing alone, are devoid of wrongful character; but when the fabric woven from this is considered as a whole and it appears contaminated by a corrupt thread running throughout the completed texture, the whole becomes a tainted product and all partaking in its creation, having voluntarily contributed to the structure, are charged with responsibility for the fabrication. The conduct of ACCO is the rotten thread of the fabric, and it so permeates the entire texture and ties together the other threads as to result in an imperfect, an illegal product —unreasonable interference with competition and power to monopolize. With the flaw of ACCO's tainted record permeating all the operations of A & P's integrated system, the activities of A & P other than those directly involving ACCO take on a polluted colored light. Manipulation of gross profit rates, at times sufficiently to do away entirely with retail profit, in competition, procurement, and enjoyment of buying preferences heretofore discussed, whether in the form of discriminatory discounts, advertising allowances or otherwise, supplementing retail earnings or overcoming deficits with earnings of manufacturing subsidiaries, the coffee department and ACCO, and other actions heretofore mentioned, even though some one or all of them standing alone might not amount to a violation of the law, when coupled and inextricably interwoven with the activities of ACCO, reflect inevitably the misuse of defendants' power in competition with others to such an extent as to create undue interference with commerce —undue restraint of trade—of such character as to result in monopoly.[1]

The issue of unfair competition, as it emerges from the A & P case, is not merely one of chain-store vs. independent-store retailing. It is the problem of integrated big business and its ability to play one sector of the economy against the other.

One test of desirable competition is whether or not it reduces the cost to the ultimate consumer. The apparent result of the operations of a chain with vertical and horizontal integration is to give its own customers lower prices than are obtainable in competing independent stores. But also to be reckoned with is the total community cost. If the low consumer prices at the chain store entail an absorption of losses by the parent company, for the benefit of its own retail outlets, and these losses are offset by profits at other levels that are taken from competing independent dealers, then the low prices at the chain store may be contributed in part by the higher prices that must be charged to consumers at the independent stores. Among those consumers who unwittingly pay that differential may be rural customers, consumers in neighborhoods not served by chains, or others whose interests will thus conflict with those of the consumers, stockholders, and officers of the integrated combine.

[1] From the A & P decision, cited above.

To be sure, no court can accurately measure the costs incurred by the community in the liquidation of independent grocers who cannot pay the charges of A & P as wholesaler and broker and at the same time meet the price competition of the chain as retailer, or the resultant losses to creditors, landlords, and the families of the independents put out of business by the double squeeze of the competition. But that there is restraint of competitive opportunity inimical to the common welfare the District Court regarded as established.[1]

It seems almost inevitable that the chain, supermarket, mail-order house, or other large retail organization should reach out to acquire better control over the sources of supply for its retail outlets. As it moves into interlocking fields of production and distribution, the chain is bound at certain points to become the vendor to independent retailers who help to absorb the full capacity of the operation. At that point the small business may be squeezed out by receiving as an outsider less favorable terms than are afforded to the chain's own outlets.

When the combine is the supplier as well as the competitor, the small competitor can easily be deprived of the opportunity to compete freely on the merit of his product and service. Such discrimination may also occur apart from the vertical integration, in the power of the chains through volume buying to command better terms than the individual merchant can obtain. It is the function of the FTC to separate the situations where such advantages are the natural and legitimate economy of larger volume orders from those in which coercive economic power has been applied in the restraint of competition.

One may gather from the long line of antitrust decisions culminating in the A & P opinion that expanding big business is continuously on probation to show that it can exist side by side with independent small business in a system of competitive enterprise. Such safeguarding against competitive encroachment must not, however, become capricious, or the confidence in business generally, large and small, will be undermined.

Greater consistency is needed in basic legislation affecting fair

[1] The A & P decision has been taken up to the Circuit Court of Appeals, where it is due to be reviewed late in 1948.

competition: in Federal vs. state legislation, the Sherman Act, the original Clayton Act, and the FTC Act, as against the Miller-Tydings and the Robinson-Patman amendments sanctioning price control. Criminal suits, under the Sherman Act, do not stipulate the measures to overcome the illegal acts. As a follow-up to the basic legislation, we need clarifying rules along with periodic revaluation of competitive practices in specific industrial situations. That is the area in which the FTC can perform a vital function as an arbiter on business competition.

## PRICE MANIPULATION AND REGULATION

Pricing remains a central problem of competition for small business. The small producer and the small retailer are under continuous pressure in contending with the economies of large-scale buying and large-scale production. We like to believe that as against these, the small businessman has offsetting advantages in simplicity of operation, flexibility, and freedom from fixed organizational requirements of larger businesses and to some extent an escape from governmental restrictions that apply to the large business. By the alert use of these advantages the small dealer is presumably able to meet the price of his larger competitor or to provide the additional services or satisfactions that gain him customers.

Nevertheless, a large segment of the small-business fraternity gives the impression of being more concerned with holding competition in leash than it is with giving full play to a flexible competitive market.

The small dealer in a small community or a neighborhood off the main line once enjoyed comparative monopoly of the neighborhood business. There was no challenge to his figuring a normal—or perhaps somewhat better than normal—margin on the business that naturally came his way. The invasion of his domain by the chain enterprise represented a rude awakening. The problems of the neighborhood dealer have been further complicated by improved transportation and by wide advertising. These made it easier for the consumer to "shop," comparing products and prices.

Because of the Sherman Antitrust Act, direct collective action aimed at price fixing has not been feasible on a nation-wide basis. On the other hand, Federal legislation dealing with interstate commerce would not ordinarily reach the limited intrastate operations of the small business. Hence, most of the protective legislation aimed at standardizing prices has been state legislation. It has become customary, under the general head of fair-trade laws, to prevent undercutting of normal margins required by the average establishment in a given line. Resale price maintenance is the form most generally taken by the legislation.

*Resale Price Maintenance*

Forty-five states now have resale price-maintenance legislation. In general, the legislation permits the manufacturer of a branded item to declare the retail price at which the commodity may be sold. When a commodity has been so contracted for, selling the item below the price fixed by the manufacturer becomes illegal, except for special exemptions relating to general clearance sales, dealer-aid programs authorized by the manufacturer, and other specific situations. The prohibition applies even to a dealer who has not made any contract with the manufacturer or his designated distributor.

The problem raised by so-called fair-trade pricing—usually associated with national brands—is best understood against the historical background of the practices that motivated the laws. To establish a reputation for low prices, the most effective means, from the standpoint of the aggressive merchandiser, was to select a well-known brand and offer it below its generally accepted price. The better known the item and the more standardized its price the more effective was its use as a "loss leader" item. Four or five standard and familiar items advertised at cost or below could readily give the impression that the dealer's prices in general were less than those charged elsewhere. Independent dealers were unable to sustain the sales at regular markups and prices for standard items on which competitors were cutting rates. The cut rate on the well-known item brought the customer into the store, and the merchant could then sell him additional items on which the consumer had no opportunity for comparison. A standard tooth paste sold below the standard rate might be the basis for selling a hair tonic or patent medicine on which profits might more than offset the loss on the "leader."

The average independent distributor did not feel that he was in a position to engage in the game of manipulating underpriced and overpriced items to come out with a net advantage. The fixing of a legal minimum price by the manufacturer suggested itself as the answer to the small retailer's problem.

The manufacturer has the option of having his item "fair-traded." Many a manufacturer has preferred to treat his product competitively, make a profit for himself, and leave it to the character of the demand to determine the resale price. Where items are fair-traded, the natural shift of emphasis in the selling policy of the manufacturer is away from efforts to bring down the cost of the item to the consumer to a concentration of effort upon keeping the brand before the eyes and ears of the public. Fair-traded distribution—requiring stabilized margins for both wholesaler and retailer and a volume of advertising adequate to sustain consumer acceptance at the fair-traded price—presents a problem with which the typical small manufacturer cannot cope in the way that his large-scale competitors can.

### *Loopholes in Fair-trade Pricing*

In the realities of the market place, the small retailer, ostensibly protected by the fixed "fair price," has no assurance that his competitive equality is thereby secure. When conditions increase the intensity of competition, both manufacturer and distributor find ready ways of circumventing retail-price maintenance.

The fair-trade price is fixed originally so that it can give the retailer the percentage of markup which he finds necessary and profitable. However, when the national brand is being hard pressed by the lower price of a rival brand, the manufacturer may reduce the fixed brand price. To do this the manufacturer may absorb some loss by billing the item at a lower figure to the retailer and letting the latter retain his markup; a producer in a dominant position may charge the retailer as before but lower the fair-trade price to the consumer, forcing the retailer to take a lower markup. The threat of the private brand or other successful price competitor leaves the retailer under fair trade little choice in a situation of this sort—one that becomes more acute on a downswing of business.

Large manufacturers, while protecting their nationally advertised brand, frequently utilize additional capacity by duplicating the product under a private brand name for sale to the large department store, chain, mail-order house, or any other customer capable of pushing its own brand. The very fact that the manufacturer has his standard brand protected by standard prices gives him the backlog that permits low-margin concessions to win the additional production that goes to private brands. The situation is not unlike the old practice under which producers whose domestic profits are protected by a high tariff go into export markets with lower prices. There is this difference, however, from export dumping: The private brand comes right into the home neighborhood to compete with the item that came from the same big barrel but under the respectable and famous brand name.

Although the interplay of national and private brands is familiarly associated with foods and drugs, some of the most striking examples have been in other lines. Among the hundreds of such instances that have been given the attention of the FTC, the marketing of Sears Roebuck "All-State" tires, which is a matter of public record, will serve as an illustration of the problem. The Goodyear Tire and Rubber Company has produced its standard tire under the national brand name of "All-Weather." It also produced the tire for Sears Roebuck, which carried it under the All-State brand. If we can take the published cost-accounting data reflected in the accompanying table at anything near their face value, the distribution expense on the standard national brand was from eight to ten times that on the tire sold to Sears Roebuck. The net billing price on the national brand was more than 50 per cent above the billing to Sears Roebuck; the net operating profit per tire was roughly one-fourth as great on Sears Roebuck sales as on those taking the national brand name. The manufacturer could justify the low-margin sale to the mail-order house as representing so much velvet over and above the basic replacement business represented by the national brand. From the standpoint of the independent retailer and consumer, however, the brand list price, considerably higher than the private brand, was contributing to the lower percentage of sales by independent stores in the total tire market.[1]

TABLE 43

GOODYEAR'S COSTS AND NET PROFITS ON AVERAGE TIRE PRICES, 1927–1933*

| | *All-Weather—Goodyear* | | *All-State—Sears Roebuck* | |
|---|---|---|---|---|
| Tire size, 4.50 × 21: | | | | |
| Net billing price | ..... | $6.66 | ..... | $4.04 |
| Distribution expense | $2.29 | ...... | $0.28 | |
| Factory cost | 3.39 | ...... | 3.51 | |
| Total cost | ..... | 5.68 | ..... | 3.79 |
| Net operating profit | ..... | $ 0.98 | ..... | $0.25 |
| Tire size, 6.00 × 21: | | | | |
| Net billing price | ..... | $14.75 | ..... | $9.11 |
| Distribution expense | $4.91 | ...... | $0.48 | |
| Factory cost | 7.55 | ...... | 8.06 | |
| Total cost | ..... | 12.46 | ..... | 8.54 |
| Net operating profit | ..... | $ 2.29 | ..... | $0.57 |

* *In the Matter of Goodyear Tire & Rubber Co., Findings as to Facts and Conclusions*, Docket No. 2116, cited by Walton Hamilton *et al.*, *Price and Price Policies*, McGraw-Hill Book Company, Inc., New York, 1938, p. 111.

The conflict between the Federal antitrust legislation aimed against trade restrictions and the price-fixing legislation of the states made additional Federal sanctions necessary to remove the legal cloud from the state legislation. The National Recovery Administration, seeking to combat the depressed prices of the early 1930's with its industry codes, was a move in that direction. After the NRA was ruled unconstitutional by the Supreme Court, Congress enacted the Miller-Tydings amendment to the Sherman Act. Thereby, commodities protected by fair-trade legislation in intrastate commerce may likewise legally maintain the fair-trade prices in their interstate commerce to and from the fair-traded states. Since all but three states and the District of Columbia

[1] The widely accepted analysis of the tire industry prepared by Warren W. Leigh of the University of Akron indicates that between 1922 and 1940 the percentage of tire sales through independent dealers was reduced from 98.1 to 46.5. In 1940, according to Leigh's estimates, 41 per cent of all tire sales were accounted for by chain stores, major oil-company outlets, and mail-order houses.

See M. P. McNair, "Fair Trade Legislation and the Retailer," *Journal of Marketing*, April, 1938, pp. 295–300.

have fair-trade legislation, the sanction has practically universal application.

The most successful area for resale price maintenance has been in drugs. The consumer has little knowledge of the ingredients of drug and cosmetic products and hesitates to take chances on a product not backed by the brand of a leading pharmaceutical house (or big name, in the case of cosmetics). The demand for drugs is relatively inflexible, and price may not be so powerful as habit in guiding demand. In the drug field even the chain stores go along with the fair-trading of the leading branded items; at the same time the drug chains feature their own lower priced brands of drug and cosmetic products. The existence of powerful trade associations working closely with the trade press has been an added factor in maintaining the discipline of fair-trade pricing in drugs.[1]

Even with these advantages, there have been important breaks in the line, especially on familiar items where no medicinal mystery or cosmetic formula for glamour is involved. Not only the chain stores but also some of the independent dealers make up their own formulas or have their own imprints on the more familiar items. Little-known brands, referred to as "off brands" in the trade, are commonly pushed by druggists who have the confidence of their customers. Moreover, fair trading has not permitted the druggist generally to confine himself to drugs and make a livelihood at their sale. More and more the druggist has taken on a large variety of miscellaneous items, from sandwiches to toys; these help the drug retailer, like other dealers, to pick up higher margins elsewhere as an offset to rigidities and limitations in that area of his business controlled under fair trade.

### *Sale below Cost*

Akin in spirit to resale price maintenance is the statutory prohibition against sales below cost, currently in the laws of 24 states. This type of legislation makes it possible in theory to bring the nonfair trade area under control. While a few of the laws forbid sales below cost by the manufacturer as well, the main emphasis is on the prevention of the wide use of "loss leaders" by the retailer.

[1] See *Report of the Federal Trade Commission on Resale Price Maintenance*, December, 1945, especially Chap. V, pp. 142–249.

In the wake of the depression experience of the early 1930's most of the industry codes adopted under the NRA declared sales below cost to be unfair competition. Although the NRA was declared unconstitutional, its provisions against sales below cost survived through enactment as state laws.

Where the term "cost" was not spelled out under the NRA codes, state laws, notably those which followed the California pattern, fortified the term by listing all elements that must enter into the computation of cost. As applied to production, they include raw materials, labor, and "all overhead expenses of the producer." For the distributor, costs means "invoice or replacement cost, whichever is lower, of the article or product to the distributor and vendor, plus the cost of doing business by said distributor and vendor." The cost of doing business, or overhead expense, as used in the typical California statute, is defined as "all costs of doing business incurred in the conduct of such business and must include without limitation the following items of expense: labor (including salaries of executives and officers), rent, interest on borrowed capital, depreciation, selling cost, maintenance of equipment, delivery costs, credit losses, all types of licenses, taxes, interest, and advertising."[1] Since strict adherence to such a law would require a level of cost accounting unknown to the very small retailer, some of the statutes provide a minimum markup ranging from 6 to 12 per cent above invoice, which is presumed to cover the cost of doing business.[2]

Most of the statutes carry the proviso that the charge as to an offense must include evidence of intent to injure competitors or suppress competition. In others, failure to maintain the markup is indicative of such intent in the absence of contrary proof.[3]

The legal basis of the sales-below-cost statutes has not been firmly established, and recently the governor of New York voiced his doubt as to the constitutionality of such measures under the police power of the states as the basis for his veto of an unfair sales bill. But whether or not the measures can get by in one state or

[1] *State Price Control Legislation*, Vol. 2, Marketing Laws Survey, Washington, D.C., 1940, p. 28.

[2] *Ibid.*, p. LIII.

[3] *Ibid.*, p. LII.

another, their significance in this discussion is that they reveal a conflict in the minds of many small businessmen between a free market price and a standard, or "fair," price to which all must adhere. Apparently a large segment of small business is becoming conditioned to a climate of administered prices, which small business generally opposed in the early days when monopoly control was the big issue. The main difference—and not an unimportant one—seems to be that whereas big business is usually prepared to do its own policing of such administered prices, small business lacks the strength to make prices stick without the aid of government as policeman.

### *Defenses against Price Discrimination*

The Clayton Antitrust Act attempted in general terms to prevent discrimination in prices among different purchasers where the effect would be the substantial lessening of competition. At the behest of the FTC, which wanted illegal discrimination and monopoly pinned down to more definite terms, the Robinson-Patman Act was passed in 1936. By this amendment to the Clayton Act (Sec. 2), discriminating in the price made to different purchasers of commodities of like grade, quality, and quantity becomes unlawful. Differentials in price between small and large sales may be only enough to make "due allowance for differences in the cost of manufacture, sale, or delivery resulting from differing methods or quantities in which such commodities are to such purchasers sold or delivered."[1] Thus, the Robinson-Patman Act attempts to reinforce the Sherman and Clayton Antitrust Acts by invoking an accounting principle to be applied in testing the fairness of terms to customers. Strictly construed, it would not permit a manufacturer or wholesaler to take additional business that he regards as "velvet" if it meant making a concession that is not proportional to difference in costs. Under the Robinson-Patman Act it has devolved upon the FTC to appraise classifications of customers of a given concern and to determine if the treatment given to each has been in accordance with the respective costs of doing business.

The Robinson-Patman Act was aimed also at numerous forms

[1] Public Law 692, 74th Congress, 2d Session, 1936.

of special allowances granted to purchasers. Among these are advertising allowances which may have grown up in the trade as a competitive inducement. For example, the practice has often been to base advertising allowances on the total volume of business done with an entire chain, whereas only a small part of the allowance actually was used for advertising. The act was also designed to discourage the practice under which large buyers receive, in addition to quantity discounts, the equivalent of brokerage fees.[1] Another practice that the FTC has checked under the Robinson-Patman Act is that of accumulating orders over a period of time and basing the discount on the total for the period rather than on specific transactions. This practice tended to favor both regular and voluntary chains operating through a central account, even where individual transactions with independent stores were larger than with the chain stores.

Thus, the aid of the government is enlisted to arbitrate a large variety of transactions in which discrimination is alleged among competitors. Conflict still exists as between the letter of the later amendments and the spirit of the antitrust laws. The FTC is undoubtedly trying to resolve the cases that come before it to stop abusive practices without preventing the normal elbowing whereby the small enterpriser seeks to hold a place in the competitive market.

## LEGAL BARRIERS TO FREE MARKET

In the search for devices to moderate the competitive struggle, small businessmen have conspired with others to hold for themselves their immediate trade area and to shut out newcomers. Among these are barriers against goods and services entering from outside the state, the imposition of heavy license or tax payments upon those attempting to break into the established circle, and, in addition, a host of special restrictions expressed in ordinances of one kind or another aimed at making more difficult a competitor's start or expansion.

[1] A nice question is here involved as to whether the large buyer, maintaining scouts for supplies, making its own traffic arrangements, and otherwise facilitating transactions for the seller, has thereby earned the equivalent of the fee that would be tendered to a broker where such an intermediary is required. It will be recalled that the differential advantage obtained through brokerage allowances were a factor in the decision against the A & P in the case discussed earlier.

*Interstate Barriers*

Freedom of commerce among the states is guaranteed by the Constitution, but the use of the police power of the state has nevertheless been widely invoked to interfere with that freedom of commerce. Some of the barriers to interstate commerce are inevitable in the diverse state and local regulations, which especially plague the small businessman who is not in a position to keep track of them. Some regulations, however, are frankly intended to penalize the outsider and keep him from competing with business inside the state. The Marketing Laws Survey on interstate trade barriers listed, in 1942, nearly 1,500 statutory provisions of the states designed for or having the effect of hampering trade among the states.[1] These are in addition to innumerable municipal ordinances and rulings of various agencies within the state that are not classified as state statutes.

A number of the barriers imposed against interstate trade have emanated as health measures. It was a short step from quarantines on entry of diseased fruits, vegetables, and livestock from another state to the expansion of inspection regulations with punitive objectives. Some states prevent the dairyman from getting his milk across the line by downgrading out-of-state milk, requiring prohibitive inspection charges, by procedures or excessive trucking fees. The egg man wishing to enter any of seven states finds that as an outsider he may not give top grading to his merchandise. If he is sending eggs into Georgia, Florida, or Arizona, he may not even grade them as fresh eggs.[2] Fertilizer may not be sold in the state until after it has gone through a special inspection process that becomes the basis of a permit to the outsider.

The itinerant merchant is barred from bringing his wares into a market unless he can prove that he is himself the grower and producer of the item. On an item like liquor, in eight states the state power to protect public morals takes the form of ascribing greater virtue to liquor dealers who are residents or to manufacturers who have distilled the product on the state's sacred soil. The power to protect public morals also reaches to the special

[1] *Interstate Trade Barriers*, Marketing Laws Survey Series, Vol. 5, p. 5.

[2] *Ibid.*, p. 25.

labeling of out-of-state products in such a manner that the incentive to bring them into the state is materially reduced.[1]

In traveling with a 5-ton truck from Alabama to South Carolina, the trucker would have to pay $400 in Alabama, $400 in Georgia, and $300 in South Carolina, and the total of $1,100 for his trip would not include an extra charge if a trailer were attached.[2]

Such exercise of the taxing power naturally falls heaviest upon the small enterpriser. The tax may not stop the entry of the large trucking company, but it is prohibitive to the self-employed trucker of whose annual earnings the license fees may be a substantial percentage.

*Other Restrictions on Business Entry*

Denying the outsider the opportunity to enter a business does not always have to come directly under the guise of interstate barrier legislation. In the battle between butter and oleomargarine in dairy states like Wisconsin or Washington, the taxing power was used to prevent the introduction of margarine. In 1937, with a 15 cents per pound tax, total revenues collected on margarine in the states of Wisconsin and Washington were $13.42. By invoking a license tax to sell margarine Wisconsin could reduce the number of dealers in that commodity from 5,007 in 1928 to 3 in 1937.[3]

More or less familiar are the laws in which the members of one trade try to prevent others from carrying the line. Thus, in a Western state the restaurant owners succeeded in preventing drugstores from selling food at their fountains unless the food booths were completely set off by partitions from the rest of the store. More common are the local ordinances limiting types and processes employed in the use of construction materials.

The mutually protected activities of trade associations and local groups to allocate territory, hold prices, and boycott those who do not fall in line parallel such activities on the part of the larger monopolies. The TNEC listed more than 150 groups in which some vestige of NRA "codes of fair competition" have been invoked to keep small the circle of those who may successfully

[1] *Ibid.*, p. 22.

[2] *Ibid.*, p. 13.

[3] See Taylor, Burtis, and Waugh, *Barriers to Internal Trade in Farm Products*, U.S. Department of Agriculture, March, 1939, Tables 1 and 2, pp. 21–22.

operate. The lines of business where there has been organized effort to restrict entry cover the whole gamut of small enterprise, including bakers, building contractors, cleaners and dyers, cobblers, parking-lot concessions, and undertakers.[1]

In the long run the small dealer is most likely to suffer, because he is the most likely to be under the necessity of picking up a new line or discovering a variation of his business that will give him a better chance to develop a successful operation. That small business, after fighting the restrictions of competition by large monopoly, should be trying to operate with the same general philosophy of setting up barriers to business entry and competitive initiative seems a backward step.

## PATENT CONTROLS, PRO AND CON

The small enterpriser seeking to manufacture a new item often must contend with intricacies of the patent law and with the manifold possibilities of manipulation aimed at his exclusion. He is in that respect comparatively helpless against competitors with financial resources for asserting their legal rights. The subject is highly involved, and we shall indicate here only the nature of the problem faced by small businesses on this score. As with other trade practices there is a need to recognize how the major changes in our economy affect the purposes for which the patent laws originally were drawn.

When the Constitution placed upon Congress the duty of promoting the progress of science and the useful arts, the immediate need was to subsidize with bounties and exclusive rights the craftsmen who would help in developing new industry catering to basic wants of a pioneer people. The granting of a patent was not specifically mentioned in the Constitution but was considered along with other special inducements to new enterprise, such as the exclusive right to operate a sawmill in a new community. The exclusive patent right was the necessary encouragement to venture in uncertain surroundings. We were thus encouraging small-business risk in its significant sense.

In the Horatio Alger tradition, the patent symbolizes the birth of a momentous idea. The hero at long last demonstrates and patents the telegraph, the steam engine, the telephone, an incan-

[1] TNEC Monograph No. 21, pp. 280–285.

descent lamp, or a far-reaching innovation in metallurgy. Today, the fact is that one may be confronted with the eight-thousandth patent on the mundane safety razor and blade. There are 150 patents on a single type of wallboard (gypsum) and 25 patents on the slot in the head of a screw. The differentiations may be so slight that one may question the innovation. But that does not eliminate its nuisance value for preemption of a market. Only a fraction of the patents actually are put to use; most of them are held by companies already surfeited with patents wherewith to block the use of similar devices by competing firms.

The development of greatest concern to small business is the use of the patent not as protection for the manufacturer of a product but as a weapon limiting the use to those who will do so under the terms of tribute and within the market pattern set by the holder of the patent right.

The interlocking of industrial techniques in our day means that a certain type of tube or a patented bearing may be needed in any one of a hundred different lines of manufacture. Whoever holds such strategic patents becomes the arbiter for many branches of manufacture, large and small.

The newcomer seeking, with or without a patent, to produce or use an item faces the threat of a patent-infringement suit from any competitor who is prone to employ that means of discouraging the newcomer. It is true that the firm threatened with infringement may be large as well as small. The head of the Ford Motor Company has testified that while his company does not itself withhold patents for its exclusive use, it has been spending $100,000 a year in protecting itself against alleged infringements claimed by others. General Motors paid $600,000 for a license on a self-starter patent —although for 15 years after the patent had been allowed no production use was made by the patentee and although General Motors "felt pretty sure the patents were invalid"—rather than run the risk of holding up production through infringement proceedings.[1] Such pin money is obviously not available to the little

[1] The testimony by James McEvoy, patent Counsel, for General Motors, described the situation as follows:

"Mr. Kettering developed the self-starter in 1911 . . . then the Remy boys started their work. . . . There are two sets: Mr. Kettering's was a single unit, and the Remy

manufacturer. The possible expense of defending his rights in patent litigation is often sufficient to deter the small man from pursuing his rights. If he is able to do so, he accepts the terms for a license from the already entrenched patentee. Success or failure may hinge on the willingness of the patentee to grant the rights to a newcomer. The exchange of exclusive rights to patents and the restrictive system of cross licensing generally have proved to be a determining factor in monopoly control of processes in which patents are involved.

The monopolistic potentialities of the modern patent and the patent system are so truly awesome that one is inclined to be less surprised by the uses made than by the restraint exercised by those in a position to push their legal rights to the limit.

The glass industry serves as an example of the centralizing effect that the patent may exert. When the glass bottle or bulb was hand blown, the art was open to anyone willing to acquire it. Thousands of craftsmen practiced it. Soon after the turn of the century, glass-blowing machinery was introduced, which revolutionized the industry. The basic patents are associated with the names of Owens, Corning, Hartford-Fairmont (later Hartford-Empire). In one branch of the glass industry alone—that of glass containers—the number of units produced was increased from 1.1 billion in 1899 to 7.7 billion in 1937. The dollar value of the output increased during the same period from $21.5 million to $160 million. Yet between 1904 and 1937 the number of companies producing glass containers declined from 155 to 40. The privilege of producing glass containers is for all practical purposes allocated by the Hartford-Empire Co., which shares control through agreements with the Owens-Illinois Glass Co. and the Corning Glass Works. Though the basic patents were acquired

---

Bros.' was a double unit, and both those large industries were built up with millions and millions of dollars invested. In 1920 five patents were issued to a man named Heaney that covered every phase of the starting and lighting system. Those patents had been held in the Patent Office for 15 years, and every year they were amended until they covered the entire situation. . . . The result was that they brought suits, the concern that owned those patents, and the General Motors Corporation, although they felt pretty sure the patents were invalid, considered it too big a risk to run, so we made a settlement, and paid $600,000 for the license." TNEC Hearings, Part 2, Patents, December, 1938, p. 371.

between 1900 and 1910, they have been kept alive through full utilization of legal rights under the patent laws. The Owens-Illinois Glass Company controlled about 29 per cent of the total output of glass containers. All but 5 per cent of the remainder is distributed among licensees of the Hartford-Empire Co., which does not itself manufacture but serves as a holding company for more than 700 patents covering production of glass containers. Cross-licensing agreements and exchange of patent privileges have likewise served to divide production of electric lamps and other forms of blown glass chiefly among General Electric, Corning Glass, and Westinghouse, along with the Hartford-Empire Co. Thus, the business in patent rights and the allocation of those rights become dominant factors in determining the structure of an important industry.[1]

The possibility under the present patent system of administering industry from a few centers of control is a standing threat not only to small business but to the private-enterprise system itself. This inherent possibility exists regardless of the most generous intentions on the part of those in the driver's seat to share their privileges with others less strategically placed. Despite this fact, one finds within the ranks of small business some of the most ardent defenders of the *status quo* in patent granting. The National Patent Council is a case in point. This organization is led by a comparatively small manufacturer, the president of an automotive-equipment concern. According to its prospectus the organization consists of some 500 smaller manufacturers, "devoted exclusively to the operation of a comprehensive national educational program adequate to defeat persistent fanatical and piratical assaults upon our patent system." To this end, nearly 300 patent lawyers and attorneys, it claims, have volunteered their services as professional associates of the council.[2] Here is one of those instances where, among small business, one man's meat is another man's poison.

That our patent system needs reform in the interest of widening

[1] See testimony of F. Goodwin Smith, president of the Hartford-Empire Co., in TNEC Hearings, Part 2, December, 1938, pp. 378–433. Also U.S. Tariff Commission, "Incandescent Electric Lamps," *Report* 133, 2d Series, 1939, cited in TNEC Monograph No. 21, p. 104.

[2] From the *Prospectus* (1946), National Patent Council, Inc., Gary, Ind., John W. Anderson, president, The Anderson Company, Gary, Ind.

economic opportunity has been stated by representatives of big as well as small business and by scientists as well as by businessmen. The system, however, is so much a part of the fabric of our productive economy that even those who are most earnest about the need for reform have hesitated to initiate it. The reforms would obviously have to be without retroactive features.

The work of the TNEC served to give additional publicity to the evils now in the patent system but contributed little in the way of sifting suggestions for reform. That task will have to be entrusted to a body of experts representing science, business, and the law to bring forth a scheme for reconstruction of the patent system—a system that has had no fundamental rethinking in legislative terms since the general mandate was placed in the Constitution to promote the progress of science and the useful arts. Prominent in such deliberations would undoubtedly be the following objectives, which are part of the suggestions made by the Science Advisory Board.

1. How to distinguish between the fundamental inventions entitled to the benefit of the full period of patent monopoly and minor devices or gadgets on which exclusive privileges could well be limited to a shorter period.

2. How to reduce the predatory nuisance factors in infringements and interference proceedings; how to increase the confidence with which a patent once issued may be acted upon without fear of delayed interference.

3. How to combine the present conflicting judicial controls and patent appeals to the jurisdiction of a single court, a judicial center adequately supported by scientific counsel and not having to depend upon the cross claims of partisan advocates.[1]

## LABOR AS A FACTOR IN COMPETITION

Small business in its labor relations may be said to occupy the extremes rather than the middle ground. The areas of industry

[1] See Science Advisory Board—Report of the Committee on the Relation of the Patent System to the Stimulation of New Industries. Cited as Exhibit 206, TNEC Hearings, Part 3, Patents, January, 1939, pp. 1139–1148.

Also George H. Willits and collaborating members of the Michigan Patent Bar: "Proposed Patent Legislation—Why It Is Needed, the Advantages of the Proposed Legislation and the Objections to It," TNEC Hearings, 1938, Part 2, Patents, pp. 714–735.

still largely unorganized are the distributive and service trades. These are the stronghold of small business. In these areas the relationship between the small enterpriser and his employees is informal and flexible. He has the opportunity to get and hold good employees by offering wages and working conditions comparable to those of his big competitor. Where he cannot compete with big business on the score of physical surroundings, he is often in a position to offset that disadvantage by a more intimate personal relationship and greater variety of activities that the employee may share with the employer.

In manufactures, as in construction, trucking, and mining, the small business is almost as frequently unionized as the large. A distinction must be made between the lines of manufacture that are predominantly in the hands of small business and those in which the small business must compete for labor with big business.

Some of the oldest, strongest, and most advanced unions are in industries that are typically small business. Examples are the apparel industry, job printing, and electrical repairs. In such situations the usual conflict of interests may exist at the bargaining table, but the problem of little business being crowded out in the labor market by big business does not arise. Moreover, in these industries union leaders have increasingly learned the importance of making their demands with an eye to the ability of the industry to absorb them.[1]

The competitive problem with respect to labor becomes most acute for small business in an industry where a considerable development of large business units has taken place and where the terms of the large industrial unions are geared to the resources of large business—with relatively little regard for their application to smaller units.

The resentment of the small businessman against the encroachment of the unions upon the owner's freedom of action has been

[1] ". . . it has been its [the union's] considered policy not to attempt to cross beyond the breaking point anywhere; the possible progressive advance of the industry is the limitation which union progress must reckon with and which intelligent unions must impose upon themselves for fear that some day they may find themselves in no man's land." (Report of the General Executive Board of the Amalgamated Clothing Workers, 13th Biennial Convention, 1940, p. 14.)

well publicized; it is understandable when one considers that the small enterpriser is an individualist, averse to imposition of formal disciplines upon his control of his business, whether by the banker, the government, or a labor organization. Easy generalization in this regard should be avoided, however. Many a small enterpriser has been a union member himself and supports labor organization. This would apply to barbers, foundrymen, printers, clothiers, and small construction contractors, among hundreds of others who move from the role of union member to that of employer. In many such lines union practices are as much the thinking of the employer as they are of the union leader. In lines where small employers predominate, they may look to the union to help maintain disciplines to prevent disastrous cross raiding of labor or excessive differentials in wage rates. The garment industry is a case in point.

The resentment of the small businessman toward the labor union in an industry that is a mixture of small and large establishments could probably be reduced if more attention were given by union leadership to the special conditions under which the smaller unit must operate. An obvious area of hostility has been created by union insistence that the small proprietor deal with an outside representative for his workers rather than deal with them directly. The nature of a small business often requires that its employees be versatile and that they be permitted to shift from one line of work to another in order to justify their earnings with a full use of man power. Featherbedding and make-work are economically as unsound for large companies as for small. But such policies hit small business much harder. The typical small enterprise is relatively more dependent upon man power and less upon capital equipment than is the large-scale enterprise. It does not have the leeway of the larger corporation in dividing skills, realigning workers, reallocating work in different plants, or otherwise offsetting a decline in worker effort through changes in organization.

Labor organizations have had substantial protection under the Clayton and Norris–LaGuardia Acts from prosecution for collusive agreements to restrict competition in processes and materials. That relative immunity was recently confirmed by the Supreme

Court (March, 1947) in a suit which involved the boycotting of types of building materials by the carpenter's union.[1] Under Sec. 8B(4) of the Labor Management Relations Act of 1947, known as the Taft-Hartley Act, it is declared an unfair practice for a labor organization or its agent

> . . . to engage in or to induce or encourage the employees of any employer to engage in a strike or a concerted refusal in the course of their employment to use, manufacture, process, transport, or otherwise handle or work on any goods, articles, materials, or commodities or to perform any services where an object thereof is (*A*) forcing or requiring any employer or self-employed person to join any labor or employer organization or any employer or other person to cease using, selling, handling, transporting or otherwise dealing in the products of any other producer, processor or manufacturer, or to cease doing business with any other person; . . . .
>
> (*D*) forcing or requiring any employer to assign particular work to employees in a particular labor organization or in a particular trade, craft, or class rather than to employees in another labor organization or in another trade, craft, or class unless such employer is failing to conform to an order or certification of the Board determining the bargaining representative for employees performing such work.

It is questionable, however, if this section aimed primarily at jurisdictional disputes and secondary boycotts can of itself serve to protect the small business from conspiracies to restrain the introduction of innovations that the union may regard as reducing the amount of work to go around.[2]

A few of the small businesses interviewed for this study by the NORC complained that they get the fringe workers—those unable to find work with the larger establishments—because of union hiring practices. The charge is not new. It could bespeak a sluggishness on the part of some small businesses in meeting prevailing standards of satisfactory wages, hours, sanitary conditions, provisions for health insurance, vacations, etc., or it may mean a lack of understanding on the part of the union of the advantages that some of their membership may find in the less rigid disciplines applicable to the small firm.

[1] *United Brotherhood of Carpenters v. United States*, 330 U.S. 395 (1947).

[2] It would not meet, for example, the situation where plumbers refused to have the materials assembled in the shop rather than on the job or painters resist the use of spray guns.

The self-interest of organized labor, as well as the working population generally, requires that the business structure retain a segment of small business that, because of its flexibility, offers opportunities for employees who are laid off or must drop out of the more fully organized lines. To allow the tiny business the freedom of an open shop helps to save the labor force from rigidities that would increase the number of the chronically unemployed. Even for those areas of small business where a genuine need exists for labor organization to prevent a disregard of decent labor standards, there should be a definite recognition that excessive rigidity in union demands must either drive out the small enterprise or impel it to join the ranks of those who oppose all forms of labor organization.

## FAIR COMPETITION AND SMALL-BUSINESS SURVIVAL

The range of trade practices and market tendencies that affect the future of small business is wide, and only a general presentation of the basic issues can be provided within the confines of a single chapter. Enough has been said, however, to reveal the nature of the problems that plague small business.

Some small business sees itself endangered by the cumulative power that can be mobilized in modern industry by the large corporation. Its sphere of action is delimited by the big-business leadership in whose wake small business often must move. To retain as much freedom of action as possible, the small business looks to the FTC and the Department of Justice to keep the channels of competition open, to keep a watchful eye on the potential squeeze that integrated big business can apply to smaller independent units.

On the other hand, in the very process of protecting itself against the greater range and often greater efficiency of big business as a direct rival, small business sometimes has fostered its own restrictions on competition, often with government aid. Apart from the public and consumer interests that are involved in such restrictive activities, there is the question of self-interest for small business itself. Time and again the very enterprisers who have attempted by legislation to restrict the field to keep out competitors find themselves the victims of such legislation. Fixed prices may prove to be ceilings as well as floors, to squeeze margins as well as protect them. They may be an invitation to substitution and to the total reduction of the market for the item or line of business thus restrained in price flexibility. The ingenuity exercised in getting around restrictions that hamper trade is likely to overcome the protective devices employed.

The sound growth of small business is, in general, not going to be increased through small enterprisers' attempting to put strait-jackets around each other or even to straitjacket the more efficient methods of larger competitors. Small business must find its own ways of keeping abreast or ahead of the times. If chain stores can reduce prices through mass buying or large manufacturers can make a place for their products by widely advertising them, then small business, too, must find the means of getting its products to the public.

Small manufacturers may, without yielding their independence, set up selling agencies to promote their brands as a group. Small dealers likewise may find it advantageous to do a certain amount of pooling of their advertising funds or their buying power.

Possibilities for cooperative action among small manufacturers and small dealers have only been tapped. Cooperative methods for growth can still leave to many small businessmen a larger degree of independence than they now enjoy when they must get on the band wagon and follow the rules laid down for them if they cannot battle single-handed.

As the character of the market changes, new means will be devised to win or hold a share in that market, and for every new attack there will be a new defense. Complete stability is neither attainable nor desirable. It is desirable, however, that the Congress periodically reexamine its position in the light of court decisions and FTC experience and that at the state level the concept of unfair competition likewise be redefined, so that reasonable people have a reasonable chance of knowing if they are steering close to the border line of competitive malpractice.

Every increase in the complexity of society means more rules, which may hamper as well as protect. The small enterprise has to learn the whole lesson on regulation. Like big business, it is under the necessity of yielding some liberties of action for the sake of a workable economic order. But small business, its own trade associations, and government regulatory agencies acting in its behalf should guard against making the dose of discipline an overdose, dulling the competitive initiative that is small business's great asset.

# IX. EDUCATION AND PUBLIC POLICY

ALL THAT HAS been said about the needs of small business, whether in management, financial aid, or the improvement of its competitive environment, bears on the subject of education for small business. To enable small business to play its full part in the development of our economy, both the small enterprise and the public it serves must be considered in the educational program. Within that public are people who may be recruited into the ranks of small business, those who deal with or compete with small business, the public agencies that through legislation and administration help to determine whether the small businessman will find his problems easier or more difficult to solve.

A prime objective for business education should be the steering of an adequate share of the best business talent into the channels of business ownership. Those who are already the owners of a small business need to participate in continuing education, to be kept fully alert to its opportunities and responsibilities. The fostering of a culture in which small business can thrive should also be part of the educational objective. In practice, public policy designed to provide maximum opportunity for small business to grow and survive will contribute a flexible, competitive economy.

To elevate small-business ownership to the level of a professional career would be highly desirable insurance against loss of ground by small business as the pace and scale of the economy increase. Small business needs to have within its own ranks the capacity and leadership to create the setting in which small business may make its maximum contribution to a free-enterprise economy.

## COMMUNITY GUIDANCE FOR NEWCOMERS

The education of the small enterpriser is a matter of enlightened self-interest for the community in which he establishes himself. That is obvious to the real-estate agency that rents or sells him his premises, to the municipality that taxes and polices his enterprise, to the workers who depend upon the enterprise for employment, and to the consumers who may look to him for his product or service.

At the close of the war, when large numbers of returning veterans were seeking to enter business, there was widespread activity by local civic organizations to help such new entrants. While the program had its main stimulus from a desire to help the veteran, many other civilians benefited.[1]

It would be unfortunate if the community interest in initiating the prospective enterpriser were to end with the short period of patriotic and immediate concern for the veteran. It stands to reason that an influx of between 50,000 and 60,000 small enterprises per month, such as prevailed in 1946, inevitably meant the entry of a large number who were inadequately prepared for the undertaking. By the end of 1946 the number of discontinuances, aside from business transfers, was running close to 15,000 per month, despite the high level of general business activity.[2]

The fact that a large number of the veterans received part of their funds for business entry from the banks by virtue of a government guaranty increases, in its way, the public stake in the continuing solvency of the investments. In any event, a periodic check of the newer small businesses should not be confined to visits from a representative of the sales-tax office or the industrial division of the health department. Obviously, the small businessman's problem is most acute not before but after he has entered business.

The local chamber of commerce and—as far as its facilities permit—the district office of the Federal or state commerce department can fruitfully serve the community as well as the small enterpriser by maintaining continued contact with the owners of these businesses in the formative period. Besides the usual clinics and forums on problems of common interest, it is desirable that an office be set up in the local chamber of commerce for personal conferences. Experienced businessmen of the community should continue to be on call, as they were in the transition period, for conferences with small enterprisers in need of guidance.

[1] The Field Development Division of the CED reported more than 3,000 local committees that made guidance available to potential entrepreneurs and those seeking to enlarge their enterprises.

[2] *Survey of Current Business*, April, 1947.

A device found useful in some communities is for successful businessmen to be available to participate as consultants on the boards of smaller and newer corporations.

This education at the community level is a two-way process, in which the community as well as the small enterpriser has something to learn. In gathering information for the business entrants, many communities have rediscovered themselves and developed information that benefits their established firms as well.

## ROLE OF THE BUSINESS COLLEGES

In raising the prestige of small business and developing among more small businessmen a professional outlook upon its problems, opportunities, and techniques, the collegiate school of business can have a significant role.

Nothing would seem more obvious than the fact that everyone who enters business, no matter how big the business, will inevitably deal with small business as customer or supplier. On that ground alone, every student of business, even the avowed student of big business, should be acquainted with the small enterprise and its peculiar problems. Nevertheless, small business has been a conspicuously neglected area in formal business education.

Where the collegiate business school emerged as an extension of the college economics department, the background was the study of wealth, value, production, consumption, and distribution as social issues. Business was not treated from the viewpoint of the enterpriser trying to retain his niche in the business sphere. The operations of large enterprise served more readily to illustrate problems of financial control and monopoly, industrial disputes, international trade, tariffs, or government and business relationships.

Where the collegiate business school faculty was recruited from the ranks of the commercial schools—as often happened in the more localized institutions—the emphasis on business skills carried over from the commercial proprietory schools, though at a more advanced level. Bookkeeping became accounting; office practice became office management; commercial arithmetic became statistics and statistical research. Higher levels of specialization emerged in such courses as business management, corporation finance, or theory of investments, superimposed on the background courses taught in the social-science departments of the liberal-arts school.

At the graduate level, the leading collegiate schools of business have recognized, at least by the titles of courses offered, a place for the study of business policy and the processes of decision-making. But in the main, the curriculum has tended to produce graduates best suited to the specialized work of a firm large enough to be formally departmentalized and to make use of business technicians.

Those who have served on business-school faculties are familiar with the scouts from large companies recruiting top-ranking students as apprentices. Some members of the faculty have been inclined to point with pride to the big-name companies that carry off its graduates. The urban collegiate school was thus, in effect, encouraging its best talent to leave the home community. Local small business got the residue. On that basis, successorship in the small businesses of the local community owed little to the influence of the collegiate business schools.

Currently educators at the higher levels of business education have become increasingly concerned over the neglect of small-business proprietorship as a career toward which a sizable fraction of the collegiate business students should be directed. A recent session of the American Association of Collegiate Schools of Business focused its attention on the problem of training students better to fit them for proprietorship.[1] Development of an awareness of this need is a first step toward an attack on the problem by experts competent to develop a curriculum suited to this purpose.

*Opportunities for Retraining*

A program aimed at professionalizing business ownership contemplates the active participation of many who are already in business.

*The Clientele.* The collegiate school of business can provide for two types of employees who are interested in the problems and responsibilities of business ownership. There is the young employee who still has a number of years to go before he can own a business, by building up sufficient savings to start a business or by possible succession upon retirement of the present owner. For such

[1] See *Proceedings* of the Annex Meeting of the Association, Chicago, May, 1946.

younger men, the process of training may extend over several years, utilizing evening hours, to fill in gaps in their general business education and increase their capacity for meeting the problems of ownership.

The second type of employee for whom collegiate business training is indicated is the more experienced person who plans to organize or to buy into a small business and who requires an intensive initiation in the special requirements of small-business management. The candidate may be a competent engineer or a salesman or a designer and yet be deficient in other training and information essential to successful entrepreneurship. He needs to be given an over-all comprehension of problems such as determining his product line; selecting his business site; making trade contacts; the organization of production; product development; gauging, creating, and holding a market for the product; arrangement of physical layout; the administration of personnel, including intelligent self-appraisal; ascertainment of where a business stands and whither it is headed; and, of course, financing the whole.

Another class of individuals whose training should concern the collegiate school of business is the active small enterpriser who seeks to improve his management or who needs to be kept abreast of the economic conditions that affect the success of his enterprise. His outlook can be broadened and methods improved through discussion sessions arranged under the guidance of the business college, with informed and successful operators of differing types of business, also with men versed in research and in governmental policy, as well as in business. Even the comparatively successful small enterpriser often finds it useful to supplement his own trial-and-error development with the discipline of systematic courses in those areas of management or in specialized fields of business operation in which he has not had opportunity to get a full grasp of the subject matter. Obviously, something more challenging than the standard classroom course must be designed to engage the interest of the entrepreneur in the role of student.[1]

Informed, capable, and socially minded businessmen should be

[1] That many a small enterpriser is eager for such education is evidenced by the liberal fees paid and large attendance at the better known institutes of the up-and-at-them inspirational type that make the rounds of metropolitan centers.

enlisted in the educational process. One aspect of that participation is already evident in the use of business executives on the advisory councils of business schools to help in curriculum building and to cooperate in supplying case materials for the study of business. Businessmen in some communities have gone further and have accepted students for part-time work or work between semesters to provide a first-hand knowledge of the business process. This may pay off in the discovery of good talent for permanent employment.

*Qualifying Business Educators*

Not the least useful way in which business may participate in the educational program is in helping to develop business teachers whose experience is not limited to the classroom. Successful proprietors who are in a position to do so and who may be so inclined should be encouraged to taper off their business activities, while still in the prime of life, to devote themselves to teaching young people as well as the more mature students seeking light on the conduct of small business.

The professionally trained classroom teacher, on the other hand, requires broader opportunities than have heretofore been open to supplement his academic experience with work experience inside business establishments. The collegiate instructor should be enabled to parallel, at a level suitable to his background, the work experience that is given to the students in cooperative training programs with department stores and industrial companies. Under auspices making for mutual confidence, classroom teachers in the field of business should increasingly be invited to sit in on executive sessions at which policy decisions of the firm are reached. Faculty members of the few collegiate business schools that now encourage the practice have proved their value and even earned permanent places on the boards of small corporations. The educator needs direct personal contact with the process whereby problems are worked out as they come up. In practice, especially among small firms, problems do not arise in so neat and symmetrical a form as would appear from the models usually supplied as illustrations in case textbooks.

While education for entrepreneurship fits neatly into the

setting of the collegiate school of business, it is obvious that most of the bread-and-butter education for small enterprise must be carried on at other levels. In the chapter on management, mention was made of educational opportunities that exist in the mutual contacts of manufacturers and distributors, suppliers and dealers, bankers and clients,[1] for counseling on individual problems. Also noted were constructive activities that may be undertaken by trade associations beyond the standardizing of records and operating techniques. The more recent reports to the Department of Commerce, Trade Association Division, indicate a substantial increase in such educational programs, both as to the number of associations so engaged and the percentage of their time devoted to that type of activity. The collegiate business school has been called upon to arrange the curriculum and to supply faculty personnel for a number of trade association institutes.

## RESEARCH FOR SMALL BUSINESS

In research, as in education and in merchandising, the individual small enterprise lacks the facilities needed for keeping abreast of technological advances. Highly generalized information is often available from the Bureau of Standards, the Bureau of Mines, and other of the technical and scientific branches of the government. What small business requires, however, is a facility to which the small business can turn for direct technological aid. The average small business cannot maintain a laboratory of its own, yet it often desperately needs such help.

A pooling of research and technological facilities is indicated as a necessary step in small-business technological progress. Some localities have set up laboratories in the interest of community development. An example is the scientific organization endowed by industrialists of Kansas City, which undertakes the solution of

[1] One service that has come to the author's attention is offered by banks in about twenty-five of the larger industrial centers. It is an Industrial Information Service, consisting of a monthly four-page bulletin, "Results from Research," supplemented by reports and bulletins, which are sent to readers who enquire about items in the bulletin. The service specializes in covering new products, materials, machines, and processes. It is designed for customers of the sponsoring bank and is restricted to the areas where these banks do business.

specific technical problems at cost; the Development Commission of the state of Wyoming, supported by basic endowment from the state treasury, is likewise available to take care of specific projects submitted to it by an individual or business group within the state. Dangers of abuse of confidences in such an arrangement are present, but they appear relatively unimportant compared with the opportunities to aid the business that is too small to maintain its own permanent facilities.

A vast quantity of business data is accumulated both by public and private agencies under the general heading of business research. The large firm, with its own research staff, is able to adapt statistical information to its own requirements, for purposes of anticipating trends, market research, guidance in inventory building, price making, product development, cost comparisons, and like facets of business-policy formation.

Little of this information is screened so that it can be used directly by the small businessman. Most small enterprisers are unaware of the existence of much information useful to them. The great majority would see little connection between the findings and their own problems. National and regional data need to be broken down into community data with the collaboration of the appropriate government field offices, the business research bureaus of the college in the area, and the local chambers of commerce or local chapters of trade associations.

Progress has been made in supplying statistical indicators of local business conditions, especially with respect to urban conditions. There are local surveys that are instructive for particular lines of business—such as annual surveys of real-estate vacancies, employment, volume of traffic, retail sales volume, and population shifts.[1] Less progress seems to have been made, however, in the follow-up of the research through business clinics and other guidance facilities for the practical utilization of the information by small firms. Outstanding exceptions are the work of the trade associations in the laundry, dry goods, furniture, and commercial banking fields, which have set up periodic conferences and have

[1] A classification of such projects by line of industry may be found in the *Survey of University Business Research Projects, 1945–46,* U.S. Department of Commerce, Office of Small Business, Washington, D.C., 1947.

published understandable manuals and news letters for the guidance of members.

Complaint has been made by officials of trade associations that the small businessman usually is unwilling to keep up his dues or bear the costs involved in giving him the benefits of research in his general field. A random questioning of small proprietors suggests that this is an open issue. The small businessman, like any other, is willing to buy and pay for what he buys when he is aware that he is making a good bargain. The failure to buy trade affiliations reflects in part a defect in the product offered or in the selling method, since the small businessman does not see fully the value of—or his need of—the services. What may be required is persistent demonstration of the practical values in the counsel offered to small enterprisers, bearing in mind that any process of mass education is necessarily a slow one. The process should become easier as the ranks of small business are progressively infiltrated by a generation that has had some formal training in the requirements of small-business management.

### CONCERN OF GOVERNMENT IN SMALL BUSINESS

As small businessmen become more widely informed on the economics of small-scale enterprise and as their outlook on the function of small business in the total economy is broadened, we may expect that they will participate more generally and with a surer hand in the making of public policy on behalf of small business. The more effectively they can help themselves the more discriminating they will be in the kind of governmental aid they seek and the legislative devices they support. At the same time, however, the acts of government inevitably exercise an influence on what the private enterprise can accomplish within the social framework. A better appreciation of the place of governmental activity in the operation of business would improve government as well as business.

Familiar to every businessman who pays taxes is the impact of fiscal policy upon the growth of all business, small as well as large. At the local level the small storekeeper, like his larger competitor, is also affected by the public handling of traffic, sanitation, recreation, law enforcement, and the other services that can contribute to the prosperity of the community as a labor and sales area. Small business likewise has a direct interest in the work of local planning commissions. The small business is affected by zoning laws, determining the balance between residential and commercial property; by the encouragement of an orderly and convenient grouping of neighborhoods, to provide adequate shipping facilities and convenient access to workers and buyers. In such matters big business may be in a position to determine its own layout; small business must depend upon community action in the common interest.

For the nation as a whole, only the government is in a position to supply certain types of mass information concerning the characteristics of the population, including income distribution and purchasing power. Many of the Federal Census data require a reworking at the state or local level, by local governments with the cooperation of local educational institutions, so that the small businessman may discern more accurately the character of the market he is serving or that is open to him. Such information can be useful to local civic associations or to the individual business for promotional purposes.

Because of the special transitional problems incident to the postwar years—the shifts in communities and the large influx of new small businesses, especially those undertaken by veterans—the government may be expected to pay increased attention to the requirements of small business for information and guidance. This is evidenced in the large number of manuals issued both by the Commerce Department of the Federal government and by the departments of commerce or business development of states that have such agencies. In its postwar program, the Department of Commerce established a network of field offices to assist local business. Their program contemplates collaboration between the Department and local business associations or colleges in the establishment of conferences, clinics, and courses for small-business guidance. Instruction in the utilization of data collected by the government on business opportunities, economic conditions, and management problems is one of the objectives. The success of this program will depend upon the readiness of local civic bodies and business groups to take over the responsibility of this program from the government agencies, leaving to the latter the collecting and distribution of such basic business data as only the government is in a position to supply.[1]

In the process of mutual education between government and small business, considerable help in understanding competitive problems and questions of business ethics has been afforded through the trade-practice conferences conducted under the auspices of the FTC. They have served to clear away some of the misunderstandings, deceptions, and discriminations to which small business has been subject and to which, in some cases, small business itself has been a party.[2]

*Political Solicitude.* Small business has long been the darling of the politician and a pet subject for oratory. Legislation has been designed both at the Federal and state levels to give special protection to small business. Some of the special aids have boomeranged in that they have tended to diminish the initiative of the small businessman and to make him depend upon artificial rigidities in pricing and licensing, in business entry and exit. The small businessman has been encouraged to mobilize his strength for punitive measures against "outsiders" and against big business without realizing the time might come when he would find himself stopped by the very measures intended for his protection.

Small businessmen are so numerous that the demands of only

[1] Demonstration of the value of the program to the Congressional Appropriations Committees is, of course, also a factor in the fulfillment of the aims.

[2] Among the subjects covered by the trade-practice conferences of the FTC the following are listed in the commission's report for 1944: Misbranding; misrepresentation in various forms, including false or misleading advertising; deceptive packaging; defamation of competitors or disparagement of their products; impersonation or misrepresentation to obtain competitors' trade secrets; price discriminations to injure, prevent, or destroy competition; discriminations and harmful practices in matters of rebates, refunds, discounts, credits, brokerage, commissions, services, etc.; commercial bribery; inducing breach of competitor's contract; false invoicing; imitation of competitor's trade-marks, trade names, brands, etc; substitution and "passing off"; deceptive use of so-called "free goods" deals; deceptive pricing; lottery schemes; use of consignment distribution to close competitors' trade outlets; use of deceptive types of containers simulating standard and generally recognized types; use of deceptive depictions (photographs, engravings, cuts, etc.) in describing industry products; selling below cost with the purpose and effect of suppressing competition, restraining trade, or creating a monopoly; use of "loss leaders" as a deceptive or monopolistic practice; bidding methods; price quoting and listing; advertising of sales; and informative labeling.

a small minority of them may loom large in the thinking of the legislator who is anxious to please. Part of the educational process that must be conducted on behalf of small business involves the more careful appraisal by public officials of the demands made upon them by lobbies of small-business minorities. For every "foreign" trucker that is kept out of the state by an excessive tax or licensing measure, there is a local trucker who is prevented from carrying his business to the legitimate extent of his natural marketing area, which may be outside his own state. The type of thinking that culminates in an ordinance preventing a drugstore from selling sandwiches may seem highly desirable to the restaurant owner, who thus appears to be eliminating additional competition. But the same type of thinking may impose upon him the necessity of installing expensive new equipment under an ordinance designed not for his convenience but for the advantage of a branch of business with construction materials or services to sell.

Education in enlightened public policy demands a close questioning by public officials of any measure restricting the right of entry or branching out or trying out of new materials or methods by the progressive and ambitious small businessman. Whether it is in the method of letting bids or in rules for labeling or in regulations for the submission of reports, the enthusiasm of the public official for rule making should not be carried to the point where the burden upon the small businessman is disproportionate to the public benefits from regulating. In this respect the public official needs to be as wary of the calculating small-business group seeking to freeze out its competitors as it is of any big business that may assert its solicitude for the public, in order to screen measures that increase expenses or difficulty of operation for the newcomer and smaller competitor.

A good part of the legislation that the public official is asked to impose may have implications of a highly technical nature with consequences far beyond those which appear on the surface. It is to be hoped that the small-business division recently set up by the Department of Commerce, working on its own and in cooperation with the Bureau of Standards and similar agencies concerned with the public welfare, will be available to the legislator for trustworthy advice on the consequences of measures for which legislation is urged. That is part of the general education for the maintenance of an intelligent democracy in which the future of small business is deeply involved.

## RECAPITULATION

Small business, as has frequently been pointed out, is less and less capable of operating successfully on a mere trial-and-error basis. The successful operation of a small business in an era of mass production is no mean achievement. It is fast arriving at the stage where its problems must be approached professionally by men qualified by training and experience to cope with those problems. The educational structure requires reexamination to make room for the needs of the small enterpriser and to help in the solution of his problems. This calls for educational activities directly focused on the career of business ownership and on the needs of small business. The services to be rendered by the educational system must reach beyond the traditional years of undergraduate life. There must be a place for the practicing or potential entrepreneur whose ordinary college days are past but who requires education in the problems which confront him as a small businessman.

Research now useful only to big business because it requires expert interpretation must be supplemented and adapted to the scope of the small businessman. Much of the information needed by small business can be furnished by the voluntary associations of the small businessmen themselves. Where it is of a nature that the government can best supply, a follow-through is called for to assure effective utilization of what government research has to offer.

The extent and variety of the ranks of small business are such that one cannot trust the wishes of any minority to represent fairly the general welfare of small business. Considerably greater care must, therefore, be exercised by the public official to make sure—insofar as is humanly practicable—that the consequences of his efforts on behalf of some small business may not be quite different from those which he seeks to foster. To this end the technical advisory services, the government agencies of counsel and research, should be utilized more fully.

# X. SUMMARY AND CONCLUSIONS

Any considered view of small business, its problems, and its significance for a democratic society must take into account its numbers and variety. Exclusive of agriculture and the professions, there are (1947) more than 3.5 million small-business firms. If the dividing line between small and large is drawn at 100 wage-earning employees, then all but 25,000 of the nation's business enterprises are small business. With more than three million centers of business initiative, the realm of small business offers a moving panorama of self-employment and responsibility for the employment of others, of competition for the patronage of customers, of new ideas and trials and errors that taken together make for a dynamic society and ensure the American economy against sterility.

Small business is cosmopolitan; every social and economic level is represented. Included are nearly two million small proprietors whose assets are mainly in their heads and hands and in small current inventories that it is their hope to enlarge. At the upper end of the scale the ranks of small business include firms with annual sales exceeding a million dollars, which may be outside the popular conception of small enterprise. Nevertheless, their characteristics and problems are akin to those of smaller establishments, and they, too, must be considered in any public policy aimed at sustaining and developing independent owner-managed enterprises.

Small business is found in virtually every sector of business endeavor. It is concentrated in distribution and services, but it contributes importantly to the national real income through manufactures, construction, and mineral extraction as well. The needs and the shades of opinion of small businessmen are almost as varied as their activities. Legislation demanded by one sector of small business is often anathema to a competing group of small enterprises. The alignment of interests is in continuing flux. An adequate public policy for small business must be elastic enough to comprehend its diverse character. The problems of special groups in small business need to be resolved, however, with a regard for the balance and prosperity of the whole economy.

*Stability and Survival*

Small business normally shows a high annual count of births and discontinuances but a fairly steady ratio of firms to total population over the years. Before the war new entries into business within a year ran as high as one-fifth of the total business population. It was not uncommon for nearly a third of those entering business to discontinue within a year. The pattern of discontinuances, as to type and length of life, has been nearly constant for at least a century. The relative importance of the turnover in the total picture can easily be overemphasized. Entries and exits of individuals with negligible capital, which build up the heavy count of births and deaths, may be compared with labor turnover; they consist largely of the self-employed who hire no help and who move in and out according to the shifts in opportunities for self-employment as against employment for others.

The war period saw a net decline of more than half a million in the number of firms in the business population. The wartime drop in number was inevitable, considering the requirements for military man power and the unavailability of merchandise in some lines. Since the war, however, the loss in numbers has been made up. The end of 1946 found the American business population at its all-time high. The large influx of new business is an impressive demonstration of the will to venture in the current American economy. One discordant note has been a postwar rise in the number of mergers where sound businesses in the middle-size range are absorbed within empires of larger scale business. That phenomenon has not, however, reached the proportions of the decade following the First World War.

The high total production achieved in two years since the war's end has increased consumer demand generally and provided new opportunities for supplying the services associated with cultural advancement, conveniences, health, and recreation—the areas of elastic demand that go with a rising standard of living. This improves the long-term prospects for the type of enterprise that is peculiarly in the province of small business. In serving these needs, small enterprise stimulates an expanding market for equipment and commodities that come mainly from the production lines of big business.

The wartime experience and the technological research that it fostered put big business in a position to reach new heights in the volume and variety of postwar output. That, in turn, means customers for small fabricators of parts that go into the assembly lines of mass production. Expanded distribution, transport, and repair services also go along with the increased output of big business. Here, too, opportunities are created for the growth of small business along with the larger operations.

*Size and Efficiency*

Available studies of the relative efficiency of large and small business are inconclusive if one seeks a definitive generalization. The break-even point and the maximum efficiency point vary as to size of firm from one industry to another. In the categories of business that permit cost comparisons over the whole size range, small units are found to be among the most efficient as well as among the least efficient producers.

Taking profits as the criterion, recent analyses of corporate earnings show the average rate of return rising for most industries to a peak at the size level represented by about $1 million of corporate assets and tapering off from there on. The exceptional cases in which the very largest firms show the highest earnings record as, for example, in cigarette manufacture—are matched by contrasting cases in which maximum earnings rates are attained by firms in the net assets classes below $100,000, as in apparel and textiles.

The evidence on costs and profits tends to the belief that in this respect the highest average efficiency is attained by the business of intermediate size rather than by the largest unit in the industry. (Intangible factors that make for survival and stability are not clarified, however, by this type of comparison.) The evidence has also pointed up a suspected fact, namely, that many small operations need to be expanded to larger volume before they can attain a satisfactory competitive position in respect to costs and profits. With war-accelerated advances in technology, many of the smaller producing units will require improved equipment and research facilities as well as larger capital to maintain a healthy position in their industry.

Small business as a whole has shown hardihood over the years; it came out of the war at a new high level of prosperity. The record by individual firms is spotty. Before the war the majority of financial statements submitted to the Bureau of Internal Revenue by small corporations (with total assets under $100,000) showed deficits after allowance for owners' salaries. This general pattern did not change until 1941. An improved general record, with more consistently profitable operation, should be a major objective in efforts to strengthen the small business sector if we are to have efficient utilization of our economic resources.

The wide range in production costs and in profits of small-business units, in industries analyzed for those factors, carries a favorable implication that the small enterprise has peculiar advantages which can be exploited successfully and disadvantages which can be overcome. Small business can do some things better than can the large business. Individualized commodities and services can be furnished by small enterprise, whereas they do not usually fit into the structure of large-scale business. Small business, in general, is more responsive to alert management.

*Management and Guidance*

The prime importance of the management factor in the success of the small enterprise is borne out by such evidence as we have from the financial statements of the Bureau of Internal Revenue, from analyses of business failures and their causes, and from studies of credit accommodations to small enterprises.

The prosperity of most small enterprises during the war was achieved with comparatively small increases in sales volume; they benefited from clearance of sluggish inventories, reduction in poor credit accounts, and elimination of unprofitable lines. A general improvement in small-business management might therefore be a potent factor in raising the general level of postwar prosperity for small business.

Most small enterprises do not have ready access to competent management guidance; moreover, the small enterpriser resists interference with his freedom of action. It is necessary to make the guidance readily available and the gains therefrom clear enough so that the small businessman will accept it and, where possible, buy it.

In addition to internal facilities for management appraisal and research, big business has access to and freely utilizes the services of outside experts in market research, industrial management, product development, and other forms of business counseling. Competent services of this type, except perhaps in the area of accounting, are beyond the financial means of the typical small firm under present conditions. Until such services can be had at practicable rates, the small business must look for its counseling requirements to the cooperation of group agencies.

The most natural source of counsel is the manufacturer or supplier of the small enterprise. Suppliers can help to raise the general level of management, for the business too small to retain its own counsel, through systematic organization of management services—through conferences and clinics and field representatives—bearing on credit policies, financial analysis, merchandising, and use of research findings.

Trade associations with small enterprises in their membership should follow the example of those who are now devoting a larger proportion of their total efforts to the education of their membership in the fields of management and research. Chambers of commerce likewise should recognize the opportunities as well as the need for counseling service, particularly in view of the abnormally large percentage of new and expanded enterprises. It would be well for general models for such programs to be worked out by a national association with adaptations to be made to the special requirements of the local or specific industry group.

Looking to the economic welfare of the community, successful executives of larger businesses should be enlisted, at least for a time, to serve as board members of smaller enterprises and to offer guidance on basic policy questions involving the organization of production and marketing, determination of the line, elimination of wasteful practices, and similar problems that bear on the success and growth of the small enterprise. This applies particularly to small enterprises still in the formative stage.

Industrial engineering and market-research agencies should

pool their efforts to devise a type of counseling service suited to and within the financial means of the small enterprise. Some parts of these programs may be worked out with trade associations or local chambers of commerce; the educational process may later provide new clientele for the counseling agency.

A field that needs to be cultivated by the small business is advertising. The small enterprise has suitable opportunities to utilize advertising of a local and specialized character; it needs to be educated to these possibilities. Newspapers and other advertising media, singly or in groups, should supplement their selling programs with educational material, so that the small enterpriser may learn how to make effective use of a small advertising budget.

A number of accounting firms and small advertising agencies currently offering their services to small firms are comprised of inexperienced personnel whose level of competence needs to be raised. It is an area in which trustworthy standards have not yet been developed. Collegiate schools of business should look into the possibility of working with those desirous of cultivating the area of small-business guidance in order to develop more effective counseling procedures.

The small manufacturing enterprise as a rule lacks laboratory facilities for scientific analysis and improvement of its product. There are a number of firms of industrial chemists, metallurgists, and other technicians who provide testing services for specific commodities. Such concerns do not, as a rule, provide counseling facilities in product development. The combination of testing services with guidance in processing and product development is a logical one. Such organizations as the American Council of Commercial Laboratories should consider the value of promoting among their members an interest in combining routine testing with technological guidance.

For technical services that can be made available to a whole industrial group, the Bureau of Standards should be authorized to serve small-business groups more aggressively with respect to information on technological developments. The government also is necessarily the only agency through which adequate information can be gathered with respect to population, national income, levels of production and business activity generally, prices and living costs, and similar data bearing on the public welfare. The large company already knows the value of such information and how to make use of it. It is a legitimate function of government to extend the usefulness of such information by facilitating its dissemination to small business. The Department of Commerce is a logical clearinghouse through which government research findings of value to small business can be fed to local civic organizations, educational institutions, trade associations, and other counseling agencies serving business. Strategically located field offices are essential for carrying out that type of cooperation with small business.

*Financial Requirements and Problems*

Sample surveys of small business establishments at the war's end indicated that they were not, in the main, concerned about short-term commercial and banking credit. As a whole, small business also felt well supplied with working capital for the immediate future. The rise in commercial bank loans to an all-time high by the end of the second postwar year indicated that small business had probably overestimated its ability to meet taxes, depreciation, reconversion, and reorganization costs without help from the banks. The rising tide of failures also attested to the weak financial structure of many small enterprises.

Bank credit, likewise, appeared more than ample at the close of the war. But small business has good reason to be more concerned with the long-run problem of ensuring credit availability when conditions are less favorable. Even more pervasive and significant, however, is the problem of supplying permanent capital for small enterprise.

Studies of the availability of bank credit deal mainly with experience in the 1930's, when banks felt anxiety for the maintenance of liquidity. The postwar outlook is brighter in that respect. Deposits are now covered by insurance. The banks hold a larger volume of liquid assets than formerly, and bank examiners are more liberal in their attitude toward longer term loans by commercial banks. The RFC, if continued, and the Federal Reserve banks are available as a rear line of defense against strain upon the lending facilities of the commercial banks.

The problem of supplying more permanent capital, and particularly equity capital for the small firm, is basic and has not been met adequately. Flotation of securities by firms in the small and even in the intermediate class has proved prohibitively expensive. The record to date of the willingness of the market to absorb small issues has been disappointing. The percentage of individual savings invested in small business ventures has been declining. In part the drying up of the sources of individual investment is attributable to high levels of taxation, resulting in smaller percentages of earnings available for business ventures or for plowing back into established enterprises. In part the trend is a natural result of the progressive concentration of the population in large urban communities; local acquaintance and kinship have become less of a factor in providing backing for new enterprise. These conditions combined have left a gap that must be filled through organized efforts to supply capital for small enterprise.

An alternative to adequate financing of small business through private channels is government lending and investment. Legislation to that end has been conceived as a peacetime extension of the wartime activities of the SWPC and the RFC. The undertaking by government to supply capital for small business holds dangers of financing under political pressure. It can mean that weak enterprises will be allowed to linger with government support to the detriment of the economy and the independence of small business. Defaulting borrowers would leave small enterprises in the lap of the government—a condition hardly consistent with the fostering of vigorous, decentralized private enterprise.

Civic development corporations have been formed in a number of communities to steer risk capital into new and expanding ventures. The results, worth while in themselves, are in the aggregate negligible when compared with over-all requirements for small-business capital. Such funds as the development corporations have provided have gone mainly into intermediate rather than small enterprises.

The possibility of localized private investment banking operating effectively in the small-business field has not materialized. This is not too surprising, since investment bankers are engaged primarily in the sale of securities rather than in management guidance, which is an essential corollary to small-business investment. The small enterpriser on his part resists capital offers if the price includes some loss of his control of the enterprise.

Some progress has been made in opening up the facilities of the commercial banks to small business for working-capital purposes through term loans running from one to five years. Yet because of its traditional concern for liquidity and the protection of depositors, the typical commercial bank is unsuited to assumption of the risks of long-term credit and investment in small business.

Nevertheless, banks are the source to which the small enterpriser naturally looks for his financial requirements. Within the framework of the banking system, a place can and should be made for specialized capital banks devoted exclusively to long-term and equity financing for enterprise that is too small to obtain its capital funds through the security markets or through institutional investment.

The plan for a network of capital banks under Federal Reserve supervision (as presented in the chapter on Financial Requirements) visualizes an evolving institution, the scope of which may be expanded or its characteristics modified with growing experience. A major objective in the proposal for a specialized bank of this type is the opportunity to work out new and effective techniques for meeting the peculiar requirements of small business and developing its potential as a financial risk. A system of capital banks would permit continuous study of the small enterprise as a credit risk and would furnish a core of well-documented information from which the creditworthiness of small business might be improved.

It is also highly desirable, with respect to business loans generally, that the small enterpriser have a clearer understanding of the elements entering into the determination of his creditworthiness. The banking fraternity should collaborate in producing a definitive manual setting forth the criteria and principles bearing upon the eligibility of a business for specific types of loans, secured and unsecured. It should indicate the accounting methods, credit ratios, and operational tests whereby a business can determine the type and magnitude of the financing that it requires and for which it may be eligible as a suitable risk. Such basic materials should be followed up by the banks—in the process of mutual education of the bank and its clients—with periodic clinics under the auspices of the local clearinghouse associations or individual banks along lines similar to those suggested for the customers of manufacturers and suppliers.

The small-town bank, as a rule, gives personal attention to the individual prospective borrower and comes to know his needs. The larger banks and those in larger cities have set up special departments for small-business clients; the latter should be strengthened with adequate facilities for personal counseling. The tendency for bank examiners to liberalize their attitude toward long-term loans has been noted. Bank examiners may well be further instructed in the sympathetic appraisal of programmed loans for periods of one or more years, with an eye to aiding in the development of appropriate standards.

Since small businesses undergo wider fluctuations in earnings from good to bad years than do larger corporations, it is highly desirable that a qualified agency, under the auspices of the ABA, the Federal Reserve System, IBA, and other interested institutions, undertake a systematic and continuing study of the experience with small-business financing over extended periods through various stages of the business cycle. They should thus seek to ascertain more definitely the character of the risks involved and the adequacy of the credit services afforded to small business under varying conditions. A goal of such research would be to make the accommodation to small business less dependent upon the changing liquidity of the individual bank and more directly attuned to the position and requirements of the business borrower.

### *Taxation of Small Business*

Whatever other devices may be developed, the savings of the enterpriser must remain the basic source of risk capital. The equity of the firm is most soundly enlarged, as a rule, through the plowing back of the earnings of the business. What the business can retain after taxes bears crucially on this problem. It is very questionable, however, if the public interest would be served by granting special subsidies or invoking discriminatory taxation on behalf of small business in order to pump funds into that particular channel. The small business in the last analysis is prosperous when business as a whole is prosperous and employment is high. Stress should therefore be laid on those tax reforms which, while in the interest of all business, would remove handicaps that bear most heavily on the growth of small business.

Most small business caters directly to the individual consumer. Such relief as can be given in the personal income tax, by the raising of exemptions and the lowering of rates, releases funds for greater consumption—particularly among those families which must use the bulk of their earnings for current consumption. To the extent, also, that individual savings gain through lowering of the surtaxes on higher incomes, additional venture capital for the growth of small business becomes available.

The small corporation—particularly one with $100,000 or less of total assets—is, in essence, a partnership in ownership and operation. To permit the advantages of the corporate form to be enjoyed by the small business without penalty, the small-business corporation should be allowed the option of making its income tax return as a partnership when the reinvestment of its earnings would be best served in that manner.

The discontinuance of the tax-exemption privilege for the securities issued by state and local governments is a long overdue measure for equity of investment; it would help to make risk capital investments relatively more attractive.

Greater latitude in stepping up the allowances for depreciation of assets during the first five years would increase the ability of small business to modernize its equipment and improve its financial position.

In view of the wide year-to-year fluctuations in its earnings, the small enterprise is unfairly penalized by inability to equalize its tax burden over the years. For both corporate and noncorporate businesses the right to carry forward losses from business operations to apply against subsequent earnings for a period of five years, with a one-year carry-back, has been recommended by the CED, along with a provision for income averaging by individuals. Both measures are necessary to remove an unfair discrimination against irregular earnings.

### *Competitive Position of Small Business*

The traditional concept of the small business as a freely competitive unit, capable of following an independent course in an open price market, has probably contained more legend than fact for a long time. The concept has, in any event, undergone significant change in recent years.

In the complex business structure of our day a large segment of small business operates within market channels and under trade practices that are laid out for it or that small business has itself helped to create. Durable goods in many instances are distributed through agencies identified with the name and product of the manufacturer. Wholesalers form defensive associations of their customers and in some instances supervise the retailers' operations. Manufacturers' brands are protected under minimum resale prices, often upon the insistence of the small merchants who handle them. Vertical integration of the processing, manufacturing, and distributing stages has meant that the small business may find itself supplied by the parent company of its chief competitor. The product of the small manufacturer may be absorbed under the private label of the large distributor. Trade associations may delimit competition among their members through intercommunication, industry codes, or protective legislation. With changes in the methods of production and distribution or the invasion of new products these alignments may shift.

In the circumstances the role of government as umpire and regulator of competitive practices has become progressively more important. At the same time the accumulation of legislation on behalf of one group interest as against another has the aggregate effect of restricting competitive opportunity for the sponsors as well as for the opposition.

The Sherman Antitrust Act has been modified by successive decisions and given variable interpretations with frequent dissenting opinions. The Clayton Act, intended to increase the safeguards against the tying up of the market, has been amended in two important respects. The Miller-Tydings amendment sanctions price fixing, and the Robinson-Patman Act attempts to delimit price differentials among customers. The FTC and the Department of Justice have found themselves at odds both with the Federal courts and with the state legislatures in interpreting the spirit and meaning of the regulations on competition.

The TNEC supplied a wealth of testimony for the United States Senate on competition and monopoly in their relation to small business. It called attention to institutions and trade practices that make for concentration of power in the market: to restrictive contracts, to price fixing, to antichain legislation, to coercion through patent controls, to interstate trade barriers and licensing to bar entry, and to a variety of other allegedly discriminatory practices that tend to destroy competition. Implicitly, the TNEC confirmed the difficulties of dogmatic generalization on the fairness or unfairness of the attacks and defenses by which competitors seek to win market advantage. Its report did not achieve a clarification of existing legislation, partly because it came on the eve of our entry into the Second World War, partly because it gave relatively minor consideration to the importance of conflicts in Federal and state legislation or as between the courts and administrative agencies. That extremely difficult task of reconciliation cannot be postponed much longer without further impairment of the position of small business within the competitive structure.

It is essential that Federal legislation relating to competition and restraints of trade—the Sherman Antitrust Act, the Clayton Act with its Miller-Tydings and Robinson-Patman amendments, and the FTC Act, along with subsidiary pieces of legislation—be reexamined and recast into a consistent body of legislation. The Congress must endeavor to lay down the governing principles and at least the broad definitions that can reasonably be applied to the economic organization of our time—by business and by the administrative agencies as well as by the courts.

The FTC should have the authority and prestige to pace the changing scene. The commission's handling of individual complaints, though important, should be regarded as only a means toward progressively clarifying the rules of competitive practice. Business firms and groups should be encouraged to lay their problems before the commission without prejudice, to obtain preliminary judgments on whether they are running afoul of the law and how they may put themselves on the right track. The work of the antitrust division of the Department of Justice should be dovetailed with that of the FTC. To provide the FTC with adequate facilities for effective performance of its umpiring and educational functions would undoubtedly call for sizable appropriations. Yet the outlay would be a small price for clearing our business structure of costly impediments that are a threat to our competitive society as a going concern.

Matching in importance the need for clarification and consistency in Federal legislation is the need for a fresh look at the regulation of competition through state laws and local ordinances. In this area the lobbyist has had a field day. One group seeks protection against the competition of another only to find that the protection is not effective; new laws are then promulgated to tighten the earlier ones; increasingly, innocent bystanders are caught in the net. Retaliatory measures are added, and in the aggregate we get a progressive contraction not only of competitive opportunity but of the volume of business.

Ideally, business itself—by group action and enlightened leadership—should cut through the maze and broaden its standards of competitive ethics without neglecting the consumer. The definitive task of implementation is inevitably the government's.

The Council of State Governments has made a significant start in its attack on the absurdities of interstate trade barriers. The states should likewise get together on a fresh approach to state regulation of competition, especially in its relation to parallel Federal legislation. Reexamination is needed of state laws on resale price maintenance, nonprofit sales, licensing provisions, antichain measures, grading regulations, restrictions on the use of new products and new processes, etc. Absolute uniformity in state laws obviously is not feasible, but in the effort to avoid abuse of power or the possible chaos of a competitive free-for-all sight should not be lost of the basic requirements for maximum competitive opportunity.

### *Small Business and Labor*

Labor, looking into recent global history, may well realize that a climate of vigorous and independent small business is the very climate in which labor organizations can operate freely. Both are symbols of a free society.

In industries where the small business predominates, there have been impressive examples of mutual understanding with management-labor cooperation in fostering the solvency and efficiency of the firms from which the wages of the workers are derived. In the mixed industries, where great industrial units exist along with small, there is need for more sympathetic attention to the fact that the small firms cannot meet all the conditions practicable in collective bargaining with large and highly departmentalized business units. Rigid craft classifications, for example, are inimical to the small business, which requires versatility of its employees and more flexible rules as to hours or other working conditions than are essential in the more formally departmentalized big plant.

Small business, in turn, cannot be supported by public opinion when its size is made an excuse for denying to the worker the benefits of stable and favorable working conditions, where the small enterprise is able to follow the lead of big business.

Collusive agreements between labor and business to shut out new products and independent enterprise must in the long run reduce the real income that labor can produce and enjoy.

*Education and Public Policy*

The problems of management, financing, and competition that confront small business require for their solution a program of training and public education. They involve those inside a small business and those who help to create the climate in which small business exists.

Professional education for business has given relatively little attention to small-business ownership as a career. Yet if small business is to survive and grow in our complex economy, it will need to recruit and hold a generous share of the best talent of the nation. Typically, educational emphasis has been on specialized technical skills of greatest use to the large enterprise. These have their value to the small-business owner as well, but a prior need in small-business operation is versatility. The training for the prospective enterpriser should be broad enough to provide an understanding of the whole of a business and its place in the economy.

Even for those who do not themselves assume the ownership of a small business, an understanding of its peculiar problems has a logical and essential place in general business training. Big business does not deal only with other giants. Patently, small businessmen are the customers, suppliers, and distributors of the big business.

The facilities of collegiate schools of business should comprehend the needs of the employee who would prepare himself for business ownership and the business owner who would like to keep abreast of good practice in management, finance, marketing, industrial relations, and product development as they impinge on the small business.

Although the schools of business and their business-research bureaus hold a strategic position for education of prospective and established small enterprisers, the great mass of small proprietors can be more readily aided through other channels. There are opportunities for mutual education of businessmen in the course of normal business relations with bankers and trade associations. The government research agencies collect a vast amount of economic, social, and scientific information, the usefulness of which may be enhanced by adapting it, directly and through local civic bodies, to the use of the small business. The Department of Commerce is the logical clearinghouse for such information.

It is sometimes argued that there are already large facilities for the education of small business of which small business does not avail itself. Up to a point the need is to acquaint the small proprietor with the existence of such aids; much of the material, however, needs to be more attractive and more intelligible to the average small businessman as well as more accessible.

Small business cannot have its stability insured. It is obliged to keep abreast of the changes that make a dynamic economy. At the same time the increasing complexity of our economy makes new demands for regulation in the common interest so that small business can have its rightful place in the competitive market.

The American economy cannot in our day operate as though it were an open prairie where each man rides at will. In a complex society all business can move more surely to its goal by the use of common roads and traffic signals. What small business may properly seek is equality of opportunity to travel the roads. It cannot make progress when the highways are obstructed with barriers and detour signs. The government must help to keep the highways clear but should not be expected to lead the small enterpriser by the hand. Adequate facilities for financing and fair access to the market are essential for the continuance of vigorous small business. The willingness of individuals to risk their substance and their ability to meet aggressive competition are at least equally essential to support a going system of private enterprise.

# APPENDIX

## APPENDIX TABLE 1

## DISTRIBUTION OF BUSINESS FIRMS AND EMPLOYMENT

### PART 1. ESTIMATED NUMBER OF OPERATING BUSINESS FIRMS, BY INDUSTRY AND SIZE*—1939†

(In thousands)

| *Industry* | *Total, all size classes* | *Number of firms with* | | | | | | | | |
|---|---|---|---|---|---|---|---|---|---|---|
| | | *0 employees* | *1–3 employees* | *4–7 employees* | *8–19 employees* | *20–49 employees* | *50–99 employees* | *100–249 employees* | *250–499 employees* | *500 or more employees* |
| Total, all industries‡ | 3,316.7 | 1,503.2 | 1,221.1 | 304.6 | 165.7 | 69.6 | 25.5 | 15.7 | 6.3 | 4.9 |
| Mining | 21.4 | 0.7 | 7.7 | 4.3 | 4.3 | 2.3 | 1.0 | 0.7 | 0.4 | 0.2 |
| Metal and coal mining | 7.3 | 0.4 | 1.9 | 1.1 | 1.4 | 1.0 | 0.6 | 0.5 | 0.3 | 0.1 |
| Crude petroleum and natural gas | 10.0 | 0.2 | 4.6 | 2.5 | 1.8 | 0.5 | 0.2 | 0.1 | § | § |
| Nonmetallic mining and quarrying | 4.1 | 0.1 | 1.2 | 0.7 | 1.1 | 0.8 | 0.1 | 0.1 | § | § |
| Contract construction | 202.1 | 77.0 | 69.2 | 29.9 | 16.7 | 6.1 | 1.7 | 1.0 | 0.4 | 0.1 |
| Manufacturing | 214.2‖ | 32.8 | 69.2 | 30.9 | 31.3 | 23.8 | 11.9 | 8.3 | 3.6 | 2.4 |
| Food and kindred products | 52.4 | 8.8 | 23.3 | 9.2 | 5.6 | 2.7 | 1.2 | 0.7 | 0.4 | 0.3 |
| Tobacco manufactures | 0.7 | § | 0.2 | 0.1 | 0.1 | 0.1 | 0.1 | § | § | § |
| Textile mill products | 5.0 | 0.1 | 0.2 | 0.2 | 0.5 | 0.9 | 1.0 | 1.1 | 0.5 | 0.5 |
| Apparel, etc. | 20.4 | 1.1 | 2.9 | 3.0 | 4.7 | 5.0 | 2.2 | 1.1 | 0.3 | 0.1 |
| Lumber and timber basic products | 22.7 | 3.2 | 9.5 | 3.5 | 2.7 | 2.3 | 0.9 | 0.4 | 0.2 | 0.1 |
| Furniture and finished lumber | 10.3 | 2.1 | 2.3 | 1.3 | 1.7 | 1.4 | 0.7 | 0.6 | 0.1 | 0.1 |
| Paper and allied products | 2.5 | § | 0.3 | 0.3 | 0.6 | 0.6 | 0.3 | 0.3 | 0.1 | 0.1 |
| Printing, publishing, etc. | 37.5 | 10.7 | 13.7 | 4.8 | 4.9 | 1.8 | 0.9 | 0.4 | 0.2 | 0.1 |
| Chemicals and allied products | 6.5 | 0.2 | 1.9 | 1.1 | 1.3 | 1.1 | 0.4 | 0.2 | 0.1 | 0.1 |
| Products of petroleum and coal | 0.8 | § | 0.2 | 0.1 | 0.1 | 0.1 | 0.1 | 0.1 | 0.1 | § |
| Rubber products | 1.6 | 0.2 | 0.6 | 0.2 | 0.2 | 0.2 | 0.1 | 0.1 | § | 0.1 |
| Leather and leather products | 2.9 | 0.1 | 0.4 | 0.3 | 0.5 | 0.5 | 0.4 | 0.5 | 0.2 | 0.1 |
| Stone, clay, and glass products | 5.5 | § | 1.2 | 0.9 | 1.1 | 1.1 | 0.5 | 0.4 | 0.2 | 0.1 |
| Iron and steel and their products | 8.1 | 0.1 | 0.6 | 1.0 | 2.0 | 1.9 | 0.9 | 1.0 | 0.4 | 0.2 |
| Transportation equipment | 1.0 | § | 0.1 | 0.1 | 0.2 | 0.2 | 0.1 | 0.1 | § | § |
| Nonferrous metals | 5.6 | 0.4 | 1.8 | 1.3 | 1.1 | 0.5 | 0.2 | 0.2 | 0.1 | 0.1 |
| Electrical machinery | 1.7 | § | 0.1 | 0.2 | 0.3 | 0.4 | 0.3 | 0.2 | 0.1 | 0.1 |
| Machinery (except electrical) | 8.4 | 0.1 | 2.1 | 1.3 | 1.6 | 1.4 | 0.7 | 0.5 | 0.5 | 0.2 |
| Automobiles and equipment | 1.2 | § | 0.2 | 0.2 | 0.3 | 0.2 | 0.1 | 0.1 | § | 0.2 |
| Miscellaneous manufacturing | 19.4 | 5.5 | 7.6 | 1.8 | 1.7 | 1.5 | 0.8 | 0.3 | 0.1 | § |
| Transportation, communication, and public utilities | 207.7 | 147.5 | 32.8 | 11.8 | 7.9 | 4.0 | 1.4 | 1.0 | 0.4 | 0.9 |
| Wholesale trade | 144.8 | 32.0 | 59.4 | 23.7 | 18.0 | 7.9 | 2.2 | 1.3 | 0.2 | 0.2 |

* For footnotes see following page.

APPENDIX TABLE 1.—(*Continued*)

| Industry | Total, all size classes | Number of firms with 0 employees | 1–3 employees | 4–7 employees | 8–19 employees | 20–49 employees | 50–99 employees | 100–249 employees | 250–499 employees | 500 or more employees |
|---|---|---|---|---|---|---|---|---|---|---|
| Retail trade | 1,601.4 | 752.8 | 631.4 | 140.7 | 55.5 | 14.7 | 3.4 | 1.6 | 0.7 | 0.7 |
| General merchandise | 36.8 | 14.9 | 13.4 | 4.1 | 1.9 | 0.7 | 0.6 | 0.5 | 0.3 | 0.3 |
| General stores with food | 37.7 | 20.8 | 12.7 | 2.9 | 1.0 | 0.2 | § | § | § | § |
| Grocery, with and without meats | 341.5 | 215.7 | 106.3 | 14.3 | 3.7 | 1.0 | 0.3 | 0.1 | 0.1 | 0.1 |
| Meat and seafood | 39.9 | 18.9 | 17.9 | 2.3 | 0.6 | 0.2 | § | § | § | § |
| Other food stores | 120.0 | 78.8 | 31.8 | 6.9 | 1.8 | 0.4 | 0.2 | 0.1 | § | § |
| Liquor | 15.3 | 6.7 | 7.4 | 1.0 | 0.2 | § | § | | | |
| Automobile dealers (new and used) | 38.4 | 5.0 | 14.2 | 8.9 | 7.0 | 2.9 | 0.5 | 0.1 | § | § |
| Other automotive | 15.1 | 4.7 | 6.1 | 1.9 | 1.6 | 0.6 | 0.2 | § | § | § |
| Apparel and accessories | 73.0 | 26.1 | 32.0 | 9.1 | 4.0 | 1.2 | 0.3 | 0.2 | 0.1 | 0.1 |
| Shoes | 13.1 | 5.1 | 6.2 | 1.1 | 0.5 | 0.1 | 0.1 | § | § | § |
| Home furnishings, equipment | 29.5 | 7.0 | 13.4 | 5.3 | 2.8 | 0.8 | 0.2 | § | § | § |
| Appliances and radio | 15.0 | 8.3 | 4.8 | 1.1 | 0.6 | 0.2 | § | § | | |
| Drugs | 52.2 | 10.7 | 28.9 | 9.7 | 2.5 | 0.3 | 0.1 | 0.1 | § | § |
| Hardware and farm implements | 37.9 | 13.6 | 18.1 | 4.6 | 1.4 | 0.2 | § | § | | |
| Lumber and building materials | 31.3 | 7.1 | 13.1 | 6.1 | 3.6 | 1.0 | 0.2 | 0.1 | § | § |
| Eating and drinking places | 295.4 | 103.6 | 135.5 | 37.5 | 14.9 | 3.2 | 0.5 | 0.2 | § | § |
| Filling stations | 226.7 | 115.2 | 100.4 | 9.1 | 1.5 | 0.2 | § | 0.1 | § | § |
| Other retail | 182.7 | 90.8 | 69.2 | 14.8 | 6.0 | 1.4 | 0.3 | 0.1 | § | § |
| Finance, insurance, and real estate | 286.4 | 112.4 | 127.7 | 26.3 | 12.7 | 4.7 | 1.4 | 0.8 | 0.3 | 0.1 |
| Service industries | 638.7 | 348.1 | 223.8 | 37.0 | 19.3 | 6.1 | 2.6 | 1.1 | 0.4 | 0.3 |
| Hotels, etc. | 27.5 | 3.2 | 13.9 | 4.7 | 3.4 | 1.2 | 0.5 | 0.3 | 0.2 | 0.1 |
| Laundries, etc. | 86.7 | 48.0 | 26.7 | 5.1 | 3.3 | 2.2 | 0.9 | 0.3 | 0.1 | 0.1 |
| Barber and beauty shops | 203.4 | 112.3 | 82.0 | 7.3 | 1.5 | 0.2 | § | § | § | |
| Other personal services | 93.0 | 62.1 | 25.9 | 3.9 | 1.0 | 0.1 | § | § | | |
| Business services | 28.2 | 10.7 | 10.2 | 3.4 | 2.2 | 0.8 | 0.3 | 0.3 | 0.1 | 0.1 |
| Automobile repair | 77.5 | 42.6 | 29.0 | 4.3 | 1.4 | 0.2 | § | § | | |
| Miscellaneous repair | 78.2 | 59.0 | 17.3 | 1.5 | 0.4 | 0.1 | § | § | § | § |
| Amusements | 44.2 | 10.2 | 18.8 | 6.8 | 6.1 | 1.4 | 0.8 | 0.1 | 0.1 | 0.1 |

* Size is measured in numbers of paid employees—not in terms of total employment including entrepreneurs and unpaid family workers.

† SOURCE: U.S. Department of Commerce, *Survey of Current Business*, May, 1944, pp. 12, 13.

‡ Owing to rounding totals do not necessarily equal the sum of components.

§ Less than 0.05.

‖ The number of manufacturing firms shown is larger than the number of establishments reported by the Bureau of the Census in 1939. This is to be explained by the fact that firms with less than $4,000 annual product are included whereas they are classified by the Census as services.

PART 2. ESTIMATED EMPLOYMENT,* BY INDUSTRY AND SIZE OF FIRM†—1939‡
(In thousands)

| Industry | Total, all size classes | Number of persons engaged, in firms with | | | | | | | | |
|---|---|---|---|---|---|---|---|---|---|---|
| | | 0 employees | 1–3 employees | 4–7 employees | 8–19 employees | 20–49 employees | 50–99 employees | 100–249 employees | 250–499 employees | 500 or more employees |
| Total, all industries | 28,707.5§ | 1,844.4 | 3,165.4 | 1,805.8 | 2,018.3 | 2,103.3 | 1,814.6 | 2,394.8 | 2,071.9 | 11,489.0 |
| Mining | 790.1 | 1.4 | 22.0 | 25.2 | 52.5 | 70.5 | 65.8 | 99.5 | 129.2 | 324.0 |
| Metal and coal mining | 569.6 | 0.8 | 5.7 | 6.8 | 17.9 | 30.5 | 41.1 | 78.1 | 111.3 | 277.4 |
| Crude petroleum and natural gas | 136.6 | 0.3 | 13.0 | 14.1 | 20.7 | 16.2 | 15.4 | 10.7 | 9.3 | 36.9 |
| Nonmetallic mining and quarrying | 83.9 | 0.3 | 3.3 | 4.3 | 13.9 | 23.8 | 9.3 | 10.7 | 8.6 | 9.7 |
| Contract construction | 1,457.8 | 113.9 | 134.8 | 159.7 | 198.4 | 185.6 | 119.6 | 153.5 | 128.5 | 263.8 |
| Manufacturing | 11,270.6 | 46.0 | 194.9 | 188.3 | 394.7 | 718.5 | 875.2 | 1,271.1 | 1,144.3 | 6,437.6 |
| Food and kindred products | 1,534.7 | 11.9 | 66.9 | 56.1 | 69.0 | 81.8 | 84.6 | 111.2 | 130.9 | 922.3 |
| Tobacco manufactures | 123.1 | 0.1 | 0.6 | 0.8 | 1.4 | 2.6 | 3.9 | 4.6 | 7.9 | 101.2 |
| Textile mill products | 1,300.7 | 0.4 | 0.8 | 1.2 | 5.7 | 27.2 | 72.0 | 173.9 | 63.6 | 955.9 |
| Apparel, etc | 939.8 | 2.1 | 9.2 | 20.2 | 63.2 | 149.7 | 150.7 | 166.0 | 113.7 | 265.0 |
| Lumber and timber basic products | 460.6 | 5.5 | 26.7 | 22.1 | 35.7 | 70.7 | 58.5 | 64.7 | 60.3 | 116.4 |
| Furniture and finished lumber | 421.6 | 3.0 | 6.6 | 7.9 | 21.8 | 42.3 | 58.5 | 92.9 | 43.1 | 145.5 |
| Paper and allied products | 290.3 | 0.1 | 0.8 | 1.5 | 7.1 | 16.9 | 47.5 | 51.8 | 32.7 | 131.9 |
| Printing, publishing, etc | 618.7 | 13.5 | 37.3 | 29.0 | 59.8 | 54.0 | 60.5 | 56.4 | 65.5 | 242.7 |
| Chemicals and allied products | 429.4 | 0.2 | 3.7 | 5.9 | 15.8 | 31.7 | 46.8 | 36.6 | 48.2 | 240.5 |
| Products of petroleum and coal | 416.2 | ...... | 0.6 | 0.7 | 1.7 | 4.0 | 4.1 | 9.9 | 17.2 | 378.0 |
| Rubber products | 183.0 | 0.2 | 1.6 | 1.4 | 2.0 | 5.1 | 7.4 | 12.6 | 12.7 | 140.0 |
| Leather and leather products | 395.1 | 0.2 | 1.3 | 2.0 | 5.6 | 16.3 | 29.6 | 71.6 | 55.1 | 213.4 |
| Stone, clay, and glass products | 408.9 | 0.3 | 3.7 | 5.5 | 14.2 | 32.3 | 35.8 | 54.8 | 58.6 | 203.7 |
| Iron and steel and their products | 1,290.1 | 0.3 | 2.1 | 6.3 | 25.6 | 56.3 | 63.6 | 156.1 | 120.6 | 859.2 |
| Transportation equipment | 244.4 | 0.1 | 0.5 | 0.8 | 4.4 | 5.6 | 8.0 | 15.2 | 15.5 | 194.3 |
| Nonferrous metals | 259.8 | 0.9 | 5.3 | 7.9 | 13.7 | 15.3 | 15.8 | 24.4 | 31.0 | 145.5 |
| Electrical machinery | 436.2 | 0.1 | 0.3 | 1.0 | 4.0 | 11.0 | 19.3 | 30.5 | 33.4 | 336.6 |
| Machinery (except electrical) | 708.3 | 0.5 | 6.3 | 7.5 | 19.7 | 43.0 | 46.4 | 76.2 | 180.9 | 327.8 |
| Automobiles and equipment | 498.4 | 0.1 | 0.6 | 1.0 | 3.1 | 6.9 | 8.9 | 12.2 | 13.8 | 451.8 |
| Miscellaneous manufacturing | 311.3 | 6.5 | 20.0 | 9.5 | 21.2 | 45.8 | 53.3 | 49.5 | 39.6 | 65.9 |
| Transportation, communication, and public utilities | 2,968.0 | 162.7 | 89.6 | 72.3 | 96.9 | 121.3 | 96.0 | 147.6 | 123.3 | 2,058.3 |
| Wholesale trade | 1,572.2 | 38.2 | 163.6 | 144.4 | 220.3 | 237.6 | 148.6 | 194.2 | 82.0 | 343.3 |
| Retail trade | 6,663.4 | 956.9 | 1,739.6 | 853.4 | 680.9 | 444.1 | 234.3 | 238.1 | 230.0 | 1,286.1 |
| General Merchandise | 948.5 | 18.8 | 37.3 | 24.7 | 23.3 | 21.9 | 42.8 | 69.1 | 101.6 | 609.0 |
| General stores with food | 119.9 | 28.2 | 36.4 | 17.6 | 12.5 | 6.5 | 1.3 | 1.7 | 2.1 | 13.6 |
| Grocery, with and without meats | 959.4 | 276.6 | 288.4 | 88.1 | 46.6 | 29.2 | 18.4 | 19.0 | 22.4 | 170.7 |
| Meat and seafood | 124.3 | 25.6 | 47.6 | 14.2 | 7.5 | 4.7 | 3.1 | 3.0 | 3.1 | 15.5 |
| Other food stores | 354.9 | 100.4 | 96.4 | 42.5 | 22.5 | 13.3 | 10.5 | 9.0 | 7.9 | 52.4 |
| Liquor | 35.8 | 7.7 | 19.3 | 5.1 | 2.4 | 0.9 | 0.4 | | | |
| Automobile dealers (new and used) | 356.1 | 6.3 | 42.2 | 55.8 | 88.8 | 86.9 | 31.7 | 12.5 | 8.6 | 23.3 |
| Other automotive | 91.8 | 5.7 | 15.8 | 11.4 | 19.1 | 17.6 | 11.8 | 2.9 | 1.7 | 5.8 |

* For footnotes see following page.

## APPENDIX TABLE 1.—(*Continued*)

| Industry | Total, all size classes | Number of persons engaged, in firms with | | | | | | | | |
|---|---|---|---|---|---|---|---|---|---|---|
| | | 0 employees | 1–3 employees | 4–7 employees | 8–19 employees | 20–49 employees | 50–99 employees | 100–249 employees | 250–499 employees | 500 or more employees |
| Apparel and accessories | 461.3 | 34.0 | 90.1 | 54.5 | 47.6 | 37.1 | 19.3 | 28.5 | 24.1 | 126.1 |
| Shoes | 71.0 | 6.4 | 15.7 | 5.9 | 5.9 | 4.0 | 3.9 | 4.6 | 5.2 | 19.4 |
| Home furnishings, equipment | 173.8 | 10.0 | 38.6 | 31.6 | 33.6 | 24.9 | 12.8 | 7.3 | 3.4 | 11.6 |
| Appliances and radio | 44.9 | 10.1 | 12.6 | 6.7 | 7.2 | 5.9 | 1.2 | 1.2 | | |
| Drugs | 247.7 | 15.5 | 84.5 | 57.4 | 29.0 | 8.0 | 3.7 | 10.1 | 6.5 | 33.0 |
| Hardware and farm implements | 120.9 | 16.8 | 49.7 | 27.3 | 16.4 | 6.4 | 2.5 | 1.8 | | |
| Lumber and building materials | 264.9 | 9.2 | 37.4 | 35.3 | 43.3 | 31.1 | 10.7 | 16.6 | 13.4 | 67.9 |
| Eating and drinking places | 1,181.1 | 145.6 | 383.9 | 232.9 | 186.3 | 97.5 | 34.6 | 25.1 | 13.1 | 62.1 |
| Filling stations | 534.9 | 130.2 | 258.5 | 54.2 | 18.5 | 7.1 | 2.9 | 12.9 | 7.9 | 42.7 |
| Other retail | 572.2 | 109.8 | 185.2 | 88.2 | 70.4 | 41.1 | 22.7 | 12.8 | 9.0 | 33.0 |
| Finance, insurance, and real estate | 1,340.0 | 125.6 | 241.1 | 138.9 | 151.8 | 142.1 | 95.9 | 120.5 | 87.5 | 236.6 |
| Service industries | 2,645.4 | 399.7 | 579.8 | 223.6 | 222.8 | 183.6 | 179.2 | 170.3 | 147.1 | 539.3 |
| Hotels, etc | 450.7 | 8.3 | 40.1 | 30.0 | 44.3 | 35.9 | 35.8 | 50.3 | 62.4 | 143.6 |
| Laundries, etc | 509.3 | 58.1 | 71.5 | 31.9 | 40.8 | 66.3 | 59.9 | 49.5 | 32.4 | 98.9 |
| Barber and beauty shops | 407.1 | 123.9 | 208.7 | 43.4 | 18.1 | 5.2 | 3.3 | 2.8 | 1.7 | |
| Other personal services | 179.8 | 70.2 | 67.1 | 23.2 | 11.6 | 3.4 | 2.3 | 2.0 | | |
| Business services | 342.4 | 13.1 | 28.1 | 19.5 | 25.0 | 23.9 | 22.5 | 42.8 | 31.7 | 135.8 |
| Automobile repair | 163.5 | 48.9 | 74.5 | 25.3 | 6.1 | 6.3 | 1.8 | 0.6 | | |
| Miscellaneous repair | 128.1 | 64.5 | 39.8 | 7.4 | 4.3 | 1.8 | 1.4 | 1.4 | 1.7 | 5.8 |
| Amusements | 464.5 | 12.7 | 50.0 | 42.9 | 72.6 | 40.8 | 52.2 | 20.9 | 17.2 | 155.2 |

* Includes paid employees, entrepreneurs, and unpaid family workers.

† Size is measured in number of paid employees—not in terms of total employment including entrepreneurs and unpaid family workers.

‡ Source: U.S. Department of Commerce, *Survey of Current Business*, May, 1944, pp. 12–13. (Above table incorporates minor revisions made after consultation with Department of Commerce staff.)

§ The comparable total from the Labor Force Census is 28,025,480. The number of paid employees reporting to the Bureau of Old-Age and Survivors Insurance in 1939 was 24,414,000. This, plus entrepreneurs and unpaid family workers reported by the Census, gives a grand total of 28,582,385.

## APPENDIX TABLE 2

REPORTED CORPORATE NET PROFIT BEFORE TAXES AND TOTAL RETURN TO OFFICERS AND OWNERS: PERCENTAGE OF EQUITY, ALL INDUSTRIES, 1932–1941*

| Assets size, thousands of dollars | 1932 | | 1934 | | 1936 | | 1937 | | 1939 | | 1941 | |
|---|---|---|---|---|---|---|---|---|---|---|---|---|
| | *Net profit* | *Total return* | *Net profit* | *Total return* | *Net profit* | *Total return* | *Net profit* | *Total return* | *Net profit* | *Total return* | *Net profit* | *Total return* |
| Under 50 | −32.8 | −6.9 | −14.7 | 17.9 | −6.2 | 35.5 | −8.2 | 34.5 | −8.2 | 33.4 | 3.0 | 46 4 |
| 50–99 | −13.8 | −3.1 | −2.2 | 9.8 | 2.7 | 18.6 | 1.8 | 18.1 | 2.0 | 17.4 | 9.9 | 29.0 |
| 100–249 | −9.7 | −3.1 | −0.6 | 6.4 | 5.0 | 14.5 | 3.9 | 13.8 | 4.3 | 13.9 | 12.2 | 24.9 |
| 250–499 | −7.1 | −3.0 | 0.4 | 4.7 | 5.8 | 11.4 | 4.9 | 10.8 | 5.2 | 11.1 | 14.2 | 22.6 |
| 500–999 | −6.1 | −3.3 | 0.9 | 3.6 | 6.1 | 9.8 | 5.3 | 9.1 | 5.4 | 9.4 | 14.9 | 20.6 |
| 1,000–4,999 | −4.1 | −3.0 | 1.5 | 2.9 | 6.4 | 8.3 | 6.0 | 7.9 | 6.2 | 8.2 | 14.7 | 17.6 |
| 5,000–9,999 | −3.8 | −2.9 | 1.7 | 2.5 | 6.6 | 7.5 | 6.0 | 7.0 | 6.1 | 7.2 | 14.7 | 16.1 |
| 10,000–49,999 | −2.4 | −1.8 | 3.0 | 3.5 | 6.6 | 7.2 | 6.9 | 7.5 | 6.8 | 7.4 | 13.0 | 13.9 |
| 50,000 and over | 0.5 | 0.7 | 3.1 | 3.2 | 5.4 | 5.6 | 5.4 | 5.6 | 4.9 | 5.1 | 9.8 | 10.0 |
| 50,000–99,999 | ..... | ..... | ..... | .... | 6.8 | 7.2 | 6.2 | 6.6 | 5.8 | 6.1 | 12.8 | 13.3 |
| 100,000 and over | ..... | ..... | ..... | .... | 5.1 | 5.3 | 5.2 | 5.4 | 4.7 | 4.9 | 9.2 | 9.3 |
| Total | −2.6 | −1.1 | 2.1 | 3.6 | 5.7 | 7.6 | 5.5 | 7.4 | 5.3 | 7.2 | 11.6 | 14.0 |

* SOURCE: U.S. Department of Commerce, *Survey of Current Business*, May, 1945, p. 8, based on data from U.S. Bureau of Internal Revenue.

## APPENDIX TABLE 3

ADJUSTED CORPORATE NET PROFIT BEFORE TAXES BY TOTAL ASSETS CLASSES, PERCENTAGE OF EQUITY, BY INDUSTRIES, 1939, 1941 *

| Industry | 1 | | 2 | | 3 | | 4 | | 5 | | 6 | | 7 | | 8 | | 9 | | 10 | |
|---|---|---|---|---|---|---|---|---|---|---|---|---|---|---|---|---|---|---|---|---|
| | *Under $50,000* | | *$50,000–$100,000* | | *$100,000–$250,000* | | *$250,000–$500,000* | | *$500,000–$1,000,000* | | *$1,000,000–$5,000,000* | | *$5,000,000–$10,000,000* | | *$10,000,000–$50,000,000* | | *$50,000,000–$100,000,000* | | *$100,000,000 and over* | |
| | *1939* | *1941* | *1939* | *1941* | *1939* | *1941* | *1939* | *1941* | *1939* | *1941* | *1939* | *1941* | *1939* | *1941* | *1939* | *1941* | *1939* | *1941* | *1939* | *1941* |
| All industries except finance | −3.4 | 14.7 | 7.6 | 21.2 | 6.0 | 19.6 | 7.3 | 20.0 | 7.8 | 20.3 | 8.2 | 20.2 | 8.1 | 20.4 | 8.0 | 17.8 | 6.7 | 16.7 | 5.1 | 11.4 |
| Mining and quarrying | −14.4† | −7.0† | −3.8† | 1.7† | −0.5† | 5.7† | 0.2† | 7.7† | 2.2† | 6.8† | 1.9 | 5.6 | 1.3 | 5.8 | 2.6 | 7.1 | 2.8 | 8.4 | 4.6 | 9.0 |
| Total manufacturing | 0.8 | 21.1 | 10.0 | 26.3 | 8.4 | 25.4 | 8.8 | 25.2 | 9.2 | 25.0 | 9.8 | 25.0 | 9.6 | 24.2 | 9.8 | 22.3 | 8.9 | 26.0 | 7.4 | 17.5 |
| Public utilities | −2.1 | 7.7 | 7.8 | 13.3 | 11.6 | 15.4 | 10.7 | 18.7 | 8.2 | 14.3 | 6.6 | 12.0 | 6.8 | 10.2 | 6.0 | 9.8 | 4.3 | 8.9 | 3.3 | 5.1 |
| Wholesale trade | 7.4 | 32.1 | 11.8 | 27.3 | 9.0 | 24.0 | 9.6 | 22.6 | 9.8 | 22.6 | 9.8 | 22.5 | 10.5 | 22.2 | 9.2 | 22.3 | § | § | 3.5 | 0.2 |
| Retail trade | −5.5 | 9.4 | 5.9 | 18.3 | 4.5 | 17.6 | 5.8 | 16.5 | 5.8 | 16.1 | 7.7 | 16.5 | 6.3 | 14.7 | 8.1 | 14.2 | § | § | 13.1 | 18.8 |
| Service | −1.4 | 21.0 | 8.8 | 19.1 | 4.7 | 10.8 | 6.2 | 11.0 | 6.6 | 10.6 | 5.4 | 10.3 | −0.2 | 1.4 | § | § | 4.6 | 7.3 | 4.4 | 6.2 |
| Finance | −9.6 | −8.9 | −1.2 | −0.1 | 0.8 | 0.9 | 0.1 | 1.8 | 0.1 | 1.9 | 2.5 | 2.1 | 2.5 | 2.7 | 4.1 | 2.0 | 3.8 | 4.1 | 3.8 | 4.8 |
| Construction | 0.6 | 27.4 | 9.0 | 32.9 | 4.8 | 28.0 | 5.5 | 26.4 | 5.0 | 25.7 | 8.3 | 25.4 | 21.2 | 32.1 | 7.4 | 21.3 | | | | |
| Agriculture, forestry, fisheries | −8.5 | 1.7 | −2.4 | 4.6 | −0.2 | 6.7 | 0.1 | 6.2 | 1.8 | 5.2 | 0.5 | 4.7 | −0.4 | 6.7 | 1.8 | 18.8 | .... | .... | 8.2 | 8.6 |
| Manufacturing industries: | | | | | | | | | | | | | | | | | | | | |
| Food and kindred products | −8.9 | −0.8 | 1.8 | 7.2 | 5.2 | 12.4 | 8.6 | 14.6 | 8.8 | 14.8 | 10.5 | 15.9 | 8.0 | 15.8 | 10.1 | 14.2 | 13.9 | 17.8 | 7.0 | 10.5 |
| Beverages | 19.1 | 20.6 | 25.2 | 25.6 | 17.4 | 26.1 | 12.5 | 22.7 | 13.5 | 21.0 | 16.2 | 20.8 | § | § | 17.4 | 20.2 | ‖ | ‖ | | |
| Tobacco manufactures | −27.3 | −15.1‡ | −1.9 | 1.4 | 3.1 | 6.8 | 4.7 | 7.4 | ‖ | ‖ | 5.5 | 4.3 | ‖ | ‖ | § | § | 15.7 | 19.8 | 17.0 | 22.0 |
| Textile mill products | −3.2 | 26.8 | 5.6 | 28.7 | 2.9 | 25.4 | 4.5 | 25.0 | 5.3 | 23.7 | 5.6 | 21.3 | 6.9 | 19.6 | § | § | 7.9 | 18.0 | | |
| Apparel and products made from fabrics | 10.0 | 31.9 | 16.8 | 32.5 | 12.5 | 28.6 | 11.0 | 24.0 | 10.4 | 23.0 | 9.8 | 21.8 | 9.2 | 15.7 | ‖ | ‖ | | | | |
| Leather and products | −3.6 | 24.4 | 10.0 | 25.0 | 5.5 | 22.8 | 8.5 | 18.0 | 7.0 | 18.1 | 7.7 | 18.5 | 8.6 | 15.7 | 8.8 | 12.8 | ‖ | ‖ | | |
| Rubber products | 8.2 | 32.9 | 23.2 | 33.0 | 18.2 | 34.1 | 13.5 | 26.7 | 14.2 | 34.5 | 13.8 | 26.6 | § | § | 10.4 | 16.7 | .... | .... | 7.4 | 17.3 |
| Lumber and timber basic products | −13.9 | 19.6 | −0.5 | 23.1 | −0.1 | 27.0 | 2.6 | 22.8 | 3.3 | 21.8 | 2.7 | 18.2 | 1.1 | 14.6 | −0.2 | 8.8 | .... | .... | 4.3 | 12.1 |
| Furniture and finished lumber products | −5.6 | 17.2 | 6.5 | 21.3 | 4.7 | 17.6 | 7.0 | 19.0 | 6.8 | 20.5 | 8.6 | 22.5 | § | § | 6.9 | 16.5 | ‖ | ‖ | | |
| Paper and allied products | 8.8 | 31.0 | 14.7 | 31.0 | 11.7 | 28.6 | 12.0 | 24.0 | 10.0 | 23.2 | 8.5 | 22.6 | 8.8 | 23.2 | 6.0 | 16.8 | § | § | 1.6 | 10.4 |

APPENDIX TABLE 3.—(*Continued*)

| Industry | 1 Under $50,000 | | 2 $50,000–$100,000 | | 3 $100,000–$250,000 | | 4 $250,000–$500,000 | | 5 $500,000–$1,000,000 | | 6 $1,000,000–$5,000,000 | | 7 $5,000,000–$10,000,000 | | 8 $10,000,000–$50,000,000 | | 9 $50,000,000–$100,000,000 | | 10 $100,000,000 and over | |
|---|---|---|---|---|---|---|---|---|---|---|---|---|---|---|---|---|---|---|---|---|
| | *1939* | *1941* | *1939* | *1941* | *1939* | *1941* | *1939* | *1941* | *1939* | *1941* | *1939* | *1941* | *1939* | *1941* | *1939* | *1941* | *1939* | *1941* | *1939* | *1941* |
| Printing and publishing... | 7.7 | 17.7 | 12.8 | 20.3 | 10.3 | 16.6 | 9.5 | 14.0 | 8.0 | 12.0 | 10.2 | 14.5 | 10.4 | 13.6 | 11.1 | 13.3 | 6.3 | 7.2 | 2.1 | 2.0 |
| Chemicals and allied products........ | −10.1 | 8.6 | 9.2 | 21.7 | 10.6 | 20.7 | 11.2 | 21.5 | 10.5 | 22.0 | 14.0 | 23.2 | 15.6 | 25.7 | 11.8 | 18.4 | 14.5 | 26.2 | 15.9 | 24.0 |
| Petroleum and coal products........ | −24.9‡ | −63.4‡ | 4.8‡ | −6.7‡ | 12.5‡ | 16.5 | 8.6 | 20.5 | ‖ | ‖ | 6.9‡ | 17.5 | ‖ | ‖ | § | § | 2.7 | 7.2 | ‖ | ‖ |
| Stone, clay, and glass products........ | −4.1 | 6.9 | 5.9 | 15.5 | 6.4 | 15.4 | 7.7 | 16.0 | 10.4 | 19.4 | 7.6 | 16.6 | 7.3 | 10.6 | 10.8 | 23.8 | 11.9 | 27.0 | ‖ | ‖ |
| Iron, steel, and products.. | 8.5 | 38.2 | 11.2 | 43.0 | 12.7 | 39.8 | 10.2 | 36.0 | 8.7 | 35.7 | 9.9 | 34.0 | 10.2 | 40.6 | 7.2 | 28.2 | 5.8 | 25.8 | 3.6 | 21.7 |
| Nonferrous metals and products........ | 13.0 | 40.3 | 12.8 | 47.7 | 15.3 | 35.0 | 13.2 | 32.8 | 11.8 | 34.0 | 12.4 | 26.6 | ‖ | ‖ | § | § | 12.6 | 24.9 | ‖ | ‖ |
| Electrical machinery...... | −5.2 | 32.7 | 7.2 | 37.2 | 13.6 | 40.7 | 14.0 | 38.0 | 13.7 | 40.0 | 13.8 | 42.4 | § | § | 12.7 | 36.7 | .... | § | 12.6 | 40.6 |
| Machinery except transportation and electrical. | −2.5 | 36.5 | 9.6 | 37.9 | 7.7 | 38.3 | 8.9 | 35.5 | 9.5 | 37.0 | 10.8 | 36.6 | 11.9 | 37.5 | 10.0 | 37.2 | § | § | 5.8 | 18.9 |
| Automobiles and equipment........ | −15.1‡ | 26.7‡ | 3.8‡ | 20.0‡ | −0.2 | 27.8‡ | 11.4 | 27.4 | 10.1 | 29.0 | 11.1 | 38.6 | § | § | 8.4 | 30.8 | § | § | 15.2 | 24.2 |
| Transportation equipment except automobiles..... | −19.8‡ | 8.0 | −17.6 | 22.5 | 2.1 | 19.0‡ | 3.0 | 21.0‡ | 5.7 | 30.2‡ | 9.7 | 29.2‡ | § | § | 11.0 | 16.6‡ | 6.3 | 26.5‡ | 0.7 | 37.7‡ |
| Miscellaneous.......... | 0.3 | 26.4 | 3.7 | 27.5 | 6.6 | 26.7 | 8.3 | 25.8 | 9.0 | 29.0 | 10.3 | 24.1 | § | § | 12.7 | 28.1 | .... | § | 12.0 | 21.3¶ |

* SOURCE *Statistics of Income*, Bureau of Internal Revenue. Adapted by Joseph L. McConnell, U.S. Department of Commerce, March, 1945.

† Capital assets have been substituted for equity.

‡ Ratio to a hypothetical equity obtained by applying the equity assets pattern (by size) of total manufacturing to the assets of the class to be adjusted.

§ Data for the firms falling in this assets class have been combined with those of the firms in the next *larger* class.

‖ Data for the firms falling in this assets class have been combined with those of the firms in the next *smaller* class.

¶ Two firms are represented. A hypothetical equity was used for one firm and the actual equity for the other.

## APPENDIX TABLE 4

ADJUSTED CORPORATE NET PROFITS BEFORE TAXES; PERCENTAGE OF EQUITY, SELECTED INDUSTRIES, 1942*

| *Industry* | *Total assets classes (000)* | | | | | | |
|---|---|---|---|---|---|---|---|
| | *Under $50* | *$50–99* | *$100–249* | *$250–499* | *$500–999* | *$1,000–4,999* | *$5,000 and over* |
| Manufacturing: | | | | | | | |
| Bakery products | 18.7 | 19.9 | 23.2 | 22.1 | 20.5 | 22.9 | 17.0 |
| Canning fruits, vegetables, and seafood | 19.2 | 29.2 | 32.6 | 31.9 | 34.4 | 32.0 | 21.9 |
| Meat products | 17.0 | 17.1 | 14.6 | 14.6 | 13.4 | 18.2 | 10.7 |
| Grain mill products, except cereal preparations† | −12.3 | 12.1 | 15.3 | 17.3 | 21.7 | 22.0 | 19.7 |
| Dairy products† | 12.0 | 13.8 | 22.5 | 22.5 | 25.9 | 26.3 | 18.9 |
| Malt liquors and malt† | −13.5 | −6.6 | 3.8 | 8.0 | 15.2 | 22.4 | 26.1 |
| Nonalcoholic beverages | 34.0 | 28.3 | 37.7 | 51.8 | 50.1 | 40.1 | 22.3 |
| Cotton manufactures | 32.3 | 32.0 | 32.3 | 35.8 | 40.2 | 37.3 | 29.9 |
| Woolen and worsted manufactures, excluding dyeing and finishing | 34.4 | 27.3 | 24.9 | 29.5 | 29.4 | 26.7 | 27.8 |
| Knit goods | 33.3 | 30.8 | 28.4 | 32.6 | 31.6 | 23.4 | 26.7 |
| Dyeing and finishing textiles, except woolen and worsted | 91.4 | 42.5 | 37.7 | 37.9 | 31.1 | 38.9 | 29.9 |
| Men's clothing | 45.1 | 30.1 | 33.6 | 28.6 | 27.9 | 30.6 | 22.9 |
| Women's clothing | 45.3 | 42.4 | 41.9 | 35.9 | 33.5 | 34.9 | |
| Leather, tanned, curried, and finished | 48.6 | 33.4 | 24.2 | 21.2 | 20.4 | 23.5 | 20.6 |
| Footwear, except rubber | 16.6 | 18.6 | 26.3 | 25.7 | 23.2 | 21.1 | 20.5 |
| Planing mills | 15.2 | 15.9 | 18.3 | 22.5 | 23.9 | 23.0 | 35.9 |
| Furniture | 20.9 | 19.8 | 18.9 | 21.1 | 21.8 | 22.6 | 22.9 |
| Newspapers | −0.8 | 8.9 | 13.7 | 14.3 | 15.1 | 16.8 | 11.3 |
| Commercial printing | 18.8 | 19.0 | 18.8 | 14.6 | 14.2 | 18.2 | 19.9 |
| Paints | 17.1 | 16.2 | 18.1 | 18.2 | 18.4 | 17.2 | 12.2 |
| Drugs, toilet preparations, etc. | 17.7 | 14.8 | 18.6 | 27.0 | 25.6 | 27.1 | 27.2 |
| Industrial chemicals | 21.8 | 26.9 | 27.4 | 28.4 | 30.0 | 26.3 | 22.1 |
| Structural clay products | −32.7 | 15.5 | 4.6 | 6.3 | 10.0 | 9.2 | 16.9 |
| Cement | ..... | ..... | ..... | ‡ | 22.9 | 13.3 | 17.1 |
| Blast furnaces and rolling mills | ..... | ..... | ..... | ‡ | 26.8 | 28.2 | 23.7 |
| Structural steel, fabricated; ornamental metalwork | 75.3 | 48.4 | 42.2 | 43.4 | 41.2 | 44.9 | 36.9 |
| Hand tools, cutlery, and hardware | 36.8 | 39.0 | 39.8 | 36.4 | 44.5 | 40.6 | 28.6 |
| General industrial machinery | 37.6 | 30.3 | 38.1 | 49.5 | 52.7 | 57.7 | 55.7 |
| Metalworking machinery, including machine tools | 76.8 | 70.2 | 83.1 | 86.5 | 78.0 | 83.5 | 95.8 |
| Public utilities: | | | | | | | |
| Taxicab companies | 104.1 | 94.8 | 68.9 | 28.2§ | | | |
| Highway freight transportation, warehousing, and storage | 26.9 | 23.7 | 21.9 | 21.2 | 20.8 | 12.8 | 9.7 |
| Radio broadcasting and television | 10.8 | 21.2 | 28.2 | 38.5 | 37.6 | 31.9 | 48.3 |
| Electric light and power† | 3.8 | 6.4 | 7.5 | 4.7 | 10.4 | 8.3 | 8.0 |

APPENDIX TABLE 4.—(*Continued*)

| *Industry* | *Total assets classes (000)* | | | | | | |
|---|---|---|---|---|---|---|---|
| | *Under $50* | *$50–99* | *$100–249* | *$250–499* | *$500–999* | *$1,000–4,999* | *$5,000 and over* |
| Wholesale trade: | | | | | | | |
| Food, including market milk dealers | 28.1 | 19.7 | 17.8 | 20.4 | 22.8 | 23.3 | 27.3 |
| Apparel and dry goods | 35.5 | 29.6 | 33.8 | 32.0 | 31.4 | 30.4 | 36.6 |
| Hardware, electrical goods, plumbing and heating equipment | 29.6 | 25.7 | 27.6 | 22.1 | 23.4 | 26.1 | 24.3 |
| Retail trade: | | | | | | | |
| Department, dry goods, and general merchandise | 13.8 | 18.2 | 15.5 | 24.0 | 24.3 | 24.5 | 21.1 |
| Limited-price variety stores | 12.4 | 25.2 | 24.6 | 31.1 | 27.9 | 40.8 | 20.6 |
| Food stores including market milk dealers | 8.0 | 13.9 | 16.5 | 21.4 | 18.6 | 19.3 | 15.1 |
| Drugstores† | 15.4 | 20.7 | 23.7 | 28.7 | 30.0 | 31.1 | 23.5 |
| Apparel and accessories | 26.9 | 26.0 | 28.5 | 29.4 | 30.0 | 27.7 | 26.9 |
| Eating and drinking places | 20.6 | 30.5 | 22.2 | 21.4 | 20.1 | 24.1 | 7.7 |
| Filling stations† | 6.4 | 8.2 | 9.2 | 7.2 | 13.5 | 9.5 | 15.2 |
| Service: | | | | | | | |
| Hotels and other lodging places† | 10.1 | 10.8 | 11.4 | 8.4 | 8.9 | 7.7 | —1.0 |
| Laundries, cleaners, and dyers | 29.1 | 18.1 | 15.0 | 12.5 | 13.6 | 10.7 | 19.7 |
| Automotive repair services and garages† | 12.6 | 9.9 | 8.8 | 3.9 | 10.9 | 5.5 | |
| Motion-picture theaters† | 69.1 | 35.8 | 32.0 | 29.3 | 32.2 | 28.7 | 16.6 |
| Finance: | | | | | | | |
| Banks and trust companies† | −6.5 | −11.7 | 0.6 | 4.6 | 5.5 | 4.9 | 5.4 |
| Construction: | | | | | | | |
| General contractors | 22.1 | 28.3 | 25.7 | 39.5 | 34.4 | 45.9 | 40.1 |

* SOURCE: U.S. Department of Commerce, *Survey of Current Business*, January, 1946, pp. 13–14.
† Adjustment involved no change in the reported profit.
‡ All firms under $1 million in assets included.
§ All firms over $250,000 in assets included.

# A NOTE ON THE COMMITTEE FOR ECONOMIC DEVELOPMENT AND ITS RESEARCH PROGRAM

THE COMMITTEE FOR ECONOMIC DEVELOPMENT was organized in August, 1942, by a group of business leaders who were convinced that attainment and maintenance of high employment after the war could not and need not be left to chance. They foresaw an opportunity to achieve unprecedented peacetime prosperity if business were ready to swing rapidly to peacetime production at the war's end and the government were prepared with policies and measures that would assist the reconversion and contribute to subsequent high production.

Recognizing that this undertaking comprised two distinct though related sets of problems, the CED provided for two areas of action: (1) a Field Development Division, to supply to businesses, large and small, in every part of the land, information and aid in planning for peacetime production and employment; (2) a Research Division, to study the economic problems of the immediate postwar transition years as well as the basic long-range problems in maintaining high production and employment.

It was generally agreed in informed quarters that high-level employment at the close of the war would require civilian jobs for seven to ten million more workers than had been employed in 1940. This meant that business had to plan a postwar volume of business greater than any prior peacetime year—in fact, an over-all increase some 30 to 45 per cent above 1940.

Through the Field Development Division, nearly 3,000 county and community committees were established. More than 65,000 businessmen served as members of these committees, responsible for getting information concerning postwar markets and job requirements to the local manufacturer, merchant, and other businesses, and responsible, likewise, for prodding the individual businessman, hard driven though he was with war work, to lay plans for peacetime.

Tested procedures for making both production and employment plans were made available by the national CED office. Specialists in industrial management, in product design, in advertising and selling, and in training of sales personnel placed their skills at the service of all cooperating businessmen, without cost, through handbooks, films, training courses, business clinics, and forums for the local committees. An outstanding achievement of the Field Development Division was a postwar market analysis, carried out with the cooperation of leading industrial firms and trade associations, covering more than 500 finished-goods products. The findings of this two-year study were given business and the public in a report, *American Industry Looks Ahead*, issued in August, 1945.

How thoroughly and carefully the local work was done was evident when, at V-J Day, the CED was the only major organization to state that, contrary to prevailing opinion, there would not be a job slump immediately following the war. Its reports from business throughout the country indicated preparedness to move rapidly into peacetime production. Its wartime "plan-jobs" assignment concluded, the Field Development Division was discontinued early in 1946.

Plans for high-level production and employment will not flourish long unless national policies prevail that make such plans feasible. To define what these national policies of government, business, and labor should be to encourage high production and employment is the special task of the CED Research Division. This is the purpose of the research studies, of which this volume is the fourteenth.

To the long-range economic questions involved in this undertaking were added the particular economic problems arising out of the war. Six studies addressed primarily to the economic problems of the transition from a war to a peace economy were completed during the war years. Of the studies concerned with the longer-range fundamental problems involved in the maintenance of high productive employment, seven have been issued. The present report on small business—the role that it plays in a free-enterprise economy and its special needs as our society is currently developing—is the eighth of the long-range studies.

The authors of these reports had already won distinction in their own fields. Perhaps more important is the fact that they had demonstrated not only the competence but also the vigor of thought that these complex problems demand. Knowing, however, that the problems that would be scrutinized—taxation, monetary policy, international trade, agriculture, and the like—are not separate ones but are integrated and must be studied in relationship one to the other, the CED has sought to make possible an exchange of information and views by the experts and, equally important, between the scholars and businessmen.

What may be a unique scheme of conferences was established, the objective being to blend the practical experience and judgment of the business world with the scholars' knowledge of the action of economic forces. A Research and Policy Committee consisting of representative successful businessmen was set up; to this group was added a Research Advisory Board, whose members are recognized as among our leading social scientists; and finally, the persons who would be responsible for the individual reports were named, to comprise the Research Staff.

The subject matter of each report is threshed out by the members of these three groups, meeting together. The author of the report therefore has the benefit of criticism and suggestion by many other competent minds. He is able to follow closely the development of the reports on other economic matters that affect his own study.

No effort is made to arrive at absolute agreement. There is no single answer to the problems that are being studied. What is gained is agreement as to the determinative factors in each problem and the possible results to be achieved by differing methods of handling the problem. The author of the report has full responsibility and complete freedom for proposing whatever action or solution seems advisable to him. There is only one rule—the approach must be from the standpoint of the general welfare and not from that of any special economic or political group; the objective must be high production and high employment in a democratic society.

The author is free to present his own conclusions and does not speak for the Research and Policy Committee or for the Research Advisory Board. In turn, the Research and Policy Committee usually prepares its own statement of national policy. This may endorse all of the recommendations arrived at by the author or it may disagree with some of them.

Implicit in the organization and support of the CED by business is the belief that leaders in each major group in our society will in future need to make every effort to appraise the policies and activities of that group as they relate to over-all national objectives and well-being. In the CED research program, a mechanism has been devised to permit responsible study by businessmen of business problems and to allow responsible proposals to be offered for national policies affecting business and the economy. After five years of work, the merit of which has been recognized by educators, government officials, labor leaders, economists, and other social scientists, it does not seem too much to say that in the CED structure, business has devised a useful tool for democracy.

The following is a description of the research studies published or under way, with the transition-period studies shown first:

A. *The Transition from War to Peace:*

1. *The Liquidation of War Production*, by A. D. H. Kaplan, The Brookings Institution (already published). The problems involved in the cancellation of war contracts and the disposal of government-owned surplus supplies, plants, and capital equipment are analyzed quantitatively as well as qualitatively. How much war plant did the government finance, and what part of it could be put into civilian production? What criteria should prevail in selecting the producers to be released first from war manufactures as the war production program is curtailed? How and when should surplus goods be sold? Rapid resumption of peacetime production, with conditions favorable to high levels of employment, is the gauge by which the recommendations are measured.
2. *Demobilization of Wartime Economic Controls*, by John Maurice Clark, Professor of Economics, Columbia University

(already published). When and how should the wartime controls be removed? The interdependency of the wartime controls of production, man power, prices, wages, rationing, credit policies, and others is made clear. How relaxation of each control may affect the peacetime economy—in terms of demand and supply, and therefore in terms of jobs and production levels—is weighed. The conditions that can be expected to prevail at different stages of the transition from a wartime to a peacetime economy are outlined, with emphasis on the variables with which we must be prepared to deal. Professor Clark does not overlook the significance of attitudes and objectives.

3. *Providing for Unemployed Workers in the Transition*, by Richard A. Lester, Associate Professor of Economics, Princeton University (already published). An estimate of the size and the duration of transition unemployment. The efficacy of public-works employment, relief employment, the adequacy of unemployment compensation, wartime savings, dismissal pay, and the like are appraised. A program is developed to provide for the maintenance of workers who may be out of jobs in the transition from war to peace.
4. *Financing Business during the Transition*, by Charles C. Abbott, Associate Professor of Business Economics, Harvard University (already published). The sources upon which business has relied for its capital are examined, along with the current financial condition of large and small corporations. These two are balanced against the likely needs of financing by industry for reconversion and expansion in the transition years following the war.
5. *Jobs and Markets*, by Melvin G. de Chazeau, Albert G. Hart, Gardiner C. Means, Howard B. Myers, Herbert Stein, and Theodore O. Yntema (already published). The problem of controlling aggregate demand in the several transition years during which the nation will endeavor to move from the high plateau of wartime production and employment to a similarly high level of peacetime productivity. The deflationary elements as well as the current

dangerous inflationary forces are examined. A program of fiscal, monetary, and price-control policies is presented to speed civilian production and to prevent inflation and depression in the return to free markets.

B. *The Longer-term Fundamental Problems:*

1. *Production, Jobs, and Taxes*, by Harold M. Groves, Professor of Economics, University of Wisconsin (already published). A study of the Federal tax structure as it affects the creation of jobs. A second volume, *Postwar Taxation and Economic Progress* (already published), concludes Professor Groves's analysis of the relationship of taxation to economic development and presents an approach to taxation that would make for constructive tax policy. The second report inquires into the problems of state and local, as well as Federal, taxation.
2. *Agriculture in an Unstable Economy*, by Theodore W. Schultz, Professor of Agricultural Economics, The University of Chicago (already published). An investigation going to the roots of the "farm problem." The significance of excess labor resources on farms, the failure of price mechanisms to induce shifts of resources out of agriculture, the differences between the farm and industrial sectors in responding to reduced demand. The importance to farmers of continued prosperity in business. A solution to the farm problem without resort to price floors or restrictions on output.
3. *International Trade and Domestic Employment*, by Calvin B. Hoover, Dean of the Graduate School of Arts and Sciences, Duke University (already published). An examination of the kind of foreign-trade policies and mechanisms we can adopt that will increase our gains from international trade and also contribute to world peace. A statement of the requirements in terms of the economies of other countries as well as our own.
4. *Controlling World Trade—Cartels and Commodity Agreements*, by Edward S. Mason, Dean, Graduate School of Public Administration, Harvard University (already published). The conditions that brought forth cartels and intergovern-

mental commodity agreements and the way in which both types of international business organization operate are presented as background to a searching appraisal of their role in the political-economic machinery of future world trade. American attitudes as well as American objectives in foreign trade are reviewed.

5. *Small Business: Its Place and Problems*, by A. D. H. Kaplan, The Brookings Institution (the present volume). An inquiry into the part that small business plays in a free-enterprise economy and as a facet of democracy. With these as basic points of reference, the position of small business in the economy today is compared with its past. An evaluation is made of social and economic factors affecting the entry of small businesses, their chances for survival and growth. What small businessmen need to do for themselves and what the community should do for small business is examined in detail.
6. *Fiscal Policy*, by Herbert Stein, CED Research Staff. An analysis of the relationship of Federal taxation and expenditures to the maintenance of stable employment and high productivity. Particular attention will be given the impact of budgetary policy since the Federal budget is likely for some years to represent a far greater percentage of the nation's income than ever before in peacetime.
7. *Monetary and Credit Policies*, by E. A. Goldenweiser, Institute for Advanced Study, Princeton University. Credit and debt policies and their relationship to booms and busts. Is it possible to keep money movements from reinforcing and exaggerating an upward or a downward swing in the economy? Can the money supply and credit policy be used effectively to counter the ups and downs? What is the significance for monetary policy of the large public debt?
8. *Management of the Public Debt*, by John K. Langum, Vice-president, Federal Reserve Bank of Chicago. The importance of the public debt in the economy from the standpoint of the total debt structure, public holdings of liquid assets, assets of financial institutions, interest charge, and relation-

ship to monetary policy. Among the factors scrutinized are the significance of the holdings of the Federal trust funds and agencies; the interest charge in relation to total Federal expenditures, tax receipts, and money flows; the changing ownership of the debt and the significance of liquidity for inflation and deflation.

9. *Analysis of Fiscal-monetary Policy between World War I and World War II*, by Bertrand Fox, Professor of Economics, Williams College. An examination of fiscal monetary policies in the interwar years, how they worked, and what we can learn from experience with them.
10. *Production versus Inflation*, by John Maurice Clark, Professor of Economics, Columbia University. Under what conditions does an increase in demand lead to an expansion of production; under what conditions does it lead to an inflation of prices? What needs to be done so that demand results in increased production and not increased prices alone? Two other CED studies—on price-wage relations and on labor-management relations—are, in part, addressed to this same problem.
11. *Labor-Management Relations*, by Douglass V. Brown, Professor of Industrial Management, and Charles A. Myers, Associate Professor of Industrial Relations, Massachusetts Institute of Technology. An examination of the growth and character of business forms along with the growth and character of unions and the labor movement. What objectives have business and unions in common, and what objectives conflict? What is the bearing of each of these on: the maintenance of high employment, uninterrupted supply as a factor of major importance to the public at large, costs and prices? This study is related also to the CED study of price-wage relations, and the study of production vs. inflation.
12. *Price-wage Relations*, by Edward S. Mason, Dean, Graduate School of Public Administration, Harvard University.
13. *What Can Individual Businesses Contribute to Stable High Production and High Employment?* by Melvin de Chazeau, Professor of Economics, The University of Chicago.

14. *Business Inventories and Their Effect on Business Movements*, by Ragnar Nurkse, Institute for Advanced Study, Princeton University.
15. *What Can State and Local Governments Do to Contribute to Business Stability?* by Clarence Heer, Professor of Economics, Duke University.
16. *Facilitating the Flow of Savings into Private Investment*, by Homer Jones, CED Research Staff.
17. *Stabilizing the Construction Industry*, by Miles L. Colean, Consulting Architect, and Robinson Newcomb, Construction Economist, Staff of the Council of Economic Advisers.
18. *Money Flows and Cash Balances*, by Morris Copeland, Federal Reserve Board. This study was initiated at the instance of the CED under the auspices of the National Bureau of Economic Research and has been taken over and continued by the Federal Reserve Board. The first report in this project—*A New Federal Financial Statement*—was issued by the NBER in December, 1947.

C. *Supplementary Papers:*

1. *World Politics Faces Economics*, by Harold Lasswell, Professor of Law, Yale University (already published). A discussion of the interrelationship of economic and political factors shaping the world political structure, with particular reference to the relations of the United States and Russia.
2. *The Economics of a Free Society*, by William Benton, Chairman of the Board, Encyclopaedia Britannica, Inc. (Published in *Fortune* magazine, October, 1944.)
3. *Personnel Problems of the Postwar Transition Period*, by Charles A. Myers, Associate Professor of Industrial Relations, Massachusetts Institute of Technology (already published). An examination of the problems that would confront employers in connection with the rehiring of servicemen and war workers, and the issues arising in the shift of the work force from wartime to peacetime production.
4. *Distribution of Income*, by William Vickrey, Department of Economics, Columbia University.
5. *What are the M in Problems of a Free Enterprise Economy?* (an economic primer), by Gardiner C. Means, Howard B. Myers, and Theodore O. Yntema, CED Research Staff.

## EXCERPTS FROM BY-LAWS OF THE COMMITTEE FOR ECONOMIC DEVELOPMENT CONCERNING THE RESEARCH PROGRAM

*Section 3. Research and Policy Committee*

It shall be the responsibility of the Research and Policy Committee to initiate studies into the principles of business policy and of public policy which will foster the full contribution by industry and commerce in the postwar period to the attainment of high and secure standards of living for people in all walks of life through maximum employment and high productivity in the domestic economy. All research is to be thoroughly objective in character, and the approach in each instance is to be from the standpoint of the general welfare and not from that of any special political or economic group.

*Publication*

The determination of whether or not a study shall be published shall rest solely with the Research Director and the Research Advisory Board. . . . A copy of any manuscript reported for publication shall be submitted to each member of the Research Advisory Board, of the Research and Policy Committee, of the Board of Trustees, and to the Chairman and Vice-chairman of the Information Committee. For each subject to be so submitted the Research Director, after consulting with the Chairman of the Research Advisory Board, shall appoint a Reading Committee of three members of the Board. Thereupon, as a special assignment each member of the Reading Committee shall read the manuscript and within fifteen days from its assignment to him shall signify his approval or disapproval for publication. If two out of the three Reading Committee members signify their approval, the manuscript shall be published at the expense of the Corporation. . . . In no case shall publication necessarily constitute endorsement by the Committee for Economic Development, the Board of Trustees, the Research and Policy Committee, or the Research Advisory Board of the manuscript's conclusions. Upon approval for publication, the Research Director shall notify all members of the Research Advisory Board and no manuscript may be published until fifteen days following such notification. The interval is allowed for the receipt of any memorandum of comment, reservation, or dissent that any member of the Research Advisory Board may wish to express. Should a member of the Research Advisory Board so request, his memorandum of comment, reservation, or dissent, which must be signed, shall be published with the manuscript. Any signed comment, reservation, or dissent which the Research Director may wish to express or have expressed by others shall at his request be published with the manuscript. . . . In the event the manuscript is not approved for publication at the Corporation's expense as above provided, the individual or group making the research shall nevertheless have the right to publish the manuscript.

*Supplementary Papers*

The Research Director may recommend to the Editorial Board for publication as a Supplementary Paper any manuscript (other than a regular research report) . . . which in his opinion should be made publicly available because it constitutes an important contribution to the understanding of a problem on which research has been initiated by the Research and Policy Committee.

An Editorial Board for Supplementary Papers shall be established consisting of five members: the Research Director, two members from the Research and Policy Committee, and two members from the Research Advisory Board. The members from the Research and Policy Committee and the members from the Research Advisory Board shall be appointed by the respective chairmen of those bodies. The Research Director shall be the chairman of the Editorial Board and shall act as Editor of the Supplementary Papers. . . . If a majority of the members of the Editorial Board vote for publication, the manuscript shall be published as one of a series of Supplementary Papers, separate and distinct from the regular research reports. . . . Publication does not constitute endorsement of the author's statements by the Committee for Economic Development, by the Board of Trustees, by the Research and Policy Committee, or by the Research Advisory Board.

# RESEARCH AND POLICY COMMITTEE

RAYMOND RUBICAM, *Chairman*
New York, New York

CHESTER C. DAVIS, *Vice Chairman*
President, Federal Reserve Bank
St. Louis, Missouri

WILLIAM BENTON
Chairman of the Board
Encyclopaedia Britannica, Inc.
and
Muzak Corporation
New York, New York

JOHN D. BIGGERS, President
Libbey-Owens-Ford Glass Company
Toledo, Ohio

JAMES F. BROWNLEE
Fairfield, Connecticut

GARDNER COWLES
President and Publisher
Des Moines Register & Tribune
Des Moines, Iowa

DONALD DAVID, Dean
Graduate School of Business Administration
Harvard University
Boston, Massachusetts

MARION B. FOLSOM, Treasurer
Eastman Kodak Company
Rochester, New York

CLARENCE FRANCIS
Chairman of the Board
General Foods Corporation
New York, New York

GEORGE L. HARRISON, President
New York Life Insurance Company
New York, New York

ROBERT HELLER, President
Robert Heller & Associates, Inc.
Cleveland, Ohio

PAUL G. HOFFMAN, President
The Studebaker Corporation
South Bend, Indiana

JAY C. HORMEL
Chairman of the Board
Geo. A. Hormel & Co.
Austin, Minnesota

ERIC A. JOHNSTON, President
Motion Picture Association of America, Inc.
Washington, D.C.

ERNEST KANZLER
Chairman of the Board
Universal C.I.T. Credit Corporation
Detroit, Michigan

FRED LAZARUS, JR., President
Federated Department Stores, Inc.
Cincinnati, Ohio

THOMAS B. MCCABE, President
Scott Paper Company
Chester, Pennsylvania

FOWLER MCCORMICK
Chairman of the Board
International Harvester Company
Chicago, Illinois

PHILIP D. REED
Chairman of the Board
General Electric Company
New York, New York

BEARDSLEY RUML
Chairman of the Board
R. H. Macy & Co., Inc.
New York, New York

HARRY SCHERMAN, President
Book-of-the-Month Club
New York, New York

WAYNE C. TAYLOR
Washington, D.C.

J. CAMERON THOMSON, President
Northwest Bancorporation
Minneapolis, Minnesota

# RESEARCH ADVISORY BOARD

# MEMBERS OF THE SUBCOMMITTEE* ON THE SPECIAL PROBLEMS OF SMALL BUSINESS

WILLIAM J. ABBOTT, JR.
Excelsior-Leader Laundry Company
St. Louis, Missouri

W. HAROLD BRENTON, President
Brenton Brothers, Incorporated
Des Moines, Iowa

WALTER D. FULLER, President
Curtis Publishing Company
Philadelphia, Pennsylvania

FLINT GARRISON
Owner and Publisher
Garrison's Magazines
New York, New York

PAUL G. HOFFMAN, President
The Studebaker Corporation
South Bend, Indiana

LOU HOLLAND, President
Holland Engraving Company
Kansas City, Missouri

JAY C. HORMEL
Chairman of the Board
Geo. A. Hormel & Co.
Austin, Minnesota

S. ABBOT SMITH, President
Thomas Strahan Company
Chelsea, Massachusetts

CECIL D. SOUTHARD, Vice President
Butler Brothers
Chicago, Illinois

WAYNE C. TAYLOR
Washington, D.C.

* Mr. William C. Foster was originally appointed as Chairman of the Subcommittee, but resigned from the committee when he was appointed Under Secretary of Commerce.

# INDEX


A

ABA (*see* American Bankers Association)
ACCO (*see* Atlantic Commission Company)
Advertising, 192
  allowance for, 206
  national, 187–189
  small-business, 238
Alien Property Custodian, 114*n.*
Amalgamated Clothing Workers of America, 128*n.*, 214*n.*
American Association of Collegiate Schools of Business, 223
American Bankers Association (ABA), 35*n.*, 145, 146
  Postwar Small Business Credit Commission, 149
American Council of Commercial Laboratories, 238
American Institute of Laundering, 112*n.*, 125
Anderson, John W., 212*n.*
Antitrust Division (*see* U.S. Department of Justice)
Antitrust laws, 1
  (*See also* names of laws)
Army Service Forces, Information and Education Division, 50
Assets, corporate, 89–91
  under $50,000, 88, 90–94, 99
  gross, 14
  liquid, 116, 239
  net capital, 14*n.*
  tangible, 78
  total, 14–15
Assets-size classes of industry, 96–98
Association of Consulting Management Engineers, 119
Atlantic Commission Company (ACCO), 195–196, 206*n.*
Atlantic and Pacific Tea Company, 193–198
Automobile industry, 16–17
Automotive Council, 127*n.*

B

Baltimore, Industrial Corporation of, 157–159
Bank für Deutsche Industrie Obligationen, 155
Bank examiners, 242
Bankruptcy, 54, 64
  big-business, 62
  small-business, 61–64, 75
Banks, 134–137, 141–144, 248
  capital, 168–171, 177, 241
    Federal Reserve supervision of, 241
    in Great Britain, 177–181
    psychology of, 170–171
  commercial, 149–150, 169, 239, 241
  Federal Reserve, 139, 142, 145–149, 160–163, 166–169
  private investment, 156, 165, 240–241
  small, 145, 242
Banques Populaires, 155
Barbee, Emmett E., 64*n.*, 65
Belgium, 155
Ben Franklin Stores, 121*n.*, 123
BIT (*see* British investment trust)
Blair, J. M., 79*n.*, 83*n.*, 84*n.*
BLS (*see* U.S. Bureau of Labor Statistics)
Bookkeeping, 112, 222
Boom years, 64, 103
Boston Chamber of Commerce, 157
Boycotts, 208, 216
Brands, 187, 243
  "off," 203
  national, 187–190, 200–201
  private, 188, 190, 200–201
British investment trust (BIT), 161*n.*

Budget Bureau (*see* U.S. Bureau of the Budget)
Buffalo, retail survival in, 69–71
Business, big, characteristics of, 18
  government regulation of, 3, 191–198, 218–219
  in relation to small business, 4, 6–7, 26, 51–52, 80–81, 87–93, 235–236, 247
  wartime, 2, 49, 114
 credit, 65
 intermediate-size, 102, 159, 165
 small, areas of, 18–19, 21, 28–41
  and chain stores, 191–198
  competition in, 182–219, 243–246
  cooperative methods in, 218
  definition of, Bureau of Labor Statistics, 13
   composite, 21–22
   by Congress, 20–21
   by market limitation, 18–19
   by method of financing, 18, 21
   by position in industry, 16–17
   by size, 10–16, 21
   by type of management, 17–18, 21
  and distribution, 244
  economic role of, 1, 3, 5–6, 233
  education for, 220–232, 237, 247–248
  efficiency of, 77–102, 235–236
  failures in, 5–6, 58–68, 234
  financing of, 135–181, 239–242
   through civic development corporations, 240
   foreign, 155–156
   through government agencies, 240
   in Great Britain, 177–181
   new proposals for, 156–171
   postwar, 148–156
   wartime, 147–148
  fluctuations in earnings of, 242
  future of, 4, 7
  and government, 228–232, 240
  insuring continuity of, 115–118
  lack of homogeneity in, 184–185
  and labor, 213–217, 246–247
  legislation concerning, 7, 19, 162–168, 172, 230–232, 240, 244–245
   state and local, 184–185, 246
  life span of, 68–74
Business, small, management guidance for, 87, 103–105, 236–242
   factors retarding, 106–108
   problems in, 108–119, 239–242
   sources of, 119–133
  mortality of, 43, 53–54, 72–76
  need for, 7–9, 233
  number and variety of, 233
  one-man, 79, 104
  operational factors in, 87, 103–105
  organization of, 17–18
  political solicitude for, 230–232
  in postwar world, 1–3, 7–9, 47–53
  prewar, 1, 23–44, 104
  public pressure on, 106
  reasons for increase in, 52–53
  research for, 226–228, 238–239
  size of, 235–236
   by assets and income, 14–16
  social value of, 4–5, 132–133, 233
  stability and survival of, 234–235
  standards and tests for, 113–114
  statistics on, 2, 5, 7–8, 11–16, 23–31, 47–48, 54–76, 233, 249–257
  taxation of, 172–175, 228, 231, 242–243
  technological progress for, 114–115, 226–228, 238–239
  unionization of, 125–127, 214–217
  wartime, 2, 32, 44–47, 49, 104, 111, 234, 236
Business cycles, 58, 62–64
Business failures, 58–74, 74–76, 165–166
 in boom years, 64
 cyclical factors in, 62–64
 informal, 66–68
 reasons for, 64–68
 in relation to size, 61–62
  (*See also* Bankruptcy; Depressions; Liquidation)
Business integration, competing with, 191–198
Business population, 101, 153*n.*, 234
 prewar trend of, 41–44
 recovery in, 46–47
 shifts in, 44
 by size, 23–38
 wartime, 44–46
Business research associations, 118

# Index


Business schools, 7, 222
  collegiate, 129
    and big business, 223
    clientele of, 223–225
    and education for small business, 222–226, 247–248
    qualification of teachers in, 225–226
Butler Bros., 121*n.*
Butter vs. oleomargerine, battle of, 208

C

Caisse Centrale, 155
California, price control legislation in, 204
Capital, ownership, proposals for supplying, 156–168
  risk, 242–243
  unsatisfied requirements for, 150–156
CED (*see* Committee for Economic Development)
Cement, relative cost of, 82–84
Census Bureau (*see* U.S. Bureau of the Census)
Census of Business, 12–13, 23, 26–31, 41
Census of Manufactures, 13, 36*n.*, 39*n.*, 81
Census Study of 1935, 141–142
Chain stores, 29, 71, 78–79, 87, 112*n.*, 116, 121, 184, 186, 206
  and competition, 191–198, 218
  legislation against, 245
  taxation of, 192
  voluntary, 121, 187, 206
Chambers of Commerce, and education for small business, 221, 227, 237
Chartered investment company, 160
Chicago, credit availability in, 142–143
Chicago Federal Reserve district, 142
Civic development corporations, 240
Clayton Antitrust Act, 192, 198, 205, 215, 244–245
Collective bargaining, 3
Commerce, free, interstate barriers to, 207–208
    and patent controls, 209–213
Committee for Economic Development (CED), 18*n.*, 119, 149, 172, 243, 259–269
  Field Development Division, 221*n.*
  Research Committee, 175
Commodity sales, 90–91
Communication, 34
Competition, 121, 182–219
  caliber of, improvements in, 105–106
  chain-store, 191–198
  conflicting trends in, 182–185
  cut-rate, 188, 199
  interstate barriers to, 207–208
  labor as factor in, 213–217
  legislation affecting, 191–198, 244–245
    state and local, 208, 246
  price, sublimation of, 189–191
  and small-business survival, 217–219
Congress (*see* U.S. Congress)
Construction, 39–41
  statistics on, 40
Consumer, 185–188, 190–191, 193, 200–201, 246
Converse, Paul D., 71*n.*
Corporations, 3, 41, 87–91, 93–94, 96, 243
  industrial development, 156–160
Cost, comparative, 79*n.*, 235
  and profits, 235–236
  sales below, 203–205
Cost accounting, uniformity in, 124, 238
Cost records, 78, 112
Costs, relative, 81–87
  by company size, 82
  by plant size, 82
Council of State Governments, 246
Cover, John A., 64*n.*
Credit, 62*n.*, 65
  bank, 134–137, 169–170, 176
    availability of, 140–149
    prospect for, 149–150
  commercial, expansion of, 149
  installment, 65
  meeting postwar need for, 148–149
  short-term, 138, 239
  from suppliers, 140
  term, 135–136, 139
Credit Artisanat (1923), 155
Credit associations, 128
Credit institutions, 136–138
Credit Mobilier, 155
Credit ratings, 135
Crum, W. L., 80*n.*, 90*n.*

D

Deficits, 88, 90, 104
Denison, E. F., 34*n*.
Denmark, special banks in, 155
Department stores, 29, 87, 112*n*., 121, 186
Depreciation allowance, 174–175, 243
Depressions, 1, 33, 35, 43, 60, 64, 75, 103, 112, 162, 204
Discontinuance of business, 55–56, 74–75, 234
  manufacturing, 71–72
  (*See also* Business failures)
Distribution, and manufactures, 187–189
  mass producer in, 185–186
  new methods of, 183–191, 235, 244
Distribution businesses, 191
  prewar, 28–32
Di Venuti, Biagio, 18*n*., 191*n*.
Drugs, price maintenance in, 203
Dun & Bradstreet, 24, 43, 45, 51, 56, 57*n*., 59*n*., 60, 69, 128*n*., 142, 144, 149, 154

E

Easton (Pennsylvania) Guarantee Fund, 157
Economic Development Council of Kansas City, 157–158
Economic power, concentration of, 3
  distribution of, 1
Education for small business, through business colleges, 222–226, 247
  through community guidance, 220–222, 248
  through government agencies, 228–232, 248
  object of, 220, 247–248
Efficiency, 191–192
  small business, hidden factors in, 100–101
    and investor, 101–102
    measurement of, 78
    relative, 77–102
Efficiency comparisons, summary of, 79–81
Employees, in construction, 40
  loyalty of, 18*n*.
Employees, in manufacturing, 36–38
  in mining, 41
  number of, in 1939, 27
  in retail trade, 30–31
  in service trades, 32, 34–36
  in wholesale trade, 30
Employment, nonagricultural, 175
  postwar, 9, 51
  self, 4–5
Engineering schools, 7
Enterprise (*see* Business; Free enterprise)
Entrepreneurship, 4, 76
  education for, 220–226
Epstein, R. C., 80*n*.
Equity capital, 140, 162
  individual, 169
Europe, small-business financing in, 155–156

F

Fair-trade legislation, 1, 188
  Federal vs. state, 202
    (*See also* Antitrust laws; names of laws)
Farming, 3, 131–132
Featherbedding, 215
Federal Deposit Insurance Corporation (FDIC), 146, 163, 167–168
Federal Housing Administration (FHA), 167–168
Federal Reserve Act, amendment of, 137
Federal Reserve index of production, 62
Federal Reserve System, 139, 145–150, 154, 160–163, 165–168, 170, 239, 242
  (*See also* Banks, Federal Reserve)
Federal Trade Commission (FTC), 18–19, 81–82, 84, 182–183, 192, 197–198, 205–206, 217–218, 230, 244–245
  Report, 116*n*.
FHA (*see* Federal Housing Administration)
Fichtner, C. C., 28*n*.
Filene, Lincoln, 158
Filene Foundation, 154
Finance, insurance, and real estate, 35–36
Finance companies, 136
  loans by, 144

Financial problems of small business, 135–138
Financial requirements of small business, foreign, 155–156
  in Great Britain, 177–181
  new proposals for, 156–171
  postwar, 148–156
  summary of, 175–177, 248
  types of, 138–140
  wartime, 147–148
Flour, relative cost of, 84–85
Fonds de Garantie, 155
Ford Motor Company, 210
Foulke, R. A., 63*n.*, 151*n.*, 154
France, special banks in, 155
Free enterprise, 4, 76
FTC (*see* Federal Trade Commission)

G

General Electric, 4, 19
General Motors, 4, 17, 79*n.*, 210
Germany, special banks in, 155
GI program for veterans, 150, 153
Glass industry, patent control in, 211–212
Good will, 78
Goodyear Tire and Rubber Company, 201–202
Government agencies, 129–131
  financing small business through, 147–149, 162–168, 239–240
  province of, 131–132
  (*See also* names of agencies)
Government regulation of business, 3, 228–232, 244
  (*See also* Legislation)
Great Britain, financing small business in, 155, 177–181
Gromfine, I. G., 146*n.*, 162*n.*
Groves, Harold M., 172
Grünwald, Kurt, 155

H

Hamilton, Walton, *et al*, 202*n.*
Hanes, Robert M., 149*n.*
Hardy, C. O., 142
Holthausen, Donald McC., 150*n.*
Hotels, profit ratio of, 99
House Committee (*see* U.S. House of Representatives)
Hutchinson, A. R., 72*n.*
Hutchinson, R. G., 72*n.*

I

IBA (*see* Investment Bankers Association)
ICFC (*see* Industrial and Commercial Finance Corporation)
Illinois, retail mortality in, 71
Income, fluctuating, and carry-over, 175
  net, 14
  in relation to service industries, 51
Indiana, retail survival in, 68–69
Independent business (*see* Business)
Industrial and Commercial Finance Corporation, Ltd. (ICFC), 178–181
Industrial concentration, 38–39
Industrial Corporation of Baltimore, 157–159
Industrial Credits companies, 155
Industrial development, community, 156–160
  through SWPC, 159
Industrial Information Service, 226*n.*
Industrial-management associations, 118
Industrial process, changes in, 183–191
Industrialization, 1
Industrieschaften, 155
Industry, assets-size classes of, 96–98
  population shifts in, 44
Insurance, 35
  of bank deposits, 239
  Federal, of small loans, 162, 167–168
  group, 126
International Ladies Garment Workers' Union, 127
Interstate barriers to free commerce, 207–208, 245
Interstate commerce, 199
Inventory, 62*n.*, 65, 78, 111
Investment, 7
  in small business, 77–79, 136, 239–242
Investment Bankers Association (IBA), 160–162, 242
Investment company for small business, 160

J

Jacoby, Neil H., 139*n.*, 144*n.*, 146*n.*
Judkins, C. J., 124*n.*

K

Kansas City, Economic Development Council of, 157–158
scientific organization in, 226–227
Kimmel, L. H., 144*n.*
Koch, Albert R., 150*n.*

L

Labor, 3
as factor in competition, 213–217
increased productivity of, 115
and small business, 246–247
Labor-management cooperation, 125–127
Labor Management Relations Act of 1947, 216
Labor relations, 115, 213–217
Lawrie, J. H., 178
Leigh, Warren W., 202*n.*
Licensing to bar entry, 206, 208, 245–246
Lindley, Judge, 193*n.*
Liquidation, 55–56, 61
Loans, bank, 148–152, 239
capital investment, 140
eligibility for, 241–242
by finance companies, 144
by government agencies, 147–149
proposed legislation for, 162–168
housing, 167–168
mortgage, 140
small, insurance of, 162, 167–168
term, 138, 140–141
expansion of, 145–147
Loss, bad-debt, 65
on installment credit, 65
and taxation, 243
Louisville Industrial Foundation, 157–159

M

McConnell, J. L., 80*n.*, 94*n.*
McEvoy, James, 210*n.*
Macmillan Committee, 155, 177
Macmillan gap, 155, 181
McNair, M. P., 202*n.*
Mail-order houses, 87, 121, 186
Management, definition of, 103*n.*
small-business, 17–18
as factor in survival, 104
problem areas in, 108–119
Management guidance, factors retarding, 106–108, 236–238
program of, 118–119
sources of, 119–133
through credit associations, 128
by educational institutions, 129
through good labor relations, 125–127
by government agencies, 129–132
through suppliers, 120–123
through trade associations, 123–125
Manuals, small-business, list of, 133–134
Manufacturer-dealer agency relationship, 183, 190
Manufacturers, 10–12, 36–38, 110, 183–191, 199–203, 244
Manufacturing, 36–38
credit availability in, 143–144
discontinuances in, 71–72
profits in, 95–99
statistics on, 37
technological progress in, 114–115
Market channels, control of, 185–191, 244
Market limitations, 18–19
Marketing Laws Survey, 204*n.*, 207
Markets, 244–245, 248
changing character of, 218
free, legal barriers to, 206–209
open price, 243
postwar, 109–111
seller's, 189
and wholesalers, 186–187
Mass production, 77–78, 103
Mergers, 116–117, 234
Merwin, Charles L., 139*n.*
Milk distribution, relative cost of, 85–87
Miller-Tydings amendment, 198, 202, 244–245
Mining and quarrying, 41, 99
Minnesota, manufacturing discontinuances in, 71–72
Mitchell, W. L., 79*n.*

Monopoly, 182, 193, 196, 244
Moody's Investors Service, 116
Mortality, business, long-term trends in, 72–74, 76
social cost of, 75–76, 106, 108
(*See also* Business failure; Discontinuance of business)
Motion-picture houses, profit ratio of, 100
Murray, James E., 19

N

National Association of Credit Men, 128
National Association of Retail Druggists, 188*n.*
National Bureau of Economic Research, 14, 139*n.*
National Industrial Conference Board (NICB), 143–144
National Opinion Research Center (NORC), 18*n.*, 107*n.*, 108*n.*, 117, 126, 149, 216
National Patent Council, 212
National Recovery Administration (NRA), 202, 204, 208
National Small Businessmen's Association, 184
New England Council, 157
New England Industrial Development Corporation, 154, 157–158, 160
New Jersey, business failures in, 65, 113*n.*
New York, price control legislation in, 204
New York State Department of Commerce, 131
Small-business Series, 134
Newcomer, Mabel, 72*n.*
NICB (*see* National Industrial Conference Board)
NORC (*see* National Opinion Research Center)
Nourse, E. G., 185*n.*
NRA (*see* National Recovery Administration)

O

Occupational standardization, 126
Office of Price Administration (OPA), 111–112, 166
Old-Age and Survivors Insurance, 55
Oleomargerine, tax on, 208
Overhead, 86

P

Paden, D. W., 46*n.*
Patent controls, 209–213, 245
Politicians, and small business, 230–232
Porter, G. Harvey, 159*n.*
Postwar Small Business Credit Commission, 149
Poughkeepsie, business mortality in, 72–74
Price control, 111–112
Price discrimination, defenses against, 205–206
Price fixing, 199–200, 217–218, 245
Price maintenance, resale, 199–200
Price manipulation and regulation, 198–206
Price supports, 3
Prices, fixed, 217–218
Pricing, 198–206
fair-trade, 199–200
loopholes in, 200–203
introductory, 194
Production, 36–41, 51, 62
mass, 183, 185–187
postwar, 234–235, 244
Profits, 58, 78
and cost, 235-236
curtailment of, 136
manufacturing, 96–99
net corporate, 96–99
rate of, 87–93
retail and service, 99–100
small-business, 172
dispersion of, 87–93
owners' compensation in, 93–95
Public utilities, 4, 34
Purchasing department, central, 183–184

Q

Quaker Maid Company, Inc., 194*n.*

R

Railroads, 4
Randolph, Jennings, 163
Randolph Bill, 163–164

Real estate, 35
Reconstruction Finance Corporation, 137, 145–148, 154, 162–168, 239–240
Reconversion Act of 1944, 13*n*., 20
Resale price maintenance, 199–200, 246
  circumvention of, 200–203
Research, 7
  business, 129, 226–228, 235–236, 248
  wartime, 114
Retail trade, 11–12, 27–32, 183–184, 186–188
  postwar increase in, 50
  profits in, 95, 99–100
  in relation to wholesale, 120–123
  sales budget guidance for, 122
  statistics on, 29–31
  survival in, 68–71
RFC (*see* Reconstruction Finance Corporation)
Robinson-Patman amendment, 198, 205–206, 244–245
Romney, George, 127*n*.
Rotholz, G., 79*n*.
Royal British Commission on Finance and Industry, 155, 177

S

Salaries, 87, 93–94
Sales below cost, 203–205
Saulnier, Raymond, 139*n*., 144*n*., 146*n*.
Sears Roebuck and Co., 201
SEC (*see* Securities and Exchange Commission)
Securities, small-business, flotation of, 136, 151–155, 240
Securities and Exchange Commission (SEC), 14, 151, 163
Service enterprises, 11–12, 32–36, 51, 191
  profits in, 96, 99–100
  statistics on, 33
Servicemen (*see* Veterans)
Sevin, Charles H., 87*n*.
Sherman Antitrust Act, 182, 192, 194, 198, 202, 205, 244–245
Small-business manuals, list of, 133–134
Smaller War Plants Corporation (SWPC), 17, 20, 129–130, 137–138, 147–148, 154, 159–162, 166, 240
Smith, F. Goodwin, 212
Smith, Tynan, 150*n*.
Social-security measures, 126
Standard & Poor's Corporation, 116
Starr, G. W., 69*n*., 70*n*.
Statistics, business, 249–257
  (*See also* Business, small, statistics on)
Steiner, G. A., 69*n*., 70*n*.
Stock Exchange, 7, 9, 17
Subsidies, 3, 166
Successorship, 116, 118
Survival rate, 104
  stability of, 73–74
Sweden, special banks in, 155
SWPC (*see* Smaller War Plants Corporation)

T

Taft-Hartley Act, 216
Tax policy for small business, 172–175
Taxation, 177, 242–243
  chain-store, 196
  recent relief from, 173–174
  reform in, 173, 242
Taxes, corporation, 174, 243
  excess-profits, 173
  excise, 173
  income, business, 174
    personal, 173, 243
  sales, 173
  and small business, 228, 231, 242–243
Taylor, Burtis, and Waugh, 208*n*.
Technological resources (*see* Research)
Temporary National Economic Committee (TNEC), 1, 13–14, 79*n*., 81*n*., 84*n*.–86*n*., 208, 209*n*.–211*n*., 213, 244–245
  Science Advisory Board, 213
Thorp, Willard, 116*n*.
TNEC (*see* Temporary National Economic Committee)
Trade associations, 1, 119, 123–125, 184, 203, 208, 219, 244
  and education, 226, 237, 248
  and research, 227–228
Transportation, 34
Truman, Harry S., President, 148

# Index


U

Unions, 125
  and small business, 18n., 19, 125–127, 214–217
U.S. Bureau of the Budget, Fiscal Division, 174n.
U.S. Bureau of the Census, 10, 15, 39, 141
U.S. Bureau of Foreign and Domestic Commerce, 11, 25, 28n.
U.S. Bureau of Internal Revenue, 87, 93–94n., 96n., 104, 139n., 236
  Statistics of Income, 14–15n., 24, 89, 91n.–92n., 96, 97n.–98n., 99, 101
U.S. Bureau of Labor Statistics (BLS), 11–13, 15, 40, 56n.
U.S. Bureau of Mines, 226
U.S. Bureau of Standards, 114, 131, 226, 231, 238
U.S. Congress, 1, 13, 130, 148, 167, 170, 202, 218, 245
U.S. Department of Agriculture, 131
U.S. Department of Commerce, 2, 10, 11, 12, 15, 16, 23–24n., 26, 34–35, 40, 43, 51n., 56, 65, 87n., 89, 94n., 96n., 113n., 116, 120, 131, 148, 159, 229, 239, 248
  Business Advisory Council, 141–142
  Business Structure Unit, 95, 97n.–98n.
  Classification of Small Business, 10–12
  Economic Series, 114n.
  Office of Business Economics, 153n.
  Office of Small Business, 130, 227n.
  Office of Trade Associations, 226
  Small Business Division, 124n.
  small-business manuals of, 133–134
U.S. Department of Justice, 194, 217, 244
  Antitrust Division, 19, 183, 245
U.S. House of Representatives, Committee on Post War Economic Policy and Planning, 149n.
  Small Business Committee, 17, 19
U.S. Senate, 244
  Small Business Committee, 13, 17–21, 28n, 144n., 151n., 160
U.S. Senate, War Investigating Committee on Manpower Problems, 127n.
U.S. Supreme Court, 215–216
U.S. Tariff Commission, 83n.–84n.
U.S. Treasury, 163, 167
University of Buffalo Studies in Business, 70n.

V

Veterans, and self-employment, 4, 8, 19, 50, 52
  and small business, 153, 221, 229
Veterans Administration, 130
Viner, Jacob, 142

W

Wages, postwar, 114–115
War, and big business, 2
  and small business, 2, 32, 44–47, 60, 109, 135, 147–148
    (*See also* World War I; World War II)
War Production Board, 166
Weissman, R. L., 154n.
West Virginia, milk distribution in, 86
Wholesale trade, 12, 30–32
  changes in, 186–187
  profits in, 95
Wholesaler, 10–11, 26–27, 50–51, 121, 183, 244
  changed position of, 186–187
Willits, George H., 213n.
World War I, 34, 58–59, 112, 116, 155, 234
World War II, 1, 103, 116, 234, 245
Wyoming, Development Commission, 227
Wyoming Industrial Research Foundation, 158
Wyoming Valley Industrial Development Fund, 157

Y

Yale Institute of Human Relations, 65
Young, Ralph A., 143n.